Complex Inequality

GENDER, CLASS, AND RACE IN THE NEW ECONOMY

Leslie McCall

ROUTLEDGE

NEW YORK • LONDON

Published in 2001 by
Routledge
29 West 35th Street
New York, NY 10001

Published in Great Britain by
Routledge
11 New Fetter Lane
London EC4P 4EE

Routledge is an imprint of the Taylor & Francis Group.

Chapter 2 is based in part on Leslie McCall. 1999. "Regional Restructuring and Wage Inequality by Gender, Class, and Race." pp. 5–88 in *Women's Progress: Perspectives on the Past, Blueprint for the Future (Fifth Women's Policy Research Conference Proceedings)*. Washington, D.C.: Institute for Women's Policy Research. Used with permission.

Chapter 5 is based in part on Leslie McCall. 1998. "Spatial Routes to Gender Wage (In)equality: Regional Restructuring and Wage Differentials by Gender and Education." *Economic Geography* 74(4): 379–404. Used with permission.

Printed in the United States of America on acid-free paper.

Library of Congress Cataloging-in-Publishing Data

McCall, Leslie, 1964–
    Complex Inequality: gender, class, and race in the new economy / Leslie McCall.
        p. cm. — (perspectives on gender)
    Includes bibliographical references and index.
    ISBN 0–415–92903–2 — ISBN 0–415–92904–0 (pbk.)
        1. Wages—Woman—United States—Case studies. 2. Sex discrimination in employment—United States—Case studies. 3. Race discrimination—United States—Case studies. 4. Social classes—United States—Case studies. 5. Equal pay for equal work—United States—Case studies. 6. Pay equity—United States—Case studies. I. Title. II. Perspectives on gender (New York, N.Y.)

HD6061.2.U6 M363 2001
331.13'3'0972—dc21   00–047064

Contents

List of Tables

Appendix

List of Figures

APPENDIX

Preface

I began this book during the sluggish recovery that followed the early 1990s recession. At that time, there were no signs that productivity and growth would ever rise again at rates similar to their peaks in the 1960s, as they have in the late 1990s, nor that the "new" inequality between the top and bottom would subside. For someone interested in inequality, the fact that the economy was restructuring—becoming more high-tech, more international, more flexible, and more service-oriented—seemed to be at the root of a new social, economic, and political environment that lowered the wages and security of most workers even as it created unprecedented concentrations of wealth. Exactly *how* and *why* this new economy had the effect it did on workers and inequality, however, was not altogether clear. The search for answers to these questions became a way of taming this new environment: if we knew the particular sources of inequality, we could develop the best strategies to reduce it.

For the most part, this picture has not changed. First, unexpectedly strong economic growth and tight labor markets are taking some of the sting off, but inflation-adjusted wages are still below their previous peaks in the 1970s, and inequality is still high relative to previous troughs in the 1970s and relative to other advanced capitalist countries. Moreover, the economy is starting to slow again. Second, there is still debate over what the causes of the new inequality are: new technology, increased competition, loss of job security? Third, there is still little public debate over how to reduce inequality. Finally, and most important for my purposes, the emphasis of research is still overwhelmingly on the new inequality and trends in rising inequality.

Now, as then, there is little discussion of what this new environment means for other forms of inequality, such as racial and especially gender inequality. In this sense, the "new" literature is very old indeed. Although I join in the search for the sources of the new inequality as part of a larger strategy to reduce inequality, I also explore these issues in a way that I hope transcends the present moment. I see the interest in the new inequality as an opportunity to examine the problem in a more comprehensive way than has been typical in recent years. In particular, I do not restrict my analysis to the new inequality only, nor to the issue of *rising* inequality. Rather, I examine the new inequality alongside the "old" inequality—gender and racial inequality—and I examine the sources of high *levels* of inequality across space rather than across time.

First, from a researcher's perspective, studying inequality across space offers a view of much more variety and variation in both levels of inequality and economic conditions than does studying inequality over the course of two or even three decades. There are literally hundreds of local economies (more than five hundred) that are at the heart of my study of economic restructuring and wage inequality. They offer a myriad of different environments in which to understand the relationship between inequality and the economy. Is inequality higher in high-tech industrial districts, immigrant-rich cities, or deindustrialized regions, and, if so, in which groups? These are just a few of the types of local economies in which I examine inequality. An additional reason to study inequality spatially is that there has always been, and no doubt will continue to be, substantial variation in levels of inequality across space. In contrast, the period of sharply rising inequality may be coming to an end, even as levels of inequality remain high.

Second, my decision to study gender and racial inequality was also motivated by interests that extend beyond the current period of rising inequality. Perhaps most important, levels of inequality between men and women and between racial groups are still quite high. One would never know it, since racial and especially gender inequality have been brushed aside in recent years as the new inequality has taken over center stage. This is probably at least in part because both gender and racial inequality have declined over the long run. It is also surely a response to the lack of popularity of gender- and race-targeted redistributive programs, especially during recessionary periods such as the early 1980s and early 1990s. To make matters worse, the scholarship that *does* focus on gender and racial inequality tends to maintain a certain continuity with discussions of discrimination that predate and overlook the new environment of restructuring and inequality. Thus, remarkably, there has been little research on the intersections of and relationships between gender, race, class (as a measure of the new inequality), and economic restructuring.

What is the consequence of such omissions? There are many, and these constitute the main theme of the book. But let us consider one key example: high levels of wage inequality between women at the top and bottom of the wage and skill distributions. Although women comprise nearly half the working population, and wage inequality is at least as high among them as it is among men, there has been virtually no research on this component of the new inequality. Why? Because scholars of the new inequality have focused on wage inequality among men, and gender stratification scholars have maintained their focus on inequality between men and women. If the latter consider inequality among women at all, it is usually in terms of racial inequality among women, not class inequality. Perhaps this omission would not matter if the patterns and sources of inequality were the same for men and women or if wage inequality among women and gender inequality were unrelated, but I present evidence that they are not.

This book, then, is an investigation of the sources of both the new inequality and the old in our new and restructuring economy. That this subject would be new and complex enough to require a book was not immediately obvious to me when I first began work on these issues in my dissertation. In fact, it took several years to realize that what I found most interesting about this subject—the overarching connections and conflicting relationships between different dimensions of inequality—could be unraveled only in a book-length study. Articles, at least in their present incarnation, are allowed to juggle only a few ideas at a time; they tend to be restricted to studies of gender inequality *or* racial inequality *or* class inequality *or* economic restructuring. If each of these had the same trajectories and sources, then the damage of this reductionist approach would be minimal. However, as I show throughout this book, this is not the case. Multidimensional structures of inequality are, perhaps by their very nature but certainly in empirical terms, very complex.

My deepest debts of gratitude therefore go to those people who helped to shape this project from its earliest stages—before it was ever to be a book—to its present form. These are the people who deserve much of the credit for the best parts of the book and, of course, none of the blame for the rest. Thanks are in order first and foremost to the person who was literally there from the very beginning to the very end, as intellectual, political, and emotional partner in life: Eric Parker. I dedicate this book to him. I am equally indebted to my impressive colleagues in sociology and women's studies at Rutgers—in particular, Judith Gerson, Patricia Roos, Leela Fernandez, and Dorothy Sue Cobble. Throughout the past five years, I have learned a great deal from them personally and from the important work they have done on topics related to this book. They provided critical feedback on many early drafts and unwavering support in countless other ways as well. Also from Rutgers (and now at the University of Minnesota), Ann Markusen provided absolutely crucial support at key moments. In particular, she read an early draft of the manuscript and returned it with comments that helped to clarify and expand the overall argument and tenor of the book.

There were other readers of the entire manuscript who provided invaluable advice on how to revise it. Myra Marx Ferree, the academic editor of this series, was always inspiring and enthusiastic. Despite an incredibly busy schedule, she provided the kind of attention and expert advice that I needed to turn my manuscript into a book. As a reviewer, Ruth Milkman conceived of a major reorganization of the book, which I tried to implement as best I could. I also thank her for her encouragement all along the way. In addition, I was lucky to have had several other reviewers whose work I have always admired: Randy Albelda, Arne Kalleberg, and Chris Tilly. They gave me detailed advice on how to turn this complex body of research into a more coherent and accessible book and how to draw out the most important of the larger themes.

As with all books that begin as dissertations, this one owes a great deal to my dissertation committee and to several other of my professors at the University of Wisconsin. In ways that I appreciate more fully as time goes by, each shaped my thinking on the issues explored in this book, as well as my career more generally, in fundamental ways. They are Jane Collins, Aimee Dechter, Robert Mare, Ann Orloff, Joel Rogers, Cynthia Truelove, and Erik Olin Wright. I also owe a lot to my fellow graduate students and Madison friends, who were a large and very influential part of my life and of my education on the issues about which I write in this book.

I would also like to thank the many people who commented on individual chapters at various stages of development, inspired me at crucial moments in the history of this project, or were supportive of my research along the way. They are: Barbara Balliet, Annette Bernhardt, Karen Booth, Susan Christopherson, Patricia Hill Collins, Kathryn Edin, Susan Hanson, Alice Kessler-Harris, Elaine McCrate, Elizabeth Mueller, dt ogilvie, Barbara Reskin, Sarah Rosenfield, Jill Rubery, Thomas Rudel, Caridad Sousa, Reeve Vanneman, Leah Vosko, Kirsten Wever, and Julie Whittaker. I have also benefited greatly from the comments of anonymous reviewers and editors on articles drawn from the larger project of which this book is a part. I thank especially the editors and reviewers of my articles in *Economic Geography*, *American Sociological Review*, and *Demography*. Special thanks go to my editor at Routledge, Ilene Kalish, who was always a breath of fresh air during the most intense periods of this process.

Finally, I acknowledge the financial support of the Rutgers University Research Council, the Institute for Research on Women at Rutgers University, and the University of Wisconsin, where much of the original data collection was supported by a dissertation fellowship. Although it was many years ago, I had tremendous help in the original collection of the data for this book, and so I would like to thank Loraine Atkins at the Wisconsin Historical Society Library and Ann Cooper, Cindy Lew, Tom Flory, and Nancy McDermott at the Center for Ecology and Demography for their assistance in that area. At the other end of this project, I was lucky to benefit from the advice of Suzanne Nichols, the publication director at the Russell Sage Foundation, where I was in blissful residence as a Visiting Scholar when I was putting the finishing touches on this book.

Leslie McCall

Introduction

Chapter One

RESTRUCTURING INEQUALITIES:
A GENDER, CLASS, AND RACE PERSPECTIVE

According to most observers at the beginning of this new century, the United States is not only in a typical period of economic expansion, but its brand of flexible restructuring has made it the most envied and dynamic economy in the world. Some project that the new American economy is even immune to future recessions. Indeed, unemployment has fallen below the level at which inflation was supposed to rise and growth was expected to moderate, and yet neither has come to pass. If this stunning turnaround from the turbulent 1980s meant that everyone was better off and the rich were better off still, the "new inequality" might go unnoticed.[1] But a broad cross section of Americans have seen their living standards stagnate or fall since at least the 1970s, while the wealthy have enjoyed rising incomes, record levels of investment in the stock market, and growing corporate profits. In fact, many forms of economic inequality in the United States are now higher and rising faster than in just about any other advanced capitalist nation. One cannot help but to conclude that economic growth no longer promises significant reductions in poverty and inequality as it once did in the twenty-five years following World War II. Instead, prosperous times are now met with persistent inequalities, to say nothing of what will happen when the economy eventually bottoms out.[2]

Although the United States is in the midst of historic economic and social changes, the problem of economic inequality is certainly not a new one. Issues of economic stratification and controversies over distributive justice have been central ones for much of America's history. Yet despite major federal policy initiatives to alleviate inequality in the

1930s and again in the 1960s, economic inequality still stands as one of the most important and visible of America's social problems. What, then, is the response to the enduring problem of inequality at the beginning of this new century? Three distinct perspectives are at the forefront of the debate over the causes of and solutions to contemporary inequality.

First, there is free-market conservatism. Free-marketers blame government programs for doing more harm than good by creating dependency on the government, stifling individual initiative, and constraining business growth. Dubbed the "Reagan Revolution," these ideas have resulted in a wholesale attack on all redistributive institutions of the New Deal and Great Society. But despite their deep commitment to social policy reform, most conservatives have little genuine interest in stemming the rising tide of inequality *per se*. Many even consider inequality a spur to innovation and a necessary condition of free-market capitalism, the intended beneficiary of deregulation. At most, conservatives who are concerned about inequality uphold education as the primary route to upward mobility and place their faith in a privatized educational system. Because the United States already has the most deregulated economy in the advanced industrial world, I use my research findings to let the relationship between the private economy and inequality speak for itself. I therefore say little more about this position as a focused and viable anti-inequality strategy.

Second, there is the U.S. variety of social democracy. Social democrats are centrally concerned with the "new inequality" and consider economic restructuring its root cause. They focus on the fact that secure and family-supporting jobs are much harder to come by now than they were just a generation ago. The rules of the game have been altered by fundamental changes in the economy, they argue, including everything from new technology and international competition to the decline of unions and the rise of temporary work. In response to growing instability and falling wages, advocates have sought to expand the employment-related institutions of the 1930s and adapt them to the needs of the new postindustrial worker. In this view, the federal government should not only provide social services for struggling workers and their families—such as dependent care, health care, unemployment insurance, and the like—but become more involved in steering the economy toward higher growth and productivity through a joint program of technological development and technical training in both the public and private sectors. More controversial would be creative initiatives to shore up institutions such as the minimum wage, unions, and other kinds of workers' associations in order to raise the living standards of low-wage postindustrial workers. What binds these positions together is a joint focus on new economic policies as well as broadly redistributive institutions—whether universal or class-based—to reverse the dislocations of recent structural economic change.[3]

Finally, given a still high degree of employment segregation, civil rights advocates, including feminists and antiracists, focus on the composition rather than the underlying structure of the economy and consider discrimination the most important source of inequality. They defend 1960s-era antidiscrimination policies and especially affirmative action against critics of the right and left who want to do away with race and gender targeting for either strategic or philosophical reasons. Although racial inequality is a more prominent public issue than gender inequality, and there has been a backlash against race targeting especially, most staunch supporters of affirmative action favor both racial and gender targeting. The bottom line is that proactive policies are still considered essential if both subordinated racial groups and white women are ever to achieve equitable access to quality education and employment. Removing discriminatory barriers at work would in turn create the conditions for greater self-sufficiency among the poor, who are disproportionately women and people of color.[4]

In this book I build on these last two perspectives but argue that neither can stand on its own. Each perspective is valuable in its own right but has only a limited grasp of the *total* problem of economic inequality because each perspective narrows its view to only a *particular* type of economic inequality. For those in favor of universal social policies—or, in their absence, class-based redistributive policies—this boils down to an exclusive focus on the new inequality. The new inequality is assumed to be a much bigger and broader problem than racial or gender inequality, thus warranting our exclusive attention. But this sort of argument begs the question: What *is* the relative importance of the new inequality versus racial inequality and gender inequality? Has the new economy made them all one and the same thing or at least radically reduced their differences? Since the only way to judge the relative importance and similarity of different types of inequality is to compare them directly, that is, in essence, the basic objective of this book.

I take advantage of the enormous diversity in the economic and social structure of localities across the United States to compare the levels and sources of gender wage inequality, racial wage inequality, and wage inequality between the college- and non-college-educated—the most commonly cited measure of the new inequality and what I term "class" inequality for short.[5] My focus is not directly on the relative merits of different policies *as such* but on their underlying premises about the causes and structure of wage inequality. In turn, I deploy my findings on the causes and structure of inequality as a springboard for a greatly expanded and certainly more nuanced discussion of the politics of inequality than has so far been offered.

Against the premise that the new inequality is of only one overarching and encompassing variety, for example, I find that there are in fact *configurations of inequality*, in which race, gender, and class intersect in a variety of ways depending on underlying economic conditions in local economies. In one configuration, relatively little class inequality exists alongside considerable gender and racial inequality, an arrangement that describes the Northern industrial centers of the 1950s and sixties. These are the very places that inspired the development of antidiscrimination and affirmative-action programs in the first place. As I show throughout this book, the conditions for such policies are still around, in those same regions as well as in some of our most advanced high-tech cities. That is, although gender and racial inequality may have declined over the long term and at the national level, they have not lost their force in key sectors and regions where the best jobs at all levels are still heavily dominated by whites and by men. Indeed, the configurations reveal that in *no* local economy are all types of wage inequality systematically and simultaneously lower or higher; complex intersections of various dimensions of inequality are the norm. Since contemporary capitalist society is capable of evolving along the lines of any one or more of the configurations I describe in this book, policy and politics can play an important role in determining—either implicitly or, one hopes, explicitly—which path is chosen and which forms of inequality are fostered or mitigated.

The existence of configurations of inequality means in addition, however, that an exclusive emphasis on gender and/or racial inequality is no more accurate than an exclusive emphasis on the new inequality. Whereas the first part of my argument holds that the universal policies and class-based redistribution of the 1930s are an insufficient remedy to the problem of inequality today, the second part contends that so are the antidiscrimination policies of the 1960s and 1970s. The key shortcoming of 1960s-era anti-inequality policies is that they were not designed, nor could they have been, to anticipate the new context of economic restructuring and the new inequality. They were enacted during the peak of twentieth-century American industrial capitalism before the onset of changes that only now are recognized as long-term and structural in nature. Unaware of what was to come, advocates focused on changing the *composition* rather than the underlying *structure* of the economy. Even to this day, much of the discussion of racial and gender earnings inequality revolves not around the impact of economic restructuring but around the barriers to individual advancement—whether equally qualified individuals (with the same human capital) are treated differently based on their race, ethnicity, or gender. What was largely missing from the 1960s, and needs to be recovered from the 1930s, is an appreciation of the impact of changes in the underlying structure of the economy and the new inequality they have spawned.

As will become increasingly clear, I am especially concerned about the lack of a structural perspective in current discussions of gender inequality.[6] By comparison, our understanding of the impact of economic restructuring on racial inequality is much further along, thanks to the seminal work of William Julius Wilson (1987, 1996; see also Morales and Bonilla 1993). The rest of the literature on the new inequality has also been more apt to investigate the racial rather than gender dimensions of the new inequality. This is probably because racial inequality began to rise in the 1980s along with all other forms of inequality except gender inequality (e.g., Moss and Tilly 1991; Bound and Holzer 1993). Perhaps the anomalous case of gender inequality—falling rather than rising—justifies its neglect in the larger literature on restructuring and inequality, but it does not justify the lack of attention to the new environment of economic restructuring in the feminist literature. Much feminist research continues to emphasize the contrast between "low-wage" women's jobs and "high-wage" men's jobs even though such a contrast is simply less salient than it once was in the 1960s and 1970s. Moreover, a focus on such distinctions has the unfortunate consequence of concealing new inequalities among women, especially skills-based wage inequalities that are as high as they are among men.

Given this major gap in the U.S. literature on gender inequality, a primary aim of this book is to bridge the divide between studies of gender inequality and studies of economic restructuring and the new inequality. In my analysis, I do not focus on the gender wage gap alone or on discrimination between equally qualified individual men and women, or view 1960s-era policies *a priori* as the most important anti-inequality policies. Instead, I judge the salience of gender and the potential impact of antidiscrimination policies against the context of economic restructuring, and find them to be vital in some circumstances but not in all. For example, in local configurations where *relatively* little wage inequality exists between men and women and yet there is *relatively* high inequality among women and among men as compared to the average labor market, a gender-based policy of comparable worth or affirmative action will not be the most effective strategy.

In fact, I go so far as to suggest that alternative universal and class-based policies make more sense even where gender inequality is relatively greater, if it occurs in a low-wage and insecure economic environment with high unemployment, high casualization, and low wages for both men and women. Such an environment calls for new institutions and employment relations aimed at sustainable job creation, wage increases, job security, and human capital formation. Not only do these policies make economic sense, they also make political sense, since widespread economic distress tends to foster scapegoating and divisiveness, which is only exacerbated by calls for race- and gender-based preferences (Wilson 1999). Although early feminist and civil rights advocates could not have foreseen the transformations ahead, the new economic era alters the context and puts into question the effectiveness of antidiscrimination strategies *on their own.*

The most effective response to the long-standing problem of inequality will therefore have to acknowledge the new inequality as well as its gendered and racial character. Unfortunately, we have no historical precedent for combining these two very different approaches to understanding and attacking the problem of inequality. Never has the United States sought to curb broad-based forms of class inequality as a result of deep-seated economic change and simultaneously assumed the responsibility of rectifying gender and racial inequality. In the 1930s, Keynesian macroeconomic growth policies were consistent with redistributive social policies, but lacking was a commitment to gender and racial equity.[7] In the 1960s, some policy-makers and civil rights activists were convinced that racial and economic justice had to be intertwined if either was to be realized (such as in Martin Luther King's 1968 Poor People's Campaign), but a strong economy separated economic from racial policy and thwarted the former (Weir 1992). I therefore suggest that since *both* structural dislocations (as in the 1930s) and relative economic prosperity (as in the 1960s) characterize the current period, the tendency to prioritize *either* economic change and class redistribution *or* racial and gender equity will serve us no better than in the past. Each approach falls short of what is needed to deal with the full extent of inequality in all its complexity.

Our challenge, then, is to conceptualize inequality as an outcome of both economic restructuring and gender and racial divisions of labor—what I will refer to as a joint economic and social analysis of inequality. The analysis is economic in the narrow sense that it delves into the underlying economic changes that have transformed U.S. society and examines the key explanations of rising inequality that have been at the forefront of recent research in labor economics. The analysis is social in the sense that it investigates the *social composition* of inequality—its full gender, racial, and class dimensions—and joins empirical research on gender and race to that on class, and vice versa. In terms of the significance of this joint economic and social approach for the *politics* of inequality, I introduce a crucial layer of analysis in investigating the underlying premises that certain policy strategies imply about the causes and structure of inequality. In asking and answering questions about the social outcomes of a range of different economic environments and scenarios, this book has something to say about economic policies of a general nature—including full employment, economic development planning, technical training, wage-setting and workers institutions—as well as about policies that are targeted toward people of color and white women.

As I mentioned above, I examine the economic sources and social composition of inequality through an analysis of local economies defined by the key dimensions of economic restructuring that most people are very familiar with by now. These include the transition to a service economy, an increase in international competition and immigration, the spread of new technologies, the casualization of the employment relationship, the loss of job security, and the decline of formal wage-setting institutions. Using the most comprehensive data sources available to measure these characteristics of local economies, my analysis centers on 1990, the year marking the end of a decade of steep wage declines and increasing wage inequality.[8] I examine more than five hundred labor markets of many varieties: industrial and postindustrial, casualized and high-tech, immigrant-rich and deindustrialized, high-growth and slack. I compare labor markets using macroquantitative as well as case study methods to arrive at distinct patterns of inequality associated with specific economic conditions in regional labor markets. Thus there are configurations of inequality associated with industrial, postindustrial, immigrant-rich, and other core economic characteristics of regional economies. I referred to several of these configurations of inequality above—areas in which gender inequality was relatively low while class and racial inequality were greater, and vice versa.

Detroit and Dallas, for example, represent, respectively, the ideal types of industrial and postindustrial configurations of inequality. The structure of wage inequality in industrial Detroit is the mirror reflection of that in postindustrial Dallas. As might be expected, wage inequality among men and racial inequality among both men and women are lower than average in the prototypical industrial city. However, as one might not expect, gender wage inequality and inequality among women are both considerably higher than average in Detroit and lower than average in postindustrial Dallas. Given these divergences, and many others revealed throughout this book, I argue that it is impossible to conclude that one paradigm or another is the more equitable in general terms, just as it is impossible to pronounce today's postindustrial society more unequal than yesterday's industrial society on all counts. Rather, we need to identify the most extreme divisions in any particular environment and tailor our anti-inequality policies and politics to rectify them.

In order to ferret out these key cleavages and conflicts, this book explores fundamentally comparative questions about the causes of and relationships between different dimensions of inequality. Are the sources of high levels of inequality among women the same as among men (Chapter 6)? Are college- and non-college-educated workers equally penalized by working in low-wage labor markets and do they benefit equally from working in high-wage labor markets (chapter 5)? Do the same factors underlie racial and class inequality among women (chapters 2, 3, and 6)? How are gender inequality and inequality among women related (Chapter 2), and does occupational gender segregation still have the same consequences for gender wage inequality as it once did (Chapter 4)? Equally important are questions about the causes of inequality: whether technology or institutions, trade or industrial shifts, immigration or contingent employment, men's wage trends or women's wage trends have contributed the most to high levels of wage inequality. The answers to these questions will go a long way toward providing the information we need—and currently do not have—to evaluate how the changing structure of the economy is changing the full structure of inequality. This information, in turn, improves our chances of formulating effective and meaningful anti-inequality policies and political strategies. In the next two sections, I address in greater detail the theoretical and then methodological dimensions of this research design, with an emphasis on the reasons for adopting a spatial strategy.

CONFIGURATIONS OF INEQUALITY

As a unifying concept, spatially defined configurations of inequality are particularly well suited to the analysis of U.S. economic and political structures, recent political-economic shifts, and the intersections of gender, class, and race. Perhaps first and foremost, a spatial strategy takes advantage of the fact that the United States is a large country with the most decentralized and deregulated political economy in the advanced industrial world. Historically, the federated U.S. system has explicitly presented ideological and structural barriers to centralized economic planning except on matters of interstate commerce and defense (Markusen 1987). Throughout the twentieth century, Southern opposition to legislation that would have interfered with local labor supply and wage rates foreclosed the possibility of strong national standards on full employment, minimum income guarantees, minimum wages, and collective bargaining rights (Quadagno 1994). Progressive innovation has therefore been left to states and localities, while these same units have served as the primary conduit for government spending on the economy (Osborne 1988).[9] Moreover, decentralization and deregulation have only intensified since the Reagan Revolution rejuvenated the drive toward "devolution" of authority from all levels of government and fostered a new wave of privatization throughout the country (Staeheli et al. 1997). How the United States is now dealing with regional differences and inequalities and how it has in the past have even become of keen interest to members of the newly formed European Union (Leibfried and Pierson 1995; Galbraith et al. 1999).

In addition to devolution of power from the nation-state in the United States, recent international economic and cultural trends have sparked a virtual explosion of interest in the "local" and the local/global continuum more generally (Smith and Katz 1993). In disciplines as seemingly far afield of economics and geography as literature and cultural studies, scholars are valorizing the "local" and the "particular" as a richer representation of how global economic and cultural markets have taken shape in a myriad of contradictory ways (e.g., Appadurai 1996; Holston 1999). In fact, nowadays it is commonplace to describe economic restructuring and the new economy as essentially about the spatially defined process of "globalization"—the worldwide spread and integration of capital, goods, and service markets—even though capitalism has been global in nature, in a highly unequally distributed way, for several centuries (Harvey 1996). When considering the economic workings of global capitalism, then, the question of whether the reorganization of production is actually any less likely to centralize in a few core and semiperipheral cities/countries or whether it is destined to further the process of fragmentation and decentralization is still an open one, as are the centrality and role of the nation-state in that process (Markusen 1999; Schoenberger 1994; Sassen 1998). And as Piore and Sable (1984) pointed out long ago, and many others have since, there are good reasons to think that both can occur at the same time. This uncertainty has spawned a spirited search for economic survival, adaptation, and innovation wherever it can be found. Yet while research on decentralization and globalization continues apace, *detailed empirical* research on the full welfare effects of local economic conditions in a landscape of uneven development lags far behind, a gap configurations of inequality are uniquely able to fill (Markusen 1996).[10]

Given these political and economic realities, this is a particularly ripe moment for the study of social inequality at the subnational level, because local communities are increasingly seen as the most exciting and effective site of social action today. Although recent interest in community-based movements has not supplanted the need for strong international and national standards and sprawling political networks across communities, cities, and nations (Dawson 1997; Mohanty 1997; Weir and Ganz 1997; Keck and Sikkink 1998), it does signal a renewed appreciation of the affective power of "place" and of localities as an especially fertile ground for interest and group formation(Keith and Pile 1993).[11] Not only do local issues and controversies seem more likely to incite activism, but the remoteness of big-money national campaigns and the liquidation of local political party organizations mean that a relatively manageable degree of independent political organization can dramatically change the composition of local governing bodies, such as school boards and city councils. Local organizations have joined together and demonstrated an ability to form diverse, broad, and at times long-lasting alliances and coalitions which encompass and reach beyond the realm of electoral politics and even beyond national borders.*

---

* Kelley 1997; Lawrence and Matsuda 1998; Sassen 1998; Wilson 1999; Orfield 1997; Savitch and Vogel 1996.

Although in this book I cannot pursue the vexing question of precisely how socioeconomic structure and political agency are related, or how this relationship is changing, or how the relationship is articulated across local/regional/national/international boundaries, I can use configurations of inequality to illustrate the crucial, but by no means obvious, connection between local economic and social structure. By identifying exactly what the key social cleavages are, configurations can serve as a sort of starting point, or springboard if you will, for the formation of truly encompassing and intersecting social movements around issues of economic justice and social inequality.

The focus on *local* inequalities also dovetails conceptually with recent feminist theoretical and ethnographic work while broadening it to include more macro-oriented and quantitative analyses of structural inequality. My spatial formulation of configurations of inequality is especially indebted to studies of the intersection of gender, race, and class.[12] I have been particularly influenced by two central developments in this burgeoning field. First is the notion that race, class, and gender are interrelated and constituted in historically and contextually specific ways. This is a relatively familiar refrain in cultural studies and most feminist research; however, as Irene Browne (1993) writes in her edited collection on *Latinas and African American Women at Work*, "quantitative approaches to the intersection of gender, race, and class are rare." Even qualitative studies that are explicitly *comparative* in their analysis of multiple and intersecting dimensions of inequality are rare.

Evelyn Nakano Glenn's (1992) excellent comparative analysis of the gender and racial division of labor across regions and racial-ethnic groups is a singular contribution in this respect. She writes: "[i]f race and gender are socially constructed systems, then they must arise at specific moments in particular circumstances and change as these circumstances change. I have suggested that one vantage point for looking at their development in the United States is in the changing division of labor in local economies" (p. 31). Glenn analyzes the direct hierarchical relationships between white women and women of color in specific occupations in which the interdependence between them is explicit. I take a more macrocomparative approach and attempt to illuminate the sources of structural inequality between white women and women of color across a large number of local economies. I delineate the sources of racial inequality and elaborate on how they frequently differ from those of gender inequality and class inequality. Like Glenn, I expose conflicts of interest between different social groups of women to challenge assumptions of universal interests among them. The growing college/noncollege divide among women becomes an especially persistent one in the discussion of local configurations of inequality.

Cross-national research on the comparative position of women in capitalist welfare states has also served as one of the intellectual inspirations of this spatially oriented project (Treiman and Roos 1983; Rosenfeld and Kalleberg 1990; Charles 1992; Orloff 1993; Blau and Kahn 1995). According to these studies, the key factor explaining variation in gender relations across countries is the character of the nation's political institutions, which ranges from social democratic to conservative corporatist to liberal (Esping-Andersen 1990). A critical contribution of feminist work on the welfare state has been to reveal the conflicts in these institutions between reducing gender inequality on the one hand and reducing family income inequality on the other (Orloff 1993). In particular, reducing labor force inequality among men has reinforced the gender division of labor at home, a prime source of gender inequality in the workplace. In a similar vein, I substitute subnational regions for national units in a comparative analysis of how economic restructuring affects gender and other forms of inequality in different ways. I essentially import and adapt the macrocomparative approach and its emphasis on institutional explanations of gender inequality to the U.S. context, a context in which most previous research has focused on micro (that is, human capital) explanations of gender and racial wage inequality. Against the backdrop of long-term structural inequality, then, I use configurations of inequality to frame the considerable degree of contextual variation I find across labor markets, as comparativists do across nations.

The second more specific development in feminist research that I build upon is not connected to the spatial design of this study as such, but is more broadly conceptual in nature. It is also evident in Nakano Glenn's (1992) study of relations of inequality between white women and women of color. As she and many other feminist theorists have demonstrated, gender cannot be understood simplistically as an uncontentious, independent category of individual and group identity—gender relations are embedded in racial and class relations, just as much as racial and class relations are mediated by gender. One of the more important implications of this formulation is that women are involved in relations of inequality not only with men, the central theme of white feminist theory, but with other women as well (Alarcon 1991). As a result, the nature of differences among women, especially racial differences, is at the heart of feminist theory and research today. Even in the social sciences, one can find a number of excellent studies on economic inequality between black and white women in the United States,[13] though even the most recent of these also tend to be micro-oriented studies in the human capital tradition (England et al. 1999). In contrast, there has been little in the way of unraveling the relationship between gender and class, in terms of either class inequality among women or gender inequality by class. In this book I take up both as central to the analysis of economic restructuring and social inequality and even counterweight the analysis more toward class differences than racial ones.

My intention, then, is to offer a new methodological framework for analyzing the full range of intersectionality, one that is concerned with multiple, overlapping, conflicting, and changing structures of inequality. In other words, the analytical complexity currently found in qualitative studies of identity and representation—which now constitute the center of women's studies—needs to be brought to bear on the neglected terrain (in feminist scholarship) of structural inequality.[14] In this endeavor I echo and respond to Nancy Fraser's exhortations to feminists to revisit the pressing issue of social inequality, which was once central to second-wave feminist studies at its inception (Fraser 1997, 2000). I take up the issue of inequality using the methods that I think offer the best insight into its structural complexity and in the process I hope to demonstrate why quantitative investigations of multiple dimensions of social inequality need to be on the feminist research agenda. This undertaking does have a cost, though. A joint and integrated analysis of gender, race, and class on this scale has never been done, and so the daunting complexity of the analysis and especially the findings was surprising, frankly, even to me. I have attempted to smooth over the twists and turns wherever possible, but a certain degree of complexity is simply intrinsic to the subject matter.

In sum, there are empirical, political, and theoretical payoffs to examining economic restructuring and social inequality at the subnational level. Political and economic decentralization are key tenets of the organization of American society that have been made all the more salient by the new devolutionism and the accelerating international mobility of capital and labor. Innovative social movements are responding to this new environment by creatively constructing alliances across divisions of class, gender, and race. Yet at the same time they are operating in an analytic vacuum about exactly how economic change is altering their communities. The macroquantitative and case-study evidence that this book provides enters this vacuum by rooting social inequality in its local economic context, linking economic analysis to its social consequences, and bridging the analysis of one dimension of inequality to the analysis of other dimensions of inequality. Configurations of inequality join economic and social analysis as a way to bridge the divide between economic and social policy—between trade, macroeconomic, and local economic development policies on the one hand, and anti-inequality and antidiscrimination policies on the other. Understanding when gender and racial inequality are not reducible to overall or class inequality, and when changing economic conditions affect gender/racial inequality as well as class inequality, will enable the development of theory and policy to deal simultaneously, as it must to be successful, with economic restructuring and the high and rising levels of inequality of all kinds that it has spawned and perpetuated.

THE MESOCOMPARATIVE METHOD

In order to investigate an oftentimes bewildering array of inequalities and an equally complex set of factors associated with economic restructuring, I bring together the strengths of the case-study and macrocomparative methods. As Paul Krugman has said, "a particularly good way to understand the American economy is by studying American cities," which is why the urban case-study approach is "growing in popularity among economists" (Krugman 1996: 205–206). And, of course, this approach is nothing new to geographers and planners. I follow in this vein by trying to isolate "naturally occurring" instances of specific labor-market conditions, such as deindustrialization and immigration, in order to determine how these characteristics are associated with different dimensions of inequality (Blanchflower and Oswald 1994; Card and Krueger 1995). This approach is premised on the fact that *labor* markets are predominantly local, in the sense that matching between individuals and jobs is uniquely produced in local labor markets;[15] that *production* is unevenly spread across geographical areas; and that much of our cognitive as well as policy orientation to economic restructuring is anchored by ongoing transformations occurring in specific *places*, such as Detroit, New York, Chicago, Silicon Valley, and Miami. One has only to witness the proliferation of case studies on these cities to appreciate this point (e.g., Wilson 1987; Zukin 1991; Sassen 1991; Portes and Stepick 1993; Saxenian 1994; Waldinger 1996).[16]

Drawing from the macrocomparative method, I also analyze variation across more than five hundred labor markets in the United States in 1990 to determine whether the patterns found in any one labor market hold up across similar cases after controlling for other factors. In the flurry of excitement over the "local" and the discovery of spatial diversity as something to exploit methodologically and conceptually, there has been little attention to two main issues: 1) how to define the geographical scale of the "local" in either a metaphorical or a literal sense (though I will be dealing with only the latter), and 2) whether broader and more general conclusions can be extrapolated from case studies of particular localities (Neil Smith 1992; Harvey 1996). While case studies of labor markets with specific characteristics abound—an influx of immigrant workers or high-tech employment, to name a few—they are rarely compared to one another or investigated in terms of their effects on more than one dimension of wage inequality.

The approach I develop examines whether the outcomes of case studies are consistent across similar cases and dimensions of inequality and whether the generalizations of national-level studies are evident throughout localities. In turn, this information should guide in the further development and design of more contextualized case studies. I begin by addressing the first issue of defining the local but then turn quickly to the more important of the two issues: the need to develop a more systematic approach to analyzing spatial variation, one that situates the strategically chosen case study within a broader interpretive, explanatory, and political framework.

What I term a "meso-level" analysis examines economic conditions and social outcomes in subnational labor markets (Massey 1984; Peck 1989, 1996). The basic elements of this approach have been employed by geographers, economists, and sociologists, but there is considerable diversity in the groups of workers studied, the aspects of local economic conditions measured, and the scale of geographical units selected. This latter issue has been a particularly contentious one among geographers who are the most invested in conceptualizing what is meant by place, locality, and, more prosaically, a regional labor market. I cannot engage the enormity of this theoretical debate here, so I focus on the more technical issue of how to define a regional labor market. Minimally, it seems to me to refer to the institutional conditions governing how workers and jobs are matched in concrete local settings, "the scale at which labor markets are lived" (Peck 1996: 112; see also Hanson and Pratt 1992). This definition is appealing because it also signals one of the most fundamental processes of social order in the making under conditions of socioeconomic change, a topic of long-standing interest to sociologists of gender and racial inequality (Wilson 1987; Reskin and Roos 1990; Kirschenman and Neckerman 1991; Fernandez Kelly 1995).

Yet because there is no satisfactory way to define labor market boundaries according to this or any other conceptualization, in practice variation in labor market outcomes is investigated across a wide range of geographical units, including broad census regions, states, metropolitan areas, and counties. The most common of these is the metropolitan area, termed the regional labor market by Morrison (1990). Although the metropolitan area has become the preferred unit of analysis, it does have drawbacks. The principal one is its inclusion of many smaller, more local, and nonoverlapping labor markets. A more obvious drawback is its exclusion of nonmetropolitan areas. As discussed in more detail in the Technical Appendix, the scale of labor market I chose was constrained by available data sources and by my interest in investigating wage variation across metropolitan as well as nonmetropolitan areas. In my analysis, then, I use the term "regional labor market" to refer to the smallest labor markets available in census microdata, which are composed of county parts, intact counties, or county groups. These may be smaller than metropolitan areas but not as small as what

Morrison considers a "local" labor market, which is organized around one or more related establishments. Nevertheless, for the sake of simplicity, I use "regional labor market," "local labor market," "regional economy," and "local economy" interchangeably to describe this "meso" unit of analysis.

The question of how to delimit a labor market spatially will perhaps never be answered to anyone's satisfaction. Fortunately, it is much easier to answer the question of why inequality ought to be studied at the meso level—with some fuzziness as to its precise scale—and what we can gain from such a study if properly conceived. In a certain sense, the answers to this question are best provided in relation to a specific research question about a specific dimension of inequality or a particular locality, and these will certainly be provided in much greater detail in the chapters to come. However, in this section my aim is to provide a general argument about the strengths and weaknesses of the mesocomparative method. I first provide a more precise definition of this method, which includes a more technical definition of configurations of inequality, and then divide the discussion into empirical and analytical reasons for adopting it in the study of restructuring and inequality.

What, then, is the mesocomparative method? First, it builds on what is simply known as the comparative method. Ragin (1987: 4) identifies the multilevel character of the comparative method as what makes it distinctive. The comparative method "proceeds at two levels simultaneously–at the level of systems and at the within-system level . . . [I]deally, system-level variables should be used to explain variation across systems in within-system relationships." This is a mouthful, but the basic point of comparative research according to Ragin is to explain *how and why relationships between two or more outcomes within systems vary across those same systems.*

If we substitute dimensions of wage inequality for "outcomes" and substitute regional labor markets for "systems," then the basic point of our endeavor is to explain *how and why relationships between two or more dimensions of inequality within labor markets vary across labor markets.* In contrast, an analysis is *not* comparative when a single outcome is the primary object of analysis. This occurs when, for example, racial inequality as an outcome is considered in separate studies from gender inequality and both of these in separate studies from overall family income inequality. This is how most labor market analysis is done, with completely separate literatures on racial inequality, gender inequality, inequality among men, and family income inequality. Continuing with this example, the comparative framework as practiced in this book involves an analysis of how gender and racial inequalities are related within a regional economy, and then how the relationship between gender and racial inequality varies across regional economies with different economic conditions. Although the burden of analysis expands exponentially with the inclusion of two or more outcomes, this step is needed to account more fully for complex, multidimensional relationships of inequality.

More formally, if any two or more dimensions of wage inequality are each associated with a particular type of regional economy, I conclude that those dimensions of inequality are themselves jointly related in a configuration of inequality. For example, if labor markets that have undergone more severe deindustrialization than the average labor market are associated with greater gender inequality but lower class inequality among men, I would group each of these elements together into a single "industrial" configuration of inequality. This particular configuration would illustrate the contrasting effects of deindustrialization on gender and class inequality and would pit these two against each other in any assessment of the welfare effects of (de)industrialization. In this way, the comparative approach emphasizes relationships among inequalities and embeds intersecting relationships among gender, race, and class inequality within the context of economic restructuring. *In short, a configuration of inequality is a unifying concept that brings together in a single formulation the relationship between constitutive dimensions of the new economy and multiple dimensions of social inequality.*

There are several empirical and analytical reasons why social scientists should be interested in this approach, some of which have already been touched on above. First, and most important, regions undergo different paths of economic development, and these different paths have consequences for labor market outcomes. Xie and Hannum (1996) demonstrate this point well in their research on inequality in China, which they show varies significantly across regions because economic development polices themselves are regionally targeted and then institutionalized over time. Card and Krueger (1995) also demonstrated this point famously in their research on the unemployment effects of the minimum wage, which they showed were minimal to nonexistent in those states with higher minimum wage laws. More generally, strategic trade theory has been developed to account for the fact that profitable high-technology and export-oriented industries require large infusions of capital, research and development, and infrastructure and therefore concentrate in a limited number of strategic locations with government assistance (Tyson 1992; Markusen and Howes 1993). And finally, we have long known that the mobility of capital is motivated by the search for place-based resource advantages, whether such advantages are "permanent," as in the case of raw material resources, or "temporary," as in the case of human resources.

As this body of research suggests, regional variation often occurs intentionally as a result of policy, but it may also occur haphazardly as a result of historical accident or rationally as a result of a geographically based accumulation strategy or equilibrium process (Harvey 1996; Fujita, Krugman, and Venables 1999). Either way, communication, information, and transportation costs are often minimized when firms in the same or related sector locate in the same region, leading to increasing economic returns for firms as a result of factors that are actually external to the firm (what economic geographers and regional economists call externality effects) (Quigley 1998). Regional variation is then enhanced by the fact that particular industry groups develop and concentrate in only a small number of regions and cannot be replicated across the country simply because there is not an unlimited demand for that industry group's products. As a result, even the most advanced industries (or, perhaps, especially the most advanced industries) become bound to places with heavy fixed capital investments (Sassen 1998). Regional heterogeneity therefore has a certain short-term stability to it and as such provides a natural opportunity to explore social and economic change and variation while holding the national policy environment constant (Card and Krueger 1995). Moreover, variation across regions is often much greater than over relatively large blocks of time and there are a larger number of units with which to explore such variation systematically (Blanchflower and Oswald 1994; Freeman and Rodgers 1999).

A second and third empirical characteristic of regions that I discuss together are that they are, by definition, 1) smaller and more comprehensible than the monolithic U.S. economy, and 2) relatively encompassing economic and social entities. In other words, they are both small and integrated enough to absorb shocks throughout their territories. Jargowsky (1997) has proven this point well by showing that neighborhood poverty is more a function of metropolitanwide levels of income and income inequality than of neighborhood-specific characteristics. Similarly, it would not be sensible to measure the effect of immigration on "overall" wage levels or wage inequality for an entire labor market, as many researchers of immigration have done, if this were not the case (Borjas et al. 1996). This does not mean that everyone is affected equally. In fact, it is crucial to recognize that different groups of workers will be affected differently. But it does formalize what everyone knows intuitively: that whole regional economies are affected by shocks such as unemployment even though not everyone is unemployed (Blanchflower and Oswald 1994). In short, I would argue that these characteristics, especially small size and identifiable character, are what make regions a popular topic of case study analysis.

Without these three empirical characteristics of regions—that they vary widely in policy, history, and composition, that they are of a small and comprehensible character, and that they have an integrated and encompassing dynamic—there would be no justification for using subnational economies as units of analysis. Fortunately these characteristics enable us to formulate a number of useful analytical questions about the nature of restructuring and inequality.

The first avenue opened up in a spatial examination of inequality is the ability to investigate the kind of within-system relationships of interest to comparativists and at the heart of configurations of inequality: How are different types of inequality related to one another? Because inequality is rising among both men and women, among families, and within racial groups, it might be assumed that all forms of inequality are higher wherever "overall" inequality is higher. But there are many reasons to be suspicious of this logic of reducing one form of inequality to another. Gender, race, ethnicity, educational background, and region position workers at different points in the wage distribution and in the labor market, and economic conditions affect different parts of the wage distribution and the labor market in different ways. What may benefit one group could intentionally or unintentionally harm another group. Thus including or excluding these groups from the analysis will affect perceptions about the seriousness of wage inequality, the sources of wage inequality, and the solutions to wage inequality.

For example, centers of Fordist manufacturing have long served as the ideal typical regional economy with high wages and low inequality among men, replaced only recently by the ideal post-Fordist industrial district (Piore and Sabel 1984). Yet until now, there has never been any investigation of whether inequality among women or gender inequality is also lower in such economies. Similarly, in terms of racial inequality, Moore and Pinderhughes (1993), Tienda (1995), and others have argued that the focus on industrialization and deindustrialization is less relevant to the economic situation of Latinos because they were never concentrated in Northern industrial regions where industrialization and deindustrialization were most intense.

Because of the potential diversity and complexity of outcomes, then, I begin with the most elementary question of whether the same factors are associated with high levels of one dimension of inequality but low levels of another dimension of inequality. To counter the focus on male and family income inequality in particular, one of my main goals is to provide a benchmark study of differences in the spatial distribution of multiple forms of inequality. Such differences would expose the inadequacy of summary measures frequently used as key independent and dependent variables in cross-metropolitan studies of poverty and other issues (e.g., Jargowsky 1997; Nielson and Alderson 1997) as well as in over-time studies. I explore these same themes and raise similar doubts about the representativeness of summary measures of gender inequality, such as occupational gender segregation and the average gender wage gap. In each set of comparisons, I argue that conceptualizing inequality as configurations of inequality decenters any single measure of average or overall inequality and shifts attention to the changing and contingent relationship between multiple and competing opportunity structures in regional economies.

The second comparative question enabled by spatial analysis is the ability to compare competing explanations of inequality. In terms of explaining gender inequality, this book's analysis will be the first empirical one on the role of recent structural economic changes, shifting the whole frame of reference from individual human capital differences between men and women to economic conditions that alter the gendered division of labor and wages. As for explanations of other dimensions of inequality, most previous regional labor-market studies tend to be incomplete in their focus on only one explanatory factor at a time and potentially misleading in not controlling for alternative explanations. By expanding the scope of typical labor-market analysis to include multiple dimensions of restructuring, we open the possibility of discovering a variety of factors implicated in the restructuring of inequalities. We can also compare the relative strength of the major explanations of inequality in accounting for spatial variation in wage inequality.

As the chapters ahead show, for example, technology does not emerge as the leading determinant of high levels of skills-based wage inequality in 1990, even though many economists now consider it by default to be the prevailing explanation of rising skills-based wage inequality over time. Instead, I have found that characteristics of what I term a *deinstitutionalized* labor market—with flexible and insecure employment conditions arising from high joblessness, casualization, and immigration—result in more wage variability and higher wage inequality, especially among women. It seems that the breakdown of employment institutions and the increase in economic insecurity among workers, especially non-college-educated workers, is a more direct cause of skills-based wage inequality than is skills-biased technological change, whose impact is *mediated* by other, more fundamental features of the local economic environment (McCall 2000a, 2000b).[17]

This brings us to the last analytical question opened by a spatial analysis. It has already been mentioned, but I want to make it more explicit: a spatial analysis enables us to investigate the causes of high *levels* of inequality. It is almost as though researchers have skipped over the analysis of levels of inequality because the current preoccupation is with rising inequality (which, by the way, ignores the countertrend of declining gender inequality, but we will leave that aside for now). Of course, understanding the nature of the time trend is extremely important, but it has come at the expense of a firm understanding of what causes high levels of inequality, a more persistent social problem. We need to know more about both the time and the spatial trend to prevent conflating the two. For instance, inequality could be rising in all postindustrial societies or rising fastest within postindustrial regions while the absolute level of inequality is still much lower in postindustrial regions than in other parts of the country. One might therefore erroneously conclude that postindustrialism is the cause of inequality and a new industrialism is the solution. A spatial analysis is able to investigate this question directly in much the same way cross-national analyses differentiate between the correlates of levels and changes in inequality.

I would like to close out this section by finally turning to some of the weaknesses of the mesocomparative analysis of inequality as I have conceived it. First, I have just argued that it is dangerous to attribute the causes of temporal patterns (rising inequality) to those of spatial patterns (high regional levels of inequality). Likewise, it would be inappropriate to draw temporal conclusions from spatial patterns. For example, if high-tech regions are not high-inequality regions (by class or between skill groups), at most this can raise questions about *how* technology is implicated in the national pattern of rising inequality. Is it generating inequality *between* high-tech and low-tech regions rather than within them? Is the effect of technology so dispersed as to be unobservable through regional analyses? In other words, since technology's impact could be revealed in a number of different ways, a null finding on the relationship between high-tech regions and the level of local inequality cannot be used as evidence against technology's role in rising inequality.

This is not to say, however, that there is no relationship whatsoever between temporal and spatial patterns. Knowing the conditions associated with high local levels of inequality *may* help us envision future outcomes if those outcomes are becoming more or less prevalent. If we know that inequality is systematically lower where joblessness is lower, for instance, this can bolster the argument in favor of full employment as an anti-inequality policy at the national level (Freeman and Rodgers 1999; Galbraith et al. 1999). If we know that gender inequality is systematically worse in high-tech regions, then promoting high-technology development without affirmative-action programs could be considered a gender-biased economic development policy that potentially sets back the clock on gender equity. These are the ways in which spatial configurations are relevant not only to localities and local politics but to national policy discussions.

A second shortcoming of cross-sectional analyses is better known: they are unable to truly discern causal processes or any dynamic processes at all; that is, they are static in nature. I do not and cannot offer the type of rich, textured case study that examines processes of change; and I do not and cannot avoid methods and language that have the effect of fixing and reifying localities. At best I can establish associations between dimensions of restructuring and components of inequality, albeit temporary or short term, and justify their directions of causality theoretically. Future panel and longitudinal studies at the regional and national level should be the basis for exploring and confirming such causal claims and dynamic processes more generally. The "how" of configurations of inequality is explored in more detail in a comparative case study of Dallas and Detroit in chapter 3 using data from 1980 and 1990, but several important questions about the mechanisms underlying differences in the configurations of inequality in these two cities still remain unanswered. This is even more true of the other cities discussed in chapter 2. Despite these limitations, the importance of spatial configurations of inequality is hopefully clear enough to raise these further questions as deserving of serious scholarly attention in future studies of restructuring and inequality.

SUMMARY OF CHAPTERS AND FINDINGS

In the chapters that follow, I present detailed evidence for the existence of spatial configurations of inequality. The next two chapters provide a descriptive analysis of gender, class, and racial wage inequality in several strategically chosen cities with distinct economic structures. These two chapters also extend the analysis from 1990 to an earlier period (1980). The first of the two chapters gives an analytical overview of configurations of inequality while the second delves more deeply into the mechanisms underlying them. In chapter 2, I define four configurations of inequality and introduce four cities that serve as ideal types for the four configurations (postindustrial Dallas, industrial Detroit, immigrant Miami, and high-tech St. Louis). For purposes of comparison, I also discuss the configurations in global cities receiving the lion's share of case-study attention—New York, Los Angeles, Silicon Valley/San Francisco, and Chicago, the first three of which are a combination of immigrant-rich and postindustrial configurations. This chapter establishes the basic contours of the configurations of inequality and focuses in particular on the college/noncollege divide, which turns out to be surprisingly important in defining the gender-related dimensions of the configurations.

In chapter 3, I turn to an in-depth comparative case study of postindustrial Dallas and industrial Detroit. I selected these two cities as a way to compare profiles of inequality in industrial and postindustrial regional economies, but I also selected them because the comparison reflects in many respects the cross-national comparison between Europe—with its more developed wage-setting institutions, higher unemployment, and lower wage inequality—and the United States—with its flexible labor markets, low unemployment, and higher wage inequality. The level and structure of inequality in Dallas is in fact a mirror reflection of that in Detroit. However, contrary to the implications of cross-national research, in neither city is inequality lower for all measures. Since gender, class, and racial differences in relative levels of inequality are prevalent *within* both cities, the contrast between the two cities points to a number of conflicts over the normative value of economic development strategies that reduce some forms of inequality while fostering others. Industrial configurations are especially problematic in that they promote gender inequality and inequality among women, while postindustrial configurations are more deeply marked by class inequalities among men and racial inequalities among both men and women. Based on these two cases, I argue that neither industrialism nor postindustrialism on its own represents the better, more equitable path of economic and social development. Rather, the weaknesses of each path need to be exposed and addressed in order to promote across-the-board equality.

The configurations discussed in chapters 2 and 3 are neither anomalies nor merely descriptive. They are based on patterns found in a systematic analysis of more than five hundred labor markets presented in chapters 4 through 6. While chapters 2 and 3 present configurations of inequality in their entirety, chapters 4, 5, and 6 narrow the focus to a particular dimension of inequality. Narrowing the focus on one end allows the focus to be expanded on the other: I examine a wider range of economic conditions than was possible in the case studies, including most of the key characteristics of economic restructuring. I group these into the three categories of industrial composition and shifts, technology and trade, and flexible and insecure employment conditions. By the end of these three chapters, I will have compared the effects of restructuring on (1) occupational gender segregation and the average gender wage gap (chapter 4), (2) the gender wage gap for the college-educated and for the non-college-educated (chapter 5), and (3) the college/non-college wage gap for men and for women (chapter 6). These more focused comparisons of just a few components of inequality at a time in chapters 4 through 6 challenge current thinking in several major areas of research on inequality.

Chapter 4 examines the impact of economic restructuring on the supposedly tight relationship between occupational gender segregation and the gender wage gap. This relationship is crucial to any discussion of gender inequality, because remedying the harmful effects of segregation on the wage gap is at the root of the two main gender equity policies of our era: comparable worth and affirmative action. My main argument is that shortly after these policies were developed, and while they were being implemented, unforeseen changes in the economy put some of their core assumptions into question. In particular, it seemed that segregation could actually persist in the face of a falling gender wage gap if wages were declining for men *in men's jobs*. Drawing insight from international research that shows a weak correlation between segregation and the wage gap across countries, I analyze their covariation across the five-hundred-plus labor markets in my sample. In the analysis, I do not follow previous research in specifying the gender composition of occupations as the explanan and the gender wage gap as the explanadum. Rather, I run two parallel models, with the wage gap as the outcome in one model and the occupational segregation index as the outcome in the second model. In doing so, I find that, like the cross-national evidence, the trajectories and causes of the two are not the same in regions across the United States. I therefore argue that the emphasis of research and policy should shift from occupational gender segregation to the dynamics of wages and wage inequality more directly.

Having focused on the average gender wage gap in chapter 4 in order to simplify the discussion, I demonstrate the inadequacies of average measures of gender wage inequality in chapter 5. I take a closer look at regional wage differentials by gender and education, and show that there are several "spatial routes" to gender wage inequality that 1) differ according to the educational background of workers, and 2) differ from the dominant temporal explanation of the narrowing gender wage gap, which emphasizes the role of men's declining wages. I discuss, for example, low-wage labor markets in which the relative wage penalty is greater for low-skilled women than for low-skilled men, thus highlighting the importance of analyzing women's wage trends separately from men's and the wages of low-skilled workers separately from those of high-skilled workers. Remarkably, I also found *no correlation* between labor markets that had a high gender wage gap for the college-educated and those that had a high gender wage gap for the non-college-educated. I conclude that what may foster equality for some groups of women will not necessarily do so for other groups of women. This makes the *average* gender wage gap—the most commonly cited statistic of women's economic status and the focus of nearly all previous research on gender wage inequality—a poor predictor of the distribution and concentration of gender inequality.

Given these education-based differences in wage trends and in gender wage inequality, I turn my attention to the growing wage gap between the college-educated and non-college-educated in chapter 6. In addition to gaining prominent popular attention as the "new class divide," the college/noncollege distinction has been at the heart of recent research in labor economics on rising earnings inequality. Comparing the sources of the gap for men and women across labor markets in 1990, I first show that the gap is actually greater among women than among men—previous literature has focused on men—and then demonstrate that nearly every dimension of labor market structure has different effects on the female gap than on the male gap. Flexible and insecure labor markets with high rates of joblessness, casualization, and immigration play an especially strong role in fostering inequality among women to a much greater degree than technology or trade-related factors, which are currently the prevailing explanations of rising inequality. Thus more attention to the problem of inequality among women seems to bring with it further support for the role of institutional conditions, and especially increasing insecurity among workers, in fostering inequality. More generally, though, these results suggest that the most taken-for-granted measures of "overall" inequality are not representative of all forms of inequality nor especially of conflicting dimensions of inequality, and therefore might provide misleading information in the discussion of how to reduce inequality.

Equipped, then, with new information on the effects of economic change on multiple and conflicting dimensions of inequality, the concluding chapter returns once again to the history and politics of inequality in the twentieth century. I first explore the dynamics of economic change and social policy formation in the 1930s, 1960s, and in the current period in greater historical detail than at the beginning of this chapter. In the current period, the United States reflects key aspects of both the 1930s and 1960s, namely deep structural dislocations and economic prosperity. We therefore need broad redistributive economic policies to alter the underlying structure of the economy, as in the 1930s, and can afford social policies to eradicate gender and racial divisions of labor, as in the 1960s. But the key justification for this dual perspective is the existence of configurations of inequality. They bring intersecting structures of inequality into clear view, showing how different paths of economic change remedy some forms of inequality but foster others. It is this reality that in the end requires and demands a joint gender, class, and racial perspective.

Part I

Chapter Two

CONFIGURATIONS OF INEQUALITY:
INTERSECTIONS OF GENDER, CLASS, AND RACE

Although generally gender, class, and racial inequality are all unacceptably high, there are highs and lows in different places. The spatial unevenness of inequality and the fact that it appears to be mostly non-random allow us to investigate two major questions about the nature of inequality. First, what are the causes of inequality? In the spatial context, this translates into a question about whether there are certain places that systematically foster inequality and others that systematically reduce it. Since some "paths" of economic development (for instance industrial, postindustrial, and so forth) are clearly concentrated in particular geographical regions, we can examine whether such paths of development are associated with low or high levels of inequality. We can also investigate whether there are multiple paths to the same outcomes; that is, whether there are several different types of regional economies that have low inequality and several different types that have high inequality. If there are multiple paths to low inequality, for example, we can compare the relative merits of alternative paths in an attempt to fashion the best policies to reduce inequality. The conditions that foster low inequality can be enhanced and replicated in other areas and anti-inequality policies can be targeted to areas with high inequality.

The second question enabled by the spatial concentration of inequality concerns the relationship between different dimensions of inequality. Do gender, class, and racial inequality follow similar or radically different patterns? If the latter, what are those patterns? In essence, the answer to this set of questions is derived from the answer to the first question about the causes of inequality, but only if we rephrase that question in a way that considers the sources of multiple dimensions of inequality. The rephrased question, then, is whether the underlying causes of inequality are the same for gender, race, class, and all other forms of inequality. If the causes are the same for multiple forms of inequality, the relationship between different dimensions of inequality is fairly straightforward. Different dimensions follow similar patterns, and we do not need to investigate each and every form of inequality because we can assume that all forms of inequality arise from essentially the same sources. A measure of "overall" inequality would be a sufficient indicator of the structure of inequality.

If, however, the causes are *not* the same for different forms of inequality, then gender, race, and class inequality should be examined on their own terms, distinct from indicators of overall inequality. From an anti-inequality perspective, this suggests that the significance of gender, race, and class varies depending on whether a particular environment fosters inequality of that type. In areas with significantly higher gender inequality and lower class and racial inequality, for example, gender might emerge as the primary marker of inequality, while the opposite would be true in areas with significantly lower gender inequality.

I bring the answers to these questions together in a *configuration of inequality*, a unifying concept that defines the economic conditions associated with unique combinations of gender, race, and class inequality. To offer empirical evidence of configurations of inequality, this chapter assembles together a wide array of descriptive measures of wage inequality, leaving the more systematic evidence to later chapters (chapters 4 through 6). The discussion centers on four cities exhibiting four different configurations of inequality. Each configuration represents a key "path" of economic development as well as a unique pattern of gender, class, and racial inequality. Although there are surely more than just these four configurations of inequality, they were the most robust to emerge from the multivariate analyses in chapters 4 through 6, and each demonstrates in a different way the need to situate the analysis of one type of inequality within the context of other forms of inequality and their underlying economic conditions.

To illustrate briefly how configurations of inequality work and why they are necessary in any discussion of the politics of inequality, consider for a moment the problem of how to interpret the meaning of a low level of inequality among women. If we find that inequality among women is significantly below average in city X, should we applaud city X and hold it up as a model of egalitarianism? The answer is: it depends. It turns out that a finding of lower inequality among women can mean one thing if it occurs alongside higher gender inequality and another if alongside lower gender inequality. In the former case of higher gender inequality, one could argue that lower inequality among women is *illu-*

sory because it results from the crowding and segregation of women in low-wage jobs; whereas, in the latter case, one could argue that lower inequality among women is genuine because it results from opportunities for women to earn higher wages at the bottom.

The interpretation of lower inequality among women also depends on the surrounding economic conditions. If inequality is lower in an economically depressed and backward region, this might be an example of what some have called "equality in poverty" or "harmonizing downward" (Armstrong 1996). Alternatively, if inequality is lower in a high-wage, high-tech region, this might be an example of genuine progress. As many more examples will show, only a rich synthesis of information on gender, race, class, and local economic conditions enables us to interpret fully the causes of inequality, the consequences of inequality, and the remedies to inequality. This is especially true for certain dimensions of inequality, such as inequality among women, whose meaning is more interdependent with other dimensions of inequality. Inequality among men, by contrast, has a more straightforward interpretation because it is not dependent on the extent of gender inequality.

I begin in the first section with a brief description of the method and measures used in the empirical analysis. This is followed in the second section by a discussion of how measures of gender, class, and racial inequality are correlated across a large number of labor markets in the United States. It is from these correlations that the general contours of the configurations are developed, first for the relationship between gender inequality and inequality among women, and then for inequality among men and racial inequality. Whereas the second section focuses exclusively on the relationships among different components of inequality, the third section introduces the cities and the economic conditions associated with them—industrial Detroit, postindustrial Dallas, high-tech St. Louis, and immigrant Miami. Each city was selected to represent one of the four configurations of inequality. Since much has been written on the major cities of New York City, Los Angeles, Chicago, and the region of Silicon Valley, the fourth section compares the structures of inequality in these cities to one another and to the ideal types represented by the four main cities. Finally, I close with some brief theoretical and policy-related comments, which will be developed in greater detail in the next and concluding chapters.

REGIONAL COMPARISONS AND MEASURES OF INEQUALITY

For many of the reasons already discussed in the first chapter, I take subnational regional labor markets in the United States as the "meso" unit of analysis in this comparative study. One of the main advantages of the regional approach is that national policies are not a factor in affecting local conditions because they should apply everywhere. A second advantage unique to the United States is that the localized process of economic development is unimpeded for the most part by the leveling effects of strong national regulations. In the relatively deregulated, deinstitutionalized, and flexible labor and competitive product markets of the United States, institutional environments are constructed locally from a unique combination of labor-market composition, industrial mix, and local economic development policies. Although income disparities between regions and states are less than between nation-states in Europe and have diminished over the long run in the United States, there is evidence of rising regional disparities since the mid-1970s, and subnational variation on a variety of economic and social indicators is at least as great as variation over periods of twenty or more years in the post-World War II period (Amos 1988; Barro and Sala-i-Martin 1990; Galbraith et al. 1999; Freeman and Rodgers 1999). Moreover, there is growing political interest in regional spaces as nation-state authority devolves and capital becomes both more localized and internationalized at the same time (Sassen 1998; Holston 1999).

Despite the difference in units of analysis, comparing levels of inequality across regions within the same country is very similar to the more common practice of comparing levels of inequality across nations. In fact, the cross-national research of Francine Blau and Lawrence Kahn (1995) provides a model for the approach I take in this chapter by examining two forms of inequality at a time, rather than the more typical practice of looking at only a single measure of inequality. They examined how the relationship between wage inequality among men and gender wage inequality varied across countries, and found that countries with less overall inequality, as measured by a more compressed wage structure among men, also have less gender inequality. They found that there was less distance between men and women because there was less distance between the top and bottom more generally. This was fortunate in that it meant that there was no conflict between reducing two forms of inequality—inequality among men and gender inequality. The two went hand in hand.

I take a similar approach to variation across subnational labor markets and ask whether lower inequality of one type is accompanied by lower inequality of another type. In contrast to Blau and Kahn's results, though, I find that measures of male wage inequality are not adequate reflections of the relative opportunities available to all groups. Indeed, we could dispense with the whole notion of a configuration of inequality if the patterns of every dimension of inequality could be assimilated to one overall measure of inequality, but in no environment did I find this to be the case. In other words, there is no model city in my estimation. Therefore my emphasis is on differences *within* regions in relative levels of gender, class, and racial inequality as well as variability *across* regions in the relationship between economic conditions and economic inequality.

In terms of measures of inequality, I will be examining a relatively large number of measures as compared to previous studies. Most are fairly common, such as the female/male, black/white, Asian/white, Latino/white, and low-percentile/high-percentile (for instance, tenth/nineteenth) hourly wage ratios. Perhaps more controversial is my use of wage ratios between college- and non-college-educated workers as a proxy for class inequality. The primary reason for this choice is the growing visibility and attention to skill differences in the new economy and in particular the recent emphasis on the college/noncollege wage gap as the central expression of these differences. Although education has always been a central marker of social class in the United States, and therefore held up as the solution to nearly every social problem, it is certainly a new sign of the times that we now regularly hear news reports of the latest trends in the college wage gap. Even President Clinton in his 1999 State of the Union address described the increasing gap between the rich and the poor as "really a skills gap."

But while the belief in higher education as the solution to inequality is widespread in the popular imagination, it also has its roots in the research literature. "Skill-biased technological change," or a relative increase in the demand for high-skilled workers, is the preferred term used by labor economists to explain falling wages among non-college-educated workers and rising wages among the college-educated (Levy and Murnane 1992). Other social scientists more apt to use the language of "class" have also seized on the growing importance of skills-based inequalities in the new economy (e.g., Bluestone and Harrison 2000). For instance, in their study of American voters, Teixeira and Rogers (2000: 15) define the "new white working class" as those who lack a four-year college degree and who are "the vast majority—three-quarters—of white adults who have not fared well over the last quarter-century." On the other side of what they call the "Great Divide" are the "quarter of white adults who have a four-year degree or more and for whom the last twenty-five years have been a time of substantial economic progress."

To maintain consistency, then, I focus on two college wage gaps: between those without a high school degree and those with a college degree or more (the LHS/COL ratio) and between those with a high school degree and those with a college degree or more (the HS/COL ratio). I selected these two measures because both refer to differences between the college- and non-college-educated (rather than between those with *some* college and those with four years or more) and there is likely to be more of a class difference between the groups. I also consider the role of education in my analysis of gender inequality. The average female/male wage ratio is calculated for the entire sample and separately for those with less than twelve years of schooling, a high school degree, some college, and a college degree or more. These distinctions turn out to be critical in the interpretation of gender inequality. Given the smaller sample sizes of racial groups in labor markets, I disaggregated the racial measures only by gender and not by education. Likewise, the measures of gender inequality are not disaggregated by race-ethnicity. These are some of the unfortunate limitations of working with data that are disaggregated by detailed region. Lastly, the measures are all hourly wage ratios, so that a high value represents greater parity and equality, whereas a low value represents greater inequality.

INTERSECTIONS OF WAGE INEQUALITY

Given the intrinsic complexities of a joint gender, class, and racial analysis, I orient the discussion around gender inequality and class inequality among women as the building blocks for the four configurations of inequality. Rather than examine the simple correlations among all the measures of inequality, I highlight the relationships between 1) measures of gender wage inequality broken down by education and 2) measures of class inequality broken down by gender. This allows us to focus on the intersection between gender and class and why it turns out to be so central to the analysis of inequality. While I take gender inequality and class inequality among women as the starting points, the question of how racial inequality and class inequality among men fit into the configurations framework is addressed throughout the discussion.

CORRELATIONS OF GENDER, CLASS, AND RACIAL WAGE INEQUALITY ACROSS LABOR MARKETS

The correlations of measures of inequality across a large number of labor markets are presented in table 2.1. A positive coefficient indicates that places with *lower* levels of gender inequality tend to have *lower* levels of class and racial inequality as well. Since coefficients can always be interpreted in two directions, a positive coefficient also indicates that places with *higher* levels of gender inequality tend to have *higher* levels of class and racial inequality as well. If all of the coefficients were positive, this would suggest that a single measure of inequality could represent all measures of inequality. In contrast, a negative coefficient indicates that places with *lower* levels of gender inequality tend to have *higher* levels of class and racial inequality (and vice versa). Negative coefficients would therefore suggest that gender inequality is not concentrated in the same areas as class and racial inequality, and thus different measures would give us different cues about the local structure of inequality. We could also draw similar conclusions from the strength of the coeffi-

Table 2.1 Correlations among Gender, Class, and Racial Wage Inequality across Labor Markets, 1989

GENDER INEQUALITY (FEMALE/MALE HOURLY WAGE RATIOS) BY EDUCATION GROUP

	LHS (1)	HS (2)	SC (3)	COL (4)	AVG (5)
Class Inequality among Women (Noncollege/College Hourly Wage Ratios)					
(1) LHS/COL	.42	.03	.05	-.36	-.07
	(.00)	(.46)	(.21)	(.00)	(.10)
(2) HS/COL	.12	.44	.22	-.60	.02
	(.00)	(.00)	(.00)	(.00)	(.69)
Class Inequality among Men (Noncollege/College Hourly Wage Ratios)					
(3) LHS/COL	-.54	-.47	-.24	.32	-.27
	(.00)	(.00)	(.00)	(.00)	(.00)
(4) HS/COL	-.34	-.62	-.32	.38	-.30
	(.00)	(.00)	(.00)	(.00)	(.00)
Racial Inequality among Women (Nonwhite/White Hourly Wage Ratios)					
(5) Black/White	-.22	-.29	-.20	-.02	-.23
	(.00)	(.00)	(.01)	(.79)	(.00)
(6) Latina/White	-.01	-.22	-.22	-.05	-.17
	(.89)	(.00)	(.00)	(.47)	(.02)
(7) Asian/White	-.09	-.40	-.27	.13	-.20
	(.19)	(.00)	(.00)	(.06)	(.00)
Racial Inequality among Men (Nonwhite/White Hourly Wage Ratios)					
(8) Black/White	-.33	-.41	-.32	.18	-.25
	(.00)	(.00)	(.00)	(.01)	(.00)
(9) Latino/White	-.28	-.30	-.23	-.06	-.26
	(.00)	(.00)	(.00)	(.38)	(.00)
(10) Asian/White	-.29	-.38	-.27	-.09	-.34
	(.00)	(.00)	(.00)	(.23)	(.00)

Note: Significance levels are in parentheses. Sample includes adult working population, ages 25–64, with hourly wages between $1.00 and $250.00. For correlations between female/male wage ratios and education-group wage ratios, the sample consists of 554 regional labor markets. For correlations between female/male wage ratios and racial wage ratios, the sample was restricted to the 200 labor markets with the largest sample sizes.

LHS = < 12 years of schooling; HS = 12 years; SC = 13-15 years; COL = 16 or more years.

For further details on the sample of 554 labor markets, see the Technical Appendix. Data taken from the 1990 5% Public Use Microdata Sample of the Census of Population.

cients. Very weak positive coefficients, which can range from 0.0 to 0.2 on a scale from 0.0 to 1.0, would indicate only a small overlap in the conditions that foster inequality of different kinds, but not very much overlap.

Glancing at the coefficients one row at a time, we see a mix of positive and negative coefficients; most of the coefficients are weak or moderate in strength but highly significant. There are a few nonsignificant coefficients in the first row, and a few in the last two columns, which is evidence of a lack of overlap among the various dimensions of inequality. I will comment on these after first discussing three important observations that the correlations reveal about the distinction between the college- and non-college-educated. This distinction turns out to be one of the central features of configurations of inequality.

First, *lower* gender inequality among the college-educated tends to be accompanied by *higher* class inequality between college- and non-college-educated women. Labor markets with higher female/male ratios among the college educated tend to be the same areas in which the ratio of noncollege to college wages is lower among women. This inverse relationship between gender and class inequality is indicated by the negative coefficients in column 4 and rows 1 and 2. These findings may seem intuitive at first (I discuss other possibilities later). As women advance to the top and reach parity with men at the top, the female wage structure stretches out, and high-skilled women inevitably climb further away from low-skilled women. *Thus whatever produces a climate of less gender inequality among the most educated workers must also be responsible for greater inequality between the most and least educated women.*

The findings are also intuitive if looked at in reverse. They suggest that class inequality among women is lower in those areas where there is greater gender inequality among the college-educated. That is, inequality among women is lower not necessarily because of disproportionate gains by less-educated women but by virtue of a more entrenched system of discrimination in which college-educated women are more deeply excluded from the top echelon of male-dominated jobs (or at least the wages associated with such jobs). These interpretations are the very possibilities that make it necessary 1) to interpret inequality among women within the context of gender inequality, which is not necessary when analyzing inequality among men, and 2) to interrogate whether the gains of well-educated women are equally shared by less-educated women.

A second important pattern to note is that *lower* gender inequality among the non-college-educated tends to be accompanied by *lower* class inequality between college- and non-college-educated women. Labor markets with higher female/male hourly wage ratios among the non-college-educated tend to be the same areas in which the educational wage ratios among women are also higher. This is indicated by the positive signs on the coefficients in columns 1 and 2 and rows 1 and 2. *From the perspective of less-educated women, this indicates greater parity with less-educated men as well as more-educated women.* These findings would be especially promising if driven by absolute gains among the majority of working women who do not have college degrees. But even if lower levels of gender inequality at the bottom are driven more by declines among men, at least these correlations point to a context in which there are more similarities between working-class men, working-class women, and middle-class women than in the average labor market. Gender boundaries would appear to be breaking down among the less educated and not leading to greater inequality among women in the process. At the very least, then, these circumstances lead to significant and multiple relative gains for non-college-educated women. A more alarming scenario is implied if these findings are looked at in reverse: there appear to be places where women at the bottom are there alone—further away from both similarly skilled men and higher skilled women.

A third important pattern to note from table 2.1 is that the distinction between the college- and non-college-educated also stands out when comparing gender inequality to class inequality among men. What differs is that the correlations run in the opposite direction to those between gender inequality and class inequality among women. Where the college wage gap among men is *lower*, gender inequality tends to be *higher* on average and for each educational group except the college-educated (note the negative coefficients in rows 3 and 4). *Thus, for most workers, those areas fostering a more equitable environment among men are among the most unequal by gender.* Among the college-educated, in contrast, gender inequality is actually lower in environments with lower inequality among men. These differences are especially noteworthy given the centrality of male inequality to recent studies of inequality and restructuring, suggesting that there may be a trade-off between gender inequality among the majority of non-college-educated workers and class inequality among men. Looked at in reverse, places that *do* achieve a lower gender wage gap among most workers are likely to see a higher college/noncollege wage gap among men and a higher gender wage gap among the college-educated. In such places, well-educated men are at a greater distance from all other groups, including college-educated women, non-college-educated men, and non-college- educated women.

These associations between class inequality among men and gender inequality are very similar to the patterns between racial and gender inequality. The racial correlations are somewhat stronger among men and between blacks and whites, but the direction of the association is generally the same across the board. Each of the six measures of racial inequality is *inversely* related to *average* levels of gender inequality (as indicated by the negative coefficients). That is, local labor markets with *less* of a gender wage gap between the average female and male worker tend to have *more* of a wage gap between racial groups. Just as there was a trade-off between gender inequality and class inequality among men, now there appears to be a trade-off between gender and racial inequality as well. As before, there are also notable differences between the college- and non-college-educated. Racial inequality tends to be higher where gender inequality among the non-college-educated is lower (a negative relationship) and lower where gender inequality among the college-educated is lower (a positive relationship).

These measures of inequality between racial groups are not as highly correlated with gender inequality, but they are consistent enough for us to speculate about at least one profile of inequality that links many of these race, gender, and class dimensions together. This particular profile illustrates well the need for contextual interpretations of inequality and for reading the "whole" structure of inequality as more than just the sum of its parts. In this profile, the simple correlations I have just reviewed point to a number of potential trade-offs, at least on the surface, between 1) *lower* racial inequality, class inequality among men, and gender inequality among the college-educated on the one hand, and 2) *lower* class inequality among women and gender inequality among the non-college-educated on the other. Lower levels of inequality in the first group do not tend to be accompanied by lower levels of inequality in the second group. But there may very well be more consistency than initially appears. Suppose for the moment that we throw low wages among less-skilled men into the mix as a factor in those areas with less gender inequality at the bottom and less class inequality among women (that is, those areas falling into group two). And recall that such areas tend to have higher inequality of all other forms listed in group one—gender inequality among the college educated, class inequality among men, and racial inequality.

Now, read together, these correlations point to the elevated position of well-educated white men relative to all other groups, and thus greater "equality in poverty" among all other groups. Instead of focusing on the better position of non-college-educated women relative to non-college-educated men and college-educated women in the second group of cities, we can focus on their absolute position at the bottom and their worse position relative to highly educated men. Instead of highlighting the conflict between gender on the one hand, and race and class, on the other, gender must be read *contextually* in relation to the larger structure of inequality. Such a reading suggests that such environments are more unequal in terms of race, class, and gender. However, when we turn to the profile that is the inverse of the one just described and is more akin to group one, it is there that we should identify gender as one of the primary markers of inequality in the local economy.

Before going on to a more formal discussion of configurations of inequality, I said I would return to the question of why some of the correlations are weak and nonsignificant and what this says about the intersection of inequalities. The weak and nonsignificant coefficients are primarily between the female skills-based wage ratios and the gender wage ratios. Note especially that the level of wage inequality between college- and non-college-educated women is *not correlated at all* with the average level of gender inequality. This means that the average gender wage gap is a poor predictor of the shape of the female wage distribution, while the gender wage gaps among the college- and non-college-educated are much stronger predictors. This may seem plausible, even obvious, if one recalls the discussion above about what intuitively seems like a zero-sum logic between gender inequality and inequality among women. As the argument goes, when college-educated women become more like college-educated men (between-group inequality declines), they become less similar to less-educated women (within-group inequality increases).

But in fact there is no reason to assume a zero-sum logic here. Wages could rise to the same degree across the female distribution, or even rise more at the bottom, so that the gender wage gap falls at both the top and bottom of the distribution. The weak-to-nonexistent correlations between the female LHS/COL wage ratio and three of the female/male wage ratios means that the significance and direction of the other correlations are by no means "natural," as does the fact that most of the racial inequality measures are not correlated with the gender wage gap among the college-educated. The lack of strength and significance in these few cases only makes the distinctiveness of the shape and strength of the other patterns stand out. In short, these findings reveal the existence of unique and contrasting profiles of inequality in regional labor markets, ones that should not be taken for granted nor hidden by aggregate measures of inequality.

CONFIGURATIONS OF GENDER AND CLASS INEQUALITY: A FIRST STEP

Drawing from the evidence above, figure 2.1 presents a graphical and more formal display of four possible relationships between gender inequality and class inequality within gender groups. To simplify the presentation, the diagrams refer to only four categories: college- and non-college-educated women, and college- and non-college-educated men. The horizontal dimension features the wage gap between men and women separately for the college- and non-college-educated. This dimension represents patterns of gender inequality and the effect of educational background on gender inequality. The vertical dimension features the wage gap between college- and non-college-educated workers separately for men and women. This dimension represents patterns of class inequality and the effect of gender on class inequality. The overall shape of each diagram conceptualizes a different configuration of inequality: Shorter horizontal and vertical lines indicate less distance between the groups and therefore less inequality, whereas longer lines indicate greater distance and greater inequality.

In figures 2.1a and 2.1b, the horizontal lines are parallel and of the same length, and the vertical lines are also parallel and of the same length. These two configurations illustrate environments of gender symmetry in the level of class inequality and class symmetry in the level of gender inequality. That is, there is no interaction between class and gender because class does not affect the level of gender inequality and gender does not affect the level of class inequality. In contrast, figures 2.1c and 2.1d have lines that are neither parallel nor of the same length. These configurations illustrate environments of asymmetry in levels of both gender and class inequality. Gender and class interact to produce different levels of gender inequality by class and different levels of class inequality by gender. Although figures 2.1a and 2.1b share similarities in form, as do figures 2.1c and 2.1d, the content and significance of each of the four configurations are unique. I elaborate on each in turn.

Figure 2.1a portrays an environment in which there is less class inequality among men and among women but greater inequality between them, regardless of educational background. The long and parallel horizontal lines of figure 2.1a indicate a greater wage gap between men and women while the short, parallel vertical lines indicate a smaller gap between the college- and non-college-educated. Although there is greater class equality for both men and women, the meaning of lower inequality among women can be fully comprehended only within the context of gender inequality. Because gender inequality is greater in this configuration, and thus women as a whole appear to be excluded from well-paying jobs, what we are left with is a genuine reduction in inequality among men and an only illusory reduction in inequality among women. The greater gender inequality produces a gender difference in the qualitative character of class inequality, and thus gender becomes doubly important—signaling greater inequality between men and women and a more skeptical reading of inequality among women. Gender is therefore the key marker of inequality in this configuration. In contrast, gender is less central in the configuration represented in figure 2.1b. Gender inequality is lower regardless of educational background, and there is no gender difference in levels of educational wage inequality. The college/noncollege wage gaps are extremely high among both men and women, making class a more important marker of inequality than gender.

Figure 2.1A   The Relationship between Gender Inequality and Inequality within Gender Groups

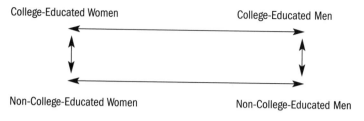

College-Educated Women   College-Educated Men

Non-College-Educated Women   Non-College-Educated Men

Figure 2.1B

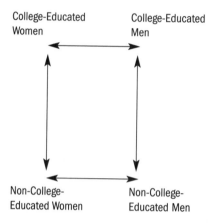

Figure 2.1C

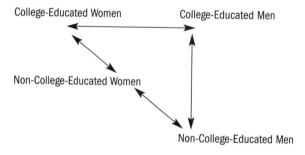

Figure 2.1D

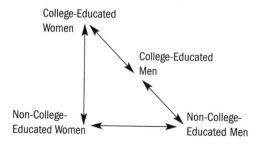

The configurations of inequality in figures 2.1c and 2.1d are quite a bit more complicated. Differences by education in patterns of gender inequality are accompanied by differences by gender in patterns of class inequality. Class and gender interact to create differences in the extent of gender inequality for the college- and non-college-educated and differences in the extent of educational wage inequality for men and women. These configurations resemble the profiles of inequality discussed above, in which the college/noncollege divide figures prominently. Figure 2.1c represents the case in which class inequality among women and gender inequality among the less-educated are both lower, but only in the context of higher inequality among men and higher gender inequality among the college-educated. This is the environment in which racial inequality is likely to be higher as well.

The inverse of this profile is represented by figure 2.1d, in which inequality among women and gender inequality among the less-educated are both much higher, while inequality among men and gender inequality among the college-educated are much lower. Racial inequality is also likely to be lower here as well. Whereas the first two figures discussed above presented either gender (in fig. 2.1a) or class (fig. 2.1b) as the primary marker of inequality, these second two figures show a more complex intersection of gender, race, and class. In one figure (2.1c), white, well-educated men are at a greater distance from all other groups. In the second figure (2.1d), less-educated women are more deeply entrenched at the bottom relative to all other groups. Thus each figure offers a different account of the significance of gender, race, and class in the overall structure of inequality.

It is a very short step from these heuristic diagrams to the configurations of inequality presented in table 2.2. This two-by-two table represents, again, the intersection of gender inequality and class inequality among women. The columns represent whether the relative level of gender inequality differs for the college- and non-college-educated (that is, whether there is an interaction between gender and class). In column 1, there is no interaction and gender inequality is either greater (cell A/fig. 2.1a) or lower (cell B/fig. 2.1b) than the average labor market for each educational group. Educational differences in the spatial layout of gender inequality are represented in column 2. Above-average levels of gender inequality among the college-educated are represented in cell C (fig. 2.1c), while below-average levels of gender inequality among them are represented in cell D (fig. 2.1d). The rows simply distinguish between lower and higher class inequality among women. As we will see in the next section, the levels of male class inequality and racial wage inequality (among men and women) in the cities I have selected generally conform to the patterns of class inequality among women found in column 1, but not to those patterns found in column 2. Even though the

Table 2.2 Configurations of Inequality

| | GENDER WAGE INEQUALITY BY EDUCATION | |
	SAME ACROSS EDUCATION GROUPS	**DIFFERENT ACROSS EDUCATION GROUPS**
Class Inequality among Women Is Low	A: Gender Inequality Is High for All Groups	C: Gender Inequality Is High for College-Educated and Low for Non-College-Educated
	(St. Louis)	(Dallas)
Class Inequality among Women Is High	B: Gender Inequality Is Low for All Groups	D: Gender Inequality Is Low for College-Educated and High for Non-College-Educated
	(Miami)	(Detroit)

Note: Rankings relative to the average regional labor market in 1990. For example, cell D indicates that some dimensions of restructuring in labor markets are associated with less gender inequality among the college-educated, greater gender inequality among the non-college-educated, and greater education-group wage inequality among women, all relative to the average labor market.

main conceptual framework is construed in terms of gender inequality and class inequality among women, the following discussion of four cities focuses on the intersection of the full set of inequalities, including inequality among men and racial inequality.

Economic Restructuring and Inequality in Four U.S. Cities

Now that we have established that the structure of inequality associated with any given place is a unique intersection of gender, class, and racial inequality, the next step is to determine the conditions that foster each profile of inequality. The complete framework suggested by a configuration of inequality incorporates relationships between multiple dimensions of inequality as well as multiple dimensions of economic restructuring. With the individual parts of the framework developed in the previous section in mind, we can now consider the full scope of configurations of inequality as they are expressed in four major cities in the United States.

The selection of these cities was guided by several criteria. First, each city had to be relatively well known as a regional economy specializing in some key segment of the economy or having some other key characteristic of the recent period of restructuring. Detroit and Miami are good examples of this criterion. Detroit is the leading symbol of the old industrial heartland with its concentration of blue-collar, unionized jobs in quintessential mass production industries. Miami, in contrast, is a major city of the New South that is home to a large influx of immigrants from the Caribbean and Latin America and also serves as a hub for economic trade throughout the Americas.

Second, it would be best to avoid regional economies that were a complex blend of factors related to economic restructuring. Most case-study research has focused on such economies, namely New York, Los Angeles, and Chicago, and I consider them later. I am more interested in *isolating* important elements of a restructuring economy in order to assess their independent effects on inequality. St. Louis was selected for this very purpose. It represents a regional agglomeration of the high end of the high-technology aerospace and defense industries and is known for little else (I restrict my analysis to St. Louis County and St. Louis city, where these industries and their supplier networks are concentrated). Most other high-tech regions, such as Seattle and Silicon Valley, are also centers of advanced-producer and high-technology services and have significant shares of immigrant workers. In St. Louis, the effects of high-technology manufacturing are not conflated with these other factors. Likewise, Dallas represents a postindustrial service economy that is dominated neither by high-technology manufacturing nor by immigrants to the same extent as many other postindustrial service cities such as New York City and San Francisco.

Third, I was especially concerned to select cities with significant populations of blacks, Latina/os, and Asians, and with distinct patterns of racial inequality. This is because the geographical imbalance in racial composition and the small sample sizes of many labor markets make the multivariate analyses of racial inequality less reliable than the analyses of other measures of inequality (but see chapter 6 and McCall 1999, 2001).

Fourth, in keeping with temporal trends, inequality should have risen between 1980 and 1990 for every within-gender measure of inequality and fallen for every between-gender measure. The consistency with trends over time highlights the extraordinary differences in the levels and structures of inequality over space.

Finally, cities were selected that could represent the economic past (Detroit) as well as different aspects of the economic future (St. Louis, Dallas, and Miami). Although the multivariate analyses in chapters 4, 5, and 6 were conducted with 1990 data, measures of inequality for each of the four cases in this chapter were calculated for 1980 and 1990. This permits a somewhat longer- term perspective on each configuration of inequality, even though I focus my attention on the spatial comparison in 1990 because the relative position of each city was the same in 1980 and 1990.

HIGH-TECH ST. LOUIS

St. Louis is a region heavily reliant on the aerospace and defense industries and was essentially spared from defense industry downsizing until the early 1990s. While my analysis of 1990 data should not be affected by major defense-industry restructuring, auto-industry employment did fall over the course of the 1980s, as it did in other industrialized regions of the Midwest. Since St. Louis had the defense industries to fall back on, the St. Louis economy in 1990 should represent the configuration of inequality associated with a local economy dominated by and specializing in high-technology manufacturing industries. Since these are not industries that can easily be replicated in other areas, our interest in St. Louis is not necessarily as a model of economic development that can be exported to other regions. Rather, our interest is in an environment that approximates some of the features of advanced industrial districts formed around large, core, technology-intensive manufacturing companies that tend to employ a disproportionately large corps of skilled production, technical, and professional (engineering) workers. These are the very conditions of demand that are supposed to spark a resurgence in technical skill acquisition and high-wage employment, which should in turn rectify the poor earnings performance of low-skilled workers and trigger a decline in inequality (e.g., Piore and Sabel 1984; Harrison 1994). This should particularly be the case for St. Louis's variety of high-technology industries, which, unlike other high-technology industries such as electronics, tend to have high union density.

The question is what *kind* of inequality (if any) is lower in a regional economy like that of St. Louis? The levels of inequality for St. Louis and Miami are presented together for purposes of comparison in figures 2.2, 2.3, and 2.4. The average levels of inequality in the metropolitan areas of the United States are also provided for comparison, and Table 2.3 summarizes the patterns of inequality relative to the U.S. metropolitan average. Judging by the inequality data, St. Louis occupies the first cell of table 2.2 (cell A/fig. 2.1a), in which gender inequality is above average regardless of educational background, and wage inequality between educational groups is lower for both men and women. As can be seen in figure 2.2, the ratio of hourly wages between workers at the bottom and workers at the top of the educational hierarchy tends to be above average for men and for women in both 1979 and 1989, an indication of less class inequality. But as can be seen in figure 2.3, the female/male ratio for St. Louis is below average for every educational group in both 1979 and 1989, an indication of greater gender inequality. The average 1989 female/male ratio (0.668) is just slightly above the lowest level of the four cities in Detroit (0.657).

In figure 2.4, racial wage ratios are also slightly below average between African Americans and whites, suggesting greater racial wage

Figure 2.2 Class Inequality in Miami and St. Louis, 1979 and 1989

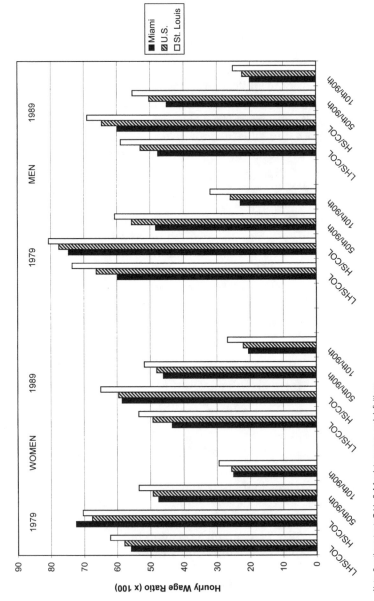

Note: See the notes to Table 2.4 for data sources and definitions.

Figure 2.3 Gender Inequality in Miami and St. Louis, 1979 and 1989

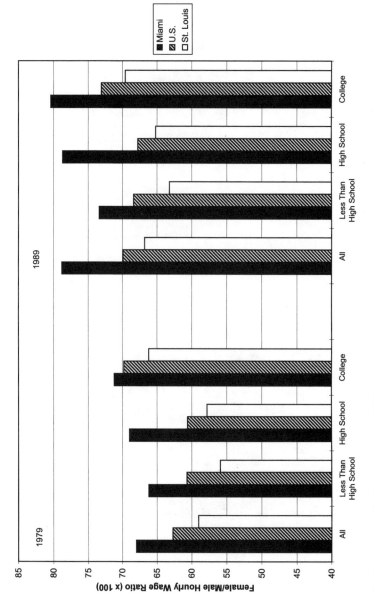

Note: See the notes to table 2.4 for data sources and definitions.

Figure 2.4 Racial Inequality in Miami and St. Louis, 1979 and 1989

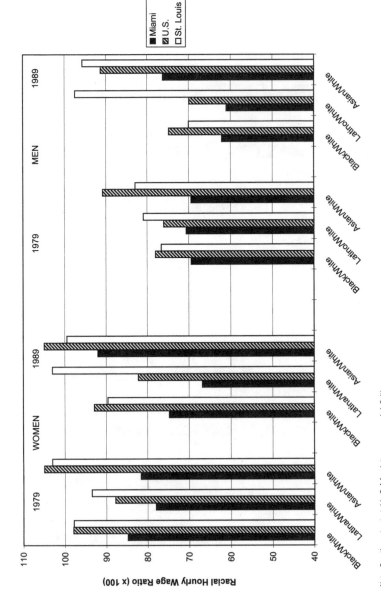

Note: See the notes to table 2.4 for data sources and definitions.

Table 2.3 Wage Inequality by Class, Race, and Gender in Four Cities Relative to the National Average for Metropolitan Areas, 1989

TYPE OF WAGE INEQUALITY	ST. LOUIS (HIGH-TECH MFG.)	MIAMI (IMMIGRANT)	DALLAS (POSTINDUSTRIAL)	DETROIT (INDUSTRIAL)
1. Class Inequality among Men	Lower	Higher	Higher	Lower
2. Class Inequality among Women	Lower	Higher	Lower	Higher
3. Racial Inequality among Men	Higher	Higher	Higher	Lower
4. Racial Inequality among Women	Higher	Higher	Higher	Lower
5. Gender Inequality (Average level)	Higher	Lower	Lower	Higher
6. Gender Inequality among College-Educated	Higher	Lower	Higher	Lower
7. Gender Inequality among Non-College-Educated	Higher	Lower	Lower	Higher

inequality among men in particular, while they are above average between whites and Latino/as, suggesting less racial wage inequality. Since a disproportionately small share of the workforce is Latino/a or Asian (1 percent of all workers) as compared to African American (13.7 percent of all workers), I emphasize the greater levels of black/white inequality in my discussion of racial inequality. Also, the black/white wage ratio deteriorated over the 1980s, and blacks are much more likely to be unemployed than are all other groups of workers (the black unemployment rate was 16.7 percent in 1990, compared to 6.4 percent overall).

In keeping with the configuration expressed in figure 2.1a, reduced class inequality among men is the main benefit of St. Louis's specialization in high-technology manufacturing. Although inequality among women is below the U.S. metro average, this stems from the exclusion of college-educated women from high-wage jobs, rather than from greater opportunities for less-educated women. St. Louis is often thought of as a typical Midwestern industrial city, but in fact Detroit pays above-average wages to college-educated women while St. Louis pays below-average, a pattern also found among women employed as managers and professionals (results for Detroit are shown in chapter 3). Lower inequality among women, then, is primarily a result of fewer opportunities for women workers across the board, and not advances among less-skilled women, as the large gender wage gap at the bottom also indicates. This discriminatory environment might theoretically contribute to lower racial inequality among women (and wage gaps are actually below average between whites and Latinas and even registered declines over the 1980s), but black/white racial wage inequality among women as well as among men is above average and greater than in 1979, though racial inequality among women is still much lower than among men (0.896 versus 0.700). Thus, with the exception of a small number of Asians and Latinos who have achieved wage parity with whites, it is mainly class inequality among white men that is diminished in St. Louis. Not surprisingly, this may be the very group policy-makers implicitly have in mind when they advocate high-technology manufacturing development to reverse the rising tide of inequality.

Immigrant Miami

While gender inequality is one of the most serious forms of inequality in St. Louis, Miami's immigrant-rich economy had the lowest level of gender inequality of the four cities in both 1979 and 1989 and one of the lowest in the country more generally. Miami resembles St. Louis in its absence of educational differences in levels of gender inequality, but this time all female/male ratios are above the national average for metropolitan areas. Gender inequality is especially low among the college-educated, with a female/male ratio of 0.800. Although higher gender wage ratios are a key indication of greater equality between men and women, they do not necessarily imply that gender is irrelevant to the local system of inequality. An environment that is more conducive to gender equality directs our attention to other components of inequality that are more extreme by national standards and may be interacting with gender in locally specific ways.

For instance, class and racial inequality are above the national average for both men and women, forming a configuration of inequality similar to the one shown in figure 2.1b. With a large nonwhite majority (two-thirds) in the labor market, this configuration is undoubtedly influenced by the immigrant and racial composition of workers. Class inequality is higher in part because inequality *within* racial groups flourishes, with a population of high-wage/high-skill as well as low-wage immigrant workers, especially among the heavily Cuban population in Miami. This can be true even as a small minority of white men and women occupy many of the top jobs in the local economy and people of color are disproportionately located in lower-paying jobs at the bottom. In addition, gender inequality is typically lower among workers of color because of disproportionately lower wages among men of color. Greater gender equality extends even to the college-educated because the racial wage gap among men is so much greater than among women (0.684 versus 0.803), a sign that average wages among college-educated men must be quite low because men of color are a large portion of that group.

This portrait contrasts with other portraits of immigrant cities, particularly in its gender-related dimensions. Immigration has figured prominently in explanations of declining wages and increasing inequality, but gender inequality has never been of much interest in these debates. Where it has, most of the research emphasizes the employment of poor immigrant women in sweatshops and low-wage factory jobs in import-sensitive industries (Hossfeld 1990; Sassen and Fernandez Kelly 1991). This portrayal of a city such as Miami is a largely correct one, especially when researchers link it to a low-wage, flexible, and informal labor market for both men and women. However, economic polarization in immigrant-rich cities is rarely understood to be a characteristic of the *female* wage distribution, since women are conceived of only in terms of being on the bottom of a dualistic hierarchy. The pattern is much more complex than this. Inequality among women is greater in cities with immigrant concentrations, particularly between the most- and least-educated (as indicated by the LHS/COL measures), and between racial groups. Meanwhile college- as well as non-college-educated women take home wages more on par with comparably educated men than they do in other cities. Although it would clearly be inaccurate to declare gender irrelevant to the structure of inequality in these cities, it would also be misleading not to bring deep class and racial divisions to the fore, among women as well as men, as the most significant markers of inequality in regional economies with concentrations of immigrant workers. A multidimensional interpretation of the structure of inequality reveals a more complex configuration of gender, race, and class than that put forward by previous claims of immigration's polarizing effects.

Industrial Detroit and Postindustrial Dallas

Conforming more to the asymmetries exhibited in figures 2.1c and 2.1d, the structures of inequality in Dallas and Detroit are considerably more complex than those in St. Louis and Miami (the graphs for Dallas and Detroit are presented in chapter 3 along with a more detailed analysis of these two configurations). Unlike the latter two cities, the degree of gender inequality varies by education, and the degree of class inequality varies by gender. Equally important, the patterns of class inequality among men and racial inequality do not follow the same structure as class inequality among women. Inequality among women is inversely related to inequality among men and racial inequality. Apart from these similarities in form between Detroit and Dallas, the configuration of inequality in Detroit is the reverse of that in Dallas. Inequality among women and gender inequality among the non-college-educated are above average in Detroit and greater than in Dallas. At the same time, class inequality among men and racial inequality are both below average in Detroit and lower than in Dallas. As if these apparent conflicts were not enough, gender inequality among the college-educated is also below average in Detroit and lower than in Dallas.

These differences in the structure of inequality stem in no small measure from differences in the structure of the economy and in the composition of the labor force, but they are not necessarily the differences that we would expect. If we think of Dallas as a prototypical postindustrial economy with a regional concentration of high-end producer services and without many of the complicating factors found in cities like New York and Los Angeles, we might expect greater equality between men and women across the educational hierarchy. This hunch is derived from two sources. First, if as a country we are now considered to be in a postindustrial stage of economic development, postindustrial regional economies should exhibit the lower levels of gender inequality that have accompanied postindustrialism at the national level. Second, and related, the image of the successful professional woman tends to be associated with the rise of urban postindustrial services. Occupational integration has supposedly taken place through the entrance of highly educated urban women into professional and managerial positions at unprecedented rates. In contrast, we have no reason to expect that college-educated women or professional and managerial women would do relatively well in a classic industrial economy such as Detroit's.

But what turns these common perceptions on their head, as I show in the next chapter, is that college-educated women's wages are pegged to the middle of a high rent-capturing male wage distribution in Detroit. Their wages are elevated relative to college-educated women in other labor markets, men of all educational levels in Detroit, and non-college-educated women in Detroit. Racial minorities *who are employed* also benefit from a traditional Fordist industrial economy with strong wage-setting institutions. In fact, Detroit is the only city of the four in which racial inequality is below average across the board. Although racism is by no means neutralized, it is clear that the level of racial inequality is significantly reduced, with both men and women of color employed in occupations benefiting from union wage premiums. For men, this means skilled and unskilled blue-collar jobs; for women, the professions and management. Without similar institutions, Latina/os and blacks in Dallas are relegated to a low-wage, flexible labor market in which unemployment is lower, job growth is greater, but racial inequality and class inequality among men is also much greater. College-educated women in Dallas are also not able fully to take advantage of high wages at the top of the occupational hierarchy. They, like other groups of women, less-educated men, and racial minorities, are at a greater distance from white, well-educated men, especially, I would assume, in the advanced and high-technology services that dominate the postindustrial base of the Dallas economy.

THE COLLEGE/NONCOLLEGE DIVIDE

There are also revealing similarities between Dallas and St. Louis on the one hand and Detroit and Miami on the other. In table 2.2, Dallas and St. Louis reside in the two cells of row 1 and specialize in high-technology industries—aerospace and defense in St. Louis and advanced-producer services and electronics in Dallas. These are the segments of the economy most likely to bolster the nation's competitive position in the international economy. The particular intersection of inequalities in these two cities suggests that regional economies specializing in the most future-oriented segments of the economy are *not* the places where well-educated professional and managerial women have closed the gap the most with similarly qualified men. And it is this glass-ceiling effect that is partly responsible for the lower but illusory levels of inequality between college- and non-college-educated women.

In contrast, college-educated women are doing well relative to college-educated men in those economies represented by the cells in row 2. By one reading, Detroit and Miami are defined by economic decline, highly insecure employment conditions, or both. Despite a recent comeback, Detroit's declining auto industry and high unemployment rates are theoretically similar in their effects on wages and bargaining to economies with concentrations of immigrant workers. Along with casualization in the local labor market, these factors contribute to greater competition among lower-skilled workers and have a tendency to lower wages in the bottom half of the wage distribution, especially among women (see chapter 6 for more on this argument). These are the conditions under which college-educated women achieve greater parity with their male peers and are more insulated from wage declines than other groups of workers. In these places, the greater relative levels of class inequality among women should highlight the problems of the low-wage labor market for women and displace the more positive impression we might have from the greater degree of gender equality among the college-educated. In neither of the rows, then, do we find an unambiguous beneficial effect of local economic conditions on the position of college-educated women, the only group to have experienced substantial real wage increases over the 1980s at the national level (see chapter 5). Thus the demand for college-educated women may be driven in part by the desire to use them as a substitute for higher-waged men in the least forward-looking sectors of the economy.

THE GLOBAL CITIES

Do these configurations of inequality shed any light on the structure of inequality in other major U.S. cities? The core urban centers of the global economy have become an increasingly popular subject of study. In particular, scholars have devoted much attention to the decline and revival of New York, Los Angeles, and Chicago. As the incubator and hub of the global information-sciences industries, Silicon Valley, together with the surrounding San Francisco metropolitan area, has also generated much interest. However, researchers in this genre have not been overly concerned with the full structure of inequality, even though it is frequently asserted that inequality is high and rising in these cities (Harrison and Bluestone 1988; Mollenkopf and Castells 1991). A related set of topics has received greater attention, such as the uneven creation of ethnic enclaves and niches, and the multilayered pattern of racial/ethnic mobility, differentiation, and inequality (Waldinger 1996; Waldinger and Bozorgmehr 1996). While I cannot match the rich and revealing detail of these case studies, which are usually focused on one city and a few detailed racial-ethnic groups at a time, I can broaden the view to encompass multiple dimensions of inequality and to include comparisons with other cities and the United States as a whole.

These cities are best known for their transformations from industrial to postindustrial centers of the global economy, for their concentrations of immigrants, and for their multiracial character more generally. Thus it makes sense that the two configurations of inequality that fit these cases best, with the exception of Chicago, are the ones associated with immigrant-rich and postindustrial service economies (see cells B and C in table 2.2, and figs. 2.1b and 2.1c). They resemble the two Southern cities of Miami and Dallas the most, though the four cities discussed in this section have unique features of their own as well.

Despite their somewhat different industrial profiles, New York and Los Angeles share many similarities in their profiles of inequality as compared to the average profile of inequality in metropolitan areas of the United States (see table 2.4). Both have extremely high levels of inequality between the top and bottom, especially between workers with a college degree and those without as much as twelve years of schooling. Nearly all forms of racial inequality are above average, particularly in New York (black/white inequality in Los Angeles is average, but unemployment is highest among blacks). On the positive side, both have average to lower levels of inequality between workers with a college and high school degree, especially among women, and the ratio of the fiftieth to the ninetieth percentiles of women is in the direction of less inequality as

Table 2.4 Gender, Race, and Class Inequality in U.S. Metropolitan Areas, New York City, Los Angeles, Chicago, and Santa Clara County, 1989

TYPE OF WAGE INEQUALITY	U.S. (1)	NYC (2)	LA (3)	CHI (4)	SC (5)
(1) Gender Inequality by Education Group (Female/Male Hourly Wage Ratios)					
Less than High School	.684	.704	.757	.680	.798
High School	.678	.722	.748	.662	.790
College	.731	.752	.749	.731	.696
Average	.699	.732	.759	.699	.728
(2) Racial Inequality among Women (Nonwhite/White Hourly Wage Ratios)					
Black/White	.929	.908	.927	.949	.918
Latino/White	.822	.716	.654	.749	.755
Asian/White	1.05	.843	.896	1.010	.911
(3) Racial Inequality among Men (Nonwhite/White Hourly Wage Ratios)					
Black/White	.748	.685	.746	.707	.738
Latino/White	.699	.596	.566	.629	.620
Asian/White	.913	.697	.770	.800	.799
(4) Class Inequality among Women (Noncollege/College and Low-Percentile/High-Percentile Hourly Wage Ratios)					
LHS/COL	.493	.481	.455	.521	.546
HS/COL	.595	.617	.629	.625	.685
50/90th	.481	.490	.485	.500	.535
10/90th	.221	.220	.211	.238	.251
(5) Class Inequality among Men (Noncollege/College and Low-Percentile/High-Percentile Hourly Wage Ratios)					
LHS/COL	.529	.263	.450	.559	.476
HS/COL	.645	.641	.633	.690	.602
50/90th	.503	.472	.481	.535	.526
10/90th	.223	.206	.187	.232	.218

Note: Sample includes adult working population, ages 25–64, with hourly wages between $1.00 and $250.00. U.S. estimates are of individuals living in metropolitan areas. New York City (NYC), Los Angeles (LA), and Chicago (CHI) estimates are of individuals living in the metropolitan areas of these cities. Santa Clara (SC) estimates are of individuals living in Santa Clara County. Analyses were run on the smoothed log wage distribution and the measures of inequality were reconverted to dollars. LHS = < 12 years schooling; HS = 12 years; SC = 13–15 years; COL = 16 or more years.

Data taken from the 1980 and 1990 5% Public Use Microdata Sample of the Census of Population.

well. Gender inequality among the non-college-educated is quite low by national standards, and gender inequality among the college-educated is slightly lower.

On balance, then, the structure of inequality in these economies conforms more to immigrant-rich Miami than to postindustrial Dallas. The high levels of inequality among women at the tails of the education and percentile distributions distinguish these two cities from other postindustrial cities such as Dallas. Greater class inequality among women is more consistent with immigrant-rich regional economies such as Miami, as are the average to lower levels of gender inequality among the college educated. Class inequality among men and racial inequality are higher than average in both immigrant-rich and postindustrial economies (in table 2.2, and cells B and C/figs. 2.1b and 2.1c), and that is replicated for the most part in both New York and Los Angeles. Extremely low levels of gender wage inequality among the non-college-educated are also consistent with both immigrant-rich and postindustrial configurations of inequality. What is unique about New York and Los Angeles, then, is that several features of the immigrant-rich and postindustrial configurations are not as strongly differentiated there as they are in Dallas and Miami. For example, college-educated women do better relative to college-educated men, but there is not as much parity as in Miami. Overall, though, these cities do conform remarkably well to the immigrant configuration of inequality and share many of the features that are the same in the immigrant and postindustrial configurations. In neither of these configurations was gender considered the main axis of inequality, but, rather, a complex interplay of gender, race, and class offered the best description of the local structure of inequality.

Although Los Angeles is composed of a unique combination of high-technology manufacturing, high-technology services, and a strong presence of immigrant workers, a similar combination in Santa Clara County produces a configuration of inequality more similar to the postindustrial profile of Dallas. Initially emphasizing the predominance of high-tech manufacturing, I had expected to find a St. Louis–type profile with greater gender inequality regardless of educational background. However, the manufacturing industries concentrated in Silicon Valley are of a nonunionized variety, employ a large share of immigrant female as well as male production and technical workers, and as a whole comprise more managers and professionals than production workers (more than 55 percent of all workers are managers or professionals). As a consequence, the lower levels of gender inequality among the less educated, especially workers without a high school degree (the female/male ratio is 0.840), is more characteristic of postindustrial and immigrant-rich economies than of high-technology manufacturing economies. On the other hand, the above-average level of gender inequality among the college-educated is typical of economies specializing in both postindustrial services and high-tech manufacturing. The relative exclusion of well-educated women from the best jobs in the local economy in turn contributes to lower levels of wage inequality among women.

There are other familiar elements of postindustrial configurations of inequality in Silicon Valley (as exhibited in cell C of table 2.2, and fig. 2.1c). The relegation of Asians and Latino/as to the bottom rungs of the labor market in both assembly and service occupations contributes to the higher degree of racial inequality between them and whites, especially among men. And educational wage inequality among men tends to be greater as well. As with the Dallas case, a complex intersection of gender, racial, and class inequality cannot be understood by the straightforward interpretation of any one component of inequality. It can be understood only within the context of grasping the limited opportunities for the majority of women and men relative to mostly white, well-educated men, who are placed in the top positions of the Silicon Valley regional economy.

While Silicon Valley, Los Angeles, and New York City have several characteristics in common, Chicago embodies a configuration completely unto itself in which inequality is generally average on almost every account. Even though Chicago has developed international ties and is the unquestionable hub of financial services in the Midwest, it is much less specialized in the advanced-producer services than New York City. In addition, Chicago's immigrant share of employment is above average (18 percent) but far below that of both New York City and Los Angeles. When placed alongside a history of high-waged manufacturing employment to a greater extent than either of these other cities, these factors may overdetermine the tendency toward higher levels of gender inequality. Countervailing factors, such as the greater importance of high-technology services relative to other Midwestern cities dominated historically by manufacturing and high unionization rates, may balance the levels of gender inequality toward the average. Gender inequality is therefore pretty much at average levels for each of the education groups. College-educated women as a whole have not apparently benefited from a history of well-developed wage-setting institutions, as they have in Detroit, but they also have not been as systematically excluded from high-paying jobs, as in St. Louis.

Given average levels of gender inequality, it is somewhat unusual that class inequality and black/white inequality among women is below average in Chicago. Skills-based wage differentials among men are only average, whereas all three measures of racial wage inequality among men are greater, and the white/Latina wage gap is also greater. In sum, Chicago's gender order is somewhat more traditional than the others, but levels of class inequality among men and women are less extreme than in the coastal global cities. Like those cities, though, which are patterned after the profile found in immigrant-rich and postindustrial regions, racial inequality emerges as one of the primary markers of inequality, especially among men, in Chicago.

CONCLUSION

Not only do different paths of economic development have different consequences for the level and structure of inequality, but gender, class, and race vary in their significance and cannot possibly be reduced to a single measure of overall earnings inequality. Configurations of inequality express this complex set of relationships between economic restructuring and gender, class, and racial inequality. In their diversity they suggest a repertoire of theoretical, political, and policy responses to the variety of conditions facing workers in today's economy. In closing, I will highlight several of the key findings and their implications for the politics of inequality, which will be discussed in greater detail in the next chapter and especially in the concluding chapter.

First, unlike inequality among men, levels of inequality among women must be interpreted in relation to levels of gender inequality. Since high levels of gender inequality could be creating the conditions for lower levels of inequality among women, sensitivity to patterns of both gender inequality and inequality among women is needed. Second, the economic conditions that tend to reduce wage dispersion among men often form the basis for greater gender inequality and/or inequality among women. We saw this in local economies specializing in industrial and high-technology manufacturing. Clearly policies that are oriented toward reducing inequality among men have the potential to intensify other forms of inequality. Third, lower inequality between college- and non-college-educated women may not coincide with lower racial inequality among women. In other words, there is no easy overlap between the pattern and sources of racial and class inequality among women. Race must be taken explicitly into consideration when contemplating policies related to reducing inequality among women. Finally, gender inequality may be reduced for the college-educated but not for the non-college-educated, calling attention to the uneven distribution of gender equality and the fact that not all groups of women are equally served by some economic development and anti-inequality strategies. In fact, the conditions that foster greater gender equality among the college-educated—high unemployment and immigration—have detrimental effects on other groups of workers by lowering wages and increasing within-group inequality.

Overall, then, there must be greater attention to the rising and high levels of inequality among women by class and race alongside the current emphasis on gender inequality by feminists, and family income and male wage inequality by most mainstream policy-makers and scholars. Every dimension of inequality should be considered in any theoretical or political assessment of the equity implications of different paths of economic development. Likewise, no single dimension should be considered the most important *a priori*. While this might sound like a blind endorsement of inclusivity, configurations of inequality emerge from the *reality* of multiple paths of economic development and conflicting outcomes from the same path, with no single path promising lower inequality of all kinds.

Chapter Three

INDUSTRIAL AND POSTINDUSTRIAL CONFIGURATIONS OF INEQUALITY: DETROIT AND DALLAS

While the last chapter established that there are differences in the level and structure of inequality across cities and traced these to differences in economic conditions, this chapter digs deeper into the mechanisms that explain why certain conditions result in the outcomes they do. I narrow my focus to Detroit and Dallas, the two cities with the most complex configurations of inequality. The configuration of inequality in one city is the exact opposite of the configuration in the other city, and in neither city is inequality relatively lower on all accounts. Each represents a mix of "good" and "bad" outcomes, and several of these outcomes are not what we would have expected. The political implications of configurations of inequality are therefore significant: there appears to be no easy choice between a low-inequality and high-inequality path of regional economic development. In contemporary parlance, this suggests as well that there is no easy choice between the "low road" and the "high road" of economic restructuring, particularly if the latter is bereft of stringent affirmative action goals. Rather, the weaknesses of each path need to be exposed and addressed in order to have any hope of achieving across-the-board improvements in inequality.

While my primary concern is with showing that any single indicator of overall inequality would conceal stark differences in the social composition of inequality, Dallas and Detroit were also strategically selected to shed light on debates over the leading causes of wage inequality. Detroit is the prototypical "old" industrial city of the North, and Dallas is one of the "new" postindustrial cities of the South. As such, several concerns about the nature of inequality in postindustrial as opposed to industrial economies can be explored through a comparison of these two cities. Although the sources of *rising* inequality should not be conflated with those of high *levels* of inequality at any given point in time, and snapshots of deindustrialized Detroit in 1980 and 1990 cannot represent the industrial configurations of inequality in the 1960s or 1970s, Detroit clearly bears the imprint of its industrial legacy, with its manufacturing base and high unionization rate, while also bearing the marks of a restructured industrial economy, with its high unemployment rate. Dallas, on the other hand, is a balanced, high growth economy that is more typical of the nation as a whole than other exceptional postindustrial regions such as Silicon Valley. The analysis of these two carefully chosen cities, then, will enable us to dig deeper into the strikingly different mechanisms that produce inequality in industrial and postindustrial economies. In addition, these two particular cities lend themselves to a greater degree of generalizability than is possible in case studies of exceptional cities such as New York, Los Angeles, and Miami.

A framework for comparing structures of inequality across regions has been suggested by recent work on cross-national differences in the institutional adjustments to global economic restructuring. As it turns out, two arguments are particularly relevant to the comparison of Detroit, an industrial city with high unemployment and strong wage-setting institutions, and Dallas, a city with low unemployment, sustained service growth, and concentrated postindustrial employment. First, several researchers comparing the United States to Europe have linked the relatively higher employment levels in the United States with its greater decline in real wages, sharper rise in inequality, and higher level of inequality, suggesting a trade-off between jobs and equality (Wood 1994; Freeman and Katz 1995). Freeman and Katz argue that, as in Europe, the "more centralized a wage-setting system, and the stronger the role of institutions in wage determination, the smaller will be the effect of shifts in supply and demand on relative wages, and, as a consequence, the greater will be their effect on relative employment."[1] Other researchers looking exclusively at wage inequality (and not employment) have found the presence of wage-setting institutions to be the crucial factor in explaining differences in levels of wage inequality between the United States and Europe and in explaining the rise of inequality within the United States (Blau and Kahn 1996; DiNardo et al. 1996).

Thus, in the language of neoclassical economics, the degree to which wages are subject to "rigid" institutional constraints or "flexible" market forces ought to have an impact on whether the wage structure is relatively compressed or not. An alternative interpretation is that when wage-setting institutions are strong, workers have more bargaining power with which to demand a larger share of profits, especially in highly productive industries. This is why the unionized manufacturing belt in the United States was held up as a model of economic growth and equality during its heyday in the 1960s. A related alternative explanation is that higher unemployment in Europe is the consequence of greater productivity growth than in the United States, especially in the service sector. Again, with strong institutions, productivity growth can be translated into higher wages for employed workers and better benefits for the unemployed (Applebaum and Schettkat 1995).

The second argument emerging from recent cross-national research on inequality concerns the social composition of wage inequality and its gender dimensions in particular. In an important series of articles, Blau and Kahn (1994, 1995) have put forth a set of findings directly linking the gender wage gap to the degree of male wage inequality, both of which are greater in the United States relative to other countries of the Organization for Economic Cooperation and Development (OECD).[2] They extend their insights on cross-national patterns to temporal trends in the United States, showing that declining gender wage inequality was impeded by rising inequality among men. Had inequality among men remained constant, the gender wage gap would have declined 25 percent more than it did between 1971 and 1988. This again points to a positive relationship between male wage inequality and gender wage inequality. Finally, Blau and Kahn find an extremely high correlation between levels of male and female wage inequality among the countries in their sample. They use this finding to justify their focus on male wage inequality as a measure of a country's "overall" level of inequality, without looking at female wage inequality separately. In sum, Blau's and Kahn's research is unusual in its focus on relationships among inequalities and as such offers a rich set of propositions with which to explore these relationships within the United States.

These two sets of arguments—about the cross-national relationship 1) between inequality, unemployment, and institutions, and 2) between male wage inequality, gender wage inequality, and female wage inequality—have the virtue of being complementary. All else being equal, countries with high unemployment as a result of strong wage-setting institutions should have lower male wage inequality, which in turn should be associated with lower gender and female wage inequality. This is a very fortunate state of affairs: it means that conditions that lower one dimension of inequality should also lower other dimensions of inequality. There would appear to be no harm in focusing attention on one dimension of inequality to the exclusion of others, because all would improve. This proposition can be explored in the relatively deregulated and decentralized U.S. economy—with its quasi-experimental universe of extremely diverse regional economies—while holding constant national labor-market policies. Although the Dallas/Detroit comparison cannot exactly replicate the United States/Europe one, it does share many of the same key characteristics, and it has the potential to inform regional politics in the United States in the same way that cross-national research has informed national and international politics around the world.

In the following sections, I first elaborate on the key differences between the Dallas and Detroit economies using data from a number of different sources. The case-study literature developed primarily by geographers and planners in the United States has tended to focus on changes in the organization of production, as in the development of flexible specialization and industrial districts, with only peripheral attention to systematic and comprehensive comparisons of inequality. When the topic of inequality is broached, researchers tend to provide only limited evidence of the growth of income polarization.[3] To balance things out, I use the next section to offer only a brief description of the salient differences between the economies of Detroit and Dallas. I then turn my focus in the rest of the chapter to the differences between the structures of inequality in the two cities. On this subject, I begin by laying out the two configurations of inequality, describing the levels of male and female wage inequality, gender wage inequality for the college- and non-college-educated, and racial wage inequality for men and women in each city. The main objective here is to demonstrate that there are differences in the relative levels of wage inequality between and *within* cities. The third section is concerned with explaining these differences and does so by examining the underlying wage structure in each city, by considering several competing explanations, and by referring to research presented later in chapters 4 through 6 that confirms the generalizability of the conclusions from these two case studies. The final section discusses the political and policy implications of configurations of inequality in general and the industrial and postindustrial types in particular.

Because the presentation of data is both detailed and complex, especially the second section's description of gender, class, and racial wage inequality, it is worth briefly outlining the findings at the outset. Broadly speaking, the main finding is that some dimensions of the configurations match cross-national patterns, and others do not. As international research would predict, Detroit exhibits higher unemployment, higher unionization rates, higher wages, and lower class inequality *among men*. Racial inequality is also lower in Detroit for both men and women, but extremely high levels of unemployment among blacks is still a major concern. So far, so good for the jobs-equality trade-off as adapted to U.S. regions.

But a more comprehensive examination reveals that many of the symmetries among inequalities found by Blau and Kahn across countries do not hold up across regions in the United States. Some forms of inequality are actually greater in Detroit. Gender-related differences are of particular interest, since both gender wage inequality and female wage inequality in Detroit are above the national average and above the levels in Dallas. Detroit has made significant headway on many fronts, but gender equality and equality among women are not among them. This is mainly because Detroit's brand of unionism was never egalitarian and encompassing enough to lift the wages of non-college-educated women workers. Gender therefore turns out to be the primary marker of inequality in the Detroit economy, whereas class becomes the primary marker in the Dallas economy. An important caveat to this argument, as will become clear, is that gender differences are mediated by the "class" divide between college- and non-college-educated women.

DALLAS AND DETROIT: THE ECONOMY AND THE LABOR FORCE

Of course any discussion of the economic differences between Detroit and Dallas must begin with the role of manufacturing. The centrality of auto production to the Detroit economy and of Detroit to the auto industry cannot be underestimated, even today. Although in 1990 the Midwest still generated more earnings from manufacturing than the Northeast, South, or West, Detroit is known primarily for its massive decline of manufacturing during the 1970s and 1980s, during which more than 50 percent of manufacturing jobs were lost.[4] The industry's declining profitability in the late 1960s forced a restructuring that not only displaced well-paid unskilled and semiskilled workers, but drove from its borders the central headquarters of several major Fortune 500 companies. Detroit had the fifth largest number of headquarters in 1960 (13) but fell from the top ten cities in 1980. On the other hand, Dallas more than doubled its number of central headquarters from 1960 to 1990 and went from a ranking of ten in 1960 to having the third-largest number in 1990 (15). This transference of fortunes is symbolic of the more general exodus of central headquarters from large metropolitan areas in the North, especially New York, to Southern metropolitan areas and to nonmetropolitan areas throughout the country.

There were several other general trends that worked themselves out in these two particular cities (see table 3.1). As is well known, manufacturing employment actually grew in Southern cities such as Dallas, which saw growth concentrated in the new high-tech electronics industries during the 1970s. Dallas even reached near-parity with Detroit in the absolute number of manufacturing jobs in 1990, but the manufacturing share of private employment in Detroit still far exceeded the share in Dallas (23.3 percent versus 14.8 percent). Perhaps more important for our purposes, an estimated 60 percent of production workers in Detroit worked in large manufacturing plants with more than five hundred employees, compared to only 25 percent in Dallas. County-level statistics on union density are unavailable, but based on this statistic alone, both the manufacturing and nonmanufacturing workforce in Detroit are no doubt far more likely to be unionized and influenced by a strong union culture. Figures for the metropolitan statistical areas of Dallas and Detroit in 1985 give a more accurate reading of the relative degree of unionization in the two cities. The union coverage rate was 26.7 percent in Detroit whereas it was only 8.0 percent in Dallas, well below the national average of 21.0 percent. Since the institutional arguments put forth by Freeman and Katz (1995), DiNardo et al. (1996), and others refer primarily to the positive role of unions and a high minimum wage in reducing levels of inequality, the stark contrast between Dallas and Detroit in terms of their unionization rates should be crucial to understanding differences in their structures of inequality.

While Detroit's deindustrialized economy remains highly industrial, Dallas's economy is dominated by postindustrial service employment. Service employment did increase modestly in Detroit over the 1980s, but the average annual rate of service employment growth in Dallas was more than three and a half times greater (6.1 percent versus 1.7 percent), while employment in the advanced producer service industries of finance, insurance, and real estate (FIRE) soared by an average annual rate of 5.1 percent in the 1970s and 3.1 percent in the 1980s. Dallas's share of employment in FIRE actually approached its share of employment in manufacturing (13.0 percent versus 14.8 percent), while the difference between the distribution of FIRE and manufacturing employment in Detroit was still severely skewed toward manufacturing (7.7 versus 23.3 percent). If other high-technology and advanced-producer services such as accounting, advertising, legal, engineering, computer, research and development, and communication services are added to FIRE, the resulting share of such employment in Dallas is twice that of Detroit (21.1 percent versus 10.5 percent). The contrast in industrial structures is further revealed in the distribution of employment by education. College-educated men held 35 percent of all jobs held by men in Dallas in 1990, compared to 26.8 percent in Detroit. Only 12 percent of jobs in Dallas were held by men with only a high school degree, compared to 27.6 percent in Detroit. The female educational distribution of employment is similar in composition.

Thus over the 1980s Dallas's growth trajectory was distinguished by its ability to attract large corporate investment, its expanding capacity in the provision of advanced producer services, and its greater demand for college-educated workers. Although Dallas does not compete in the same league as New York, Los Angeles, or San Francisco, it certainly qualifies as a regional business and financial center with national and international scope. In fact its status as a "moderate" outlier and its mix of high-technology manufacturing make developments there all the

Table 3.1   Economic and Demographic Characteristics of Dallas and Detroit

	DALLAS	DETROIT
Industrial Composition		
Share of 1990 Private Sector Employment in:		
Manufacturing[a]	14.8%	23.3%
Finance, Insurance, and Real Estate[a]	13.0	7.7
High-Technology and Advanced-Producer Services[b]	21.1	10.5
Average Annual Employment Growth in Services, 1980s[a]	6.1	1.7
Share of Production Workers in Large Manufacturing Plants with more than 500 Employees, 1987[c]	25.0	60.0
Union Coverage Rate, 1985[d]	8.0	26.7
Unemployment, 1990[b]	6.2	12.5
Educational Composition		
College-Educated Men as Share of All Employed Men, 1990[b]	35.0	26.8
High-School-Educated Men as Share of All Employed Men, 1990[b]	12.0	27.6
Immigrant and Racial Composition		
Immigrants as Share of Employed, 1990[b]	11.8	6.4
Latino/as as Share of Employed, 1990[b]	10.4	1.7

Notes:
a. Regional Economic Information System (U.S. Department of Commerce 1994b).
b. Public Use Microdata Sample (5%) of the Census of Population for 1990.
c. 1987 Economic Census (U.S. Department of Commerce 1994a).
d. Current Population Survey (Curme et al. 1990).

more representative of the emerging postindustrial regional economy in which manufacturing plays an important but much smaller role. By 1989, even Dallas's unemployment rate was average by national standards (6.2 percent—still only half that of Detroit), a result of slowed growth in the 1980s after a booming 1970s.

In addition to these differences in industrial structure, an equally important set of distinctions to draw between Detroit and Dallas is demographic, and in particular, the racial and immigrant composition of each city's workforce and the significant population shifts in and out of these regions. Among U.S. cities in the late 1980s, Detroit had the largest net negative level of outmigration.[5] Meanwhile Dallas drew in large numbers of white, black, and Latino internal migrants as well as Latino/a immigrants over the 1985-to-1990 period. It ranked among the top ten areas with the largest numbers of new residents from these groups. As a result of these shifts, the percentage of immigrants in the Dallas workforce more than doubled from 4.9 percent in 1980 to 11.8 percent in 1990, while it remained the same in Detroit (6.4 percent). The share of

Latino/a workers in Dallas is also much larger (10.4 percent versus 1.7 percent) and these workers are on the whole less educated than their counterparts in Detroit. At the other end of the educational hierarchy, though, Dallas has attracted large numbers of black college graduates and was one of the "New South" cities with the largest proportions of black residency in suburban areas. It was far less segregated racially than Detroit, one of the most segregated regions in the country.

In all these respects, Dallas resembles other immigrant-rich postindustrial cities that "continue to create employment opportunities in professional and high skilled jobs [while] the low skilled jobs are increasingly filled by immigrants from abroad" (Frey 1995: 296). Although the proportion of immigrant workers in Dallas does not approach that in Miami, New York City, or Los Angeles, their presence in low-wage services and manufacturing is consistent with patterns in these cities and others throughout the Southwest. It also contrasts sharply with the process of deindustrialization that has disproportionately affected blacks and Puerto Ricans in the North (Moore and Pinderhughes 1993; Morales and Bonilla 1993).

In sum, the differences between Dallas and Detroit must be understood as more than simply a function of additive differences in their labor supply, industrial mix, and racial composition. Each city represents a complex interaction of shifts in labor supply, product market demand, technology, and institutions. For example, one of the main characteristics distinguishing Detroit from Dallas is its higher level of unemployment, but this cannot be separated from the historical development and decline of the U.S. auto industry and the collective bargaining institutions that generated a positive high-wage spillover in other industries. Likewise, the fact that Dallas has an export advantage in high growth, high-technology service and manufacturing industries in a low-unemployment environment represents industrial as well as institutional and technological differences between the two cities. Finally, differences in racial and immigrant composition are part and parcel of the supply and demand of labor played out over the very different historical periods of Fordism and post-Fordism, the latter characterized by a greater influx of immigrants. Thus, as an integrated whole, Dallas and Detroit each represent the key features associated with postindustrial and industrial economies, respectively.

CONFIGURATIONS OF GENDER, CLASS, AND RACIAL INEQUALITY

We expect the structure of the economy to be associated with the structure of inequality, a notion at the basis of almost all comparative research, but the analysis of inequality has lagged far behind the more extensive analysis of different regional production regimes, industrial districts, and the like. This section corrects that bias and looks at inequality in much greater detail than in previous research. The dimensions of inequality that I examine are clear enough—gender, race, and class—but some of the measures I use are somewhat unconventional, especially for describing "class" divisions. I use "class" to refer to wage inequality between the college- and non-college-educated and between workers at the top and bottom percentiles of the wage distribution. I also use "class" to refer to differences between the gender wage gap for the college- versus non-college-educated. Although they do not imply any direct class relationship, college and percentile wage gaps have become the most common measures of stratification between groups in the economics literature on restructuring and inequality. For consistency's sake, then, I use them here as well (for a lengthier discussion of this issue, see chapters 2 and 6).

Recall that in this section I focus simply on how inequality is configured, and then in the following section I discuss why we observe these particular configurations and whether they are anomalies or systematically reproduced in other regional economies with similar economic structures. The final section considers the political implications of these configurations of inequality.

CLASS INEQUALITY AMONG WOMEN AND AMONG MEN

Measures of class inequality for U.S. metro areas, Dallas, and Detroit are displayed in figure 3.1 for the years 1979 and 1989 (and table 2.3 in the previous chapter summarizes the relative standing of Detroit and Dallas on these measures).[6] The figure includes many of the standard measures of wage inequality: the ratio of average hourly wages between workers with and without a college education (referred to as the HS/COL and LHS/COL ratios) and between workers at the tenth, fiftieth, and ninetieth percentiles of the wage distribution (referred to as the tenth/ninetieth and fiftieth/ninetieth ratios). A higher ratio means that those at the bottom are earning a larger share of the earnings of those at the top. When the ratios are multiplied by 100, they can be interpreted in percentage terms. For example, the highest bar in figure 3.1 is for the 1979 male HS/COL ratio in Detroit. It shows that high school-educated men earned about 80 percent of what college-educated men earned in the Detroit area in 1979. This same figure fell below 70 percent in 1989. While these absolute values are informative, my focus will be on the levels of wage inequality in one city relative to the other and to the average level for metropolitan areas in the United States.

Figure 3.1 clearly shows that all measures of male inequality rose during the 1980s, yet it also shows that the level of male inequality in Detroit is substantially less than in Dallas and in the nation as a whole. Wage inequality among men in Detroit was between 4.5 percent (HS/COL) and 15.3 percent (LHS/COL) lower than the national aver-

Figure 3.1 Class Inequality in Dallas and Detroit, 1979 and 1989

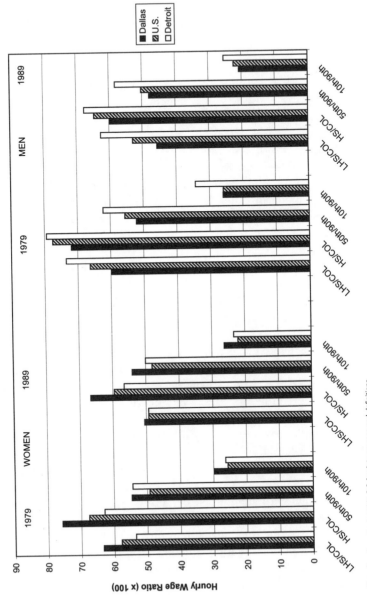

Note: See the notes to table 3.2 for data sources and definitions.

age and between 11.4 percent (HS/COL) and 26.9 percent (LHS/COL) lower than in Dallas. The divergence between Detroit, Dallas, and the national average fell somewhere in between these bounds for the other measures. The considerable disparity between Detroit and Dallas, as well as between Detroit and the national average, is greatest for the LHS/COL ratio, followed by the percentile ratios, and is lowest for the HS/COL ratio. *This suggests that Detroit's economy is particularly favorable to male workers with the lowest levels of formal schooling, and Dallas's economy is particularly unfavorable to such men.*

In contrast to male wage inequality, female wage inequality is lower in Dallas than in Detroit and is generally lower than in the nation as a whole. The level of inequality among women is between 2.5 percent (LHS/COL) and 15.3 percent (HS/COL) lower in Dallas than in Detroit. Thus, Detroit's economic structure fosters more dispersion among women around the broad middle sections of the wage distribution, while there is less severe dispersion between the tails. Despite this more complicated pattern, inequality among women in Detroit is still on the whole substantially greater than in Dallas. Relative to the national average, the level of inequality among women is also lower in Dallas. For example, the tenth/ninetieth ratio is 15.9 percent lower in Dallas than in the average metropolitan labor market.

While it is clear that inequality among women is greater in Detroit than in Dallas, Detroit's standing relative to the national average is less straightforward. The percentile wage gaps showed less inequality than in the nation as a whole in both 1980 and 1990 because dispersion is not as extreme in the tails, at the very top and the very bottom, of Detroit's female wage structure. In this respect, both male and female workers at the bottom end of the labor market benefit from a more compressed wage structure in Detroit. The educational measures are perhaps more reflective of differences in the broad middle of the distribution, and they present a different picture. Both measures of skills-based wage inequality among women in Detroit exceeded the national average in 1980, and the degree of HS/COL inequality was also above average in 1990, while the LHS/COL ratio was about the same as the national average in 1990.

While the relative positions of Dallas and Detroit are consistent across all measures of female wage inequality, the fact that Detroit's position vis-à-vis the national average changed considerably over the course of the 1980s is interesting for several reasons. First, it reveals that the nation as a whole is catching up to the historically higher relative levels of inequality in Detroit. In the aggregate, the nation is becoming as unequal as Detroit was *in the past.* This is fascinating in light of Detroit's standing as a relatively egalitarian, high-wage, working-class city. Second, it offers a set of stark contrasts to the situation in Dallas. In

1989, after a decade of substantial increases in inequality, the level of wage dispersion among women in Dallas was roughly equivalent to Detroit's level *in 1979*. Only one of the 1989 measures of female wage inequality in Dallas, the LHS/COL gap, significantly exceeds the corresponding figure for Detroit in 1979. Consequently, Dallas and Detroit are more similar on this measure than on any of the others. Interestingly, this is a reversal of what we found among men. *The Dallas economy is more favorable to high-school-educated women, whereas the least educated fare about the same in Dallas and Detroit.*

In sum, gender differences in the level and structure of inequality offer contradictory support for the relevance of cross-national arguments to interregional patterns in the United States. In the two cases of Detroit and Dallas, male and female wage inequality are inversely related.[7] These results suggest that areas lower in "overall" inequality based on measures of male inequality, such as those with high unemployment and more developed wage-setting institutions, are not equally conducive to lower levels of female wage inequality. Conversely, areas such as Dallas that have undergone a set of postindustrial transformations in a relatively deinstitutionalized economy and typically reflect the trend toward increasing inequality, are more likely to exhibit lower levels of inequality among women. As important as it is becoming, however, inequality among women has always been eclipsed by the greater concern for inequality among men and gender wage inequality. This should begin to change with advancing gender wage equality, to which I now turn.

GENDER WAGE INEQUALITY
Figure 3.2 displays the average female/male hourly wage ratio for three educational groups in 1979 and 1989.[8] In keeping with how the gender wage gap is typically measured, higher female/male ratios reflect higher levels of gender equality, and the interpretation of the ratios in percentage form is the same as in figure 3.1. The most striking contrast between Dallas and Detroit is immediately apparent in the distinction between the gender ratio for workers with and without a college degree. Dallas has lower levels of inequality among noncollege groups and higher levels among college-educated groups. Detroit's profile is the exact opposite, with extraordinarily high inequality among the non-college educated and low inequality among the college-educated. These patterns are consistent with the ranking of Dallas and Detroit relative to the national average as well. The educational differences in and across the two cities were actually more pronounced in 1989, when the distinction between the college- and non-college-educated was becoming less noticeable at the national level. In fact, the educational breakdowns of the gender wage gap in 1989 at the national level are often deployed as

Figure 3.2 Gender Inequality in Dallas and Detroit, 1979 and 1989.

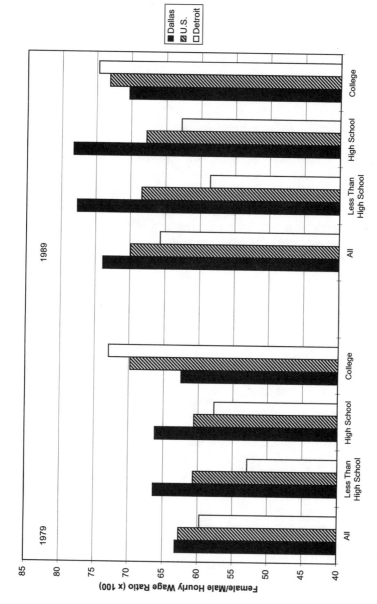

Note: See the notes to table 3.2 for data sources and definitions.

evidence of equally distributed gender discrimination across the educational spectrum. These regional data allow us to redirect attention to how inequality is in fact mediated by class and influenced in different ways by various aspects of economic restructuring.

As for "overall" or average levels of gender wage inequality, they are greater in Detroit in both 1979 and 1989. Because Detroit has a relatively small share of college-educated workers, its average gender wage ratio is not heavily influenced by the greater degree of equity between college-educated men and women. In Dallas, on the other hand, the disproportionate share of college-educated workers raises its average level of inequality closer to the college level in the city. Still, the main determinant of Dallas's lower average gender inequality is the much greater wage parity between the majority of men and women who do not have college degrees (a difference in the female/male wage ratio of between 9.3 and 19.1 percentage points greater than in Detroit and the nation at large). Using Detroit as an example, therefore, it could not be said that gender wage inequality is lower in regions with a more compressed male wage structure (that is, lower male wage inequality), as the cross-national evidence might suggest. Surprisingly, only the college-educated benefit among women, a finding that will be explored in greater detail below.

RACIAL WAGE INEQUALITY

Figure 3.3 reports racial wage ratios separately for men and women and indicates that racial inequality is substantially greater in Dallas than in Detroit and in the nation as a whole. Racial inequality also grew over the 1980s in both cities and again at the national level. The only exceptions were that the level of Asian/white wage inequality was about the same in 1979 and 1989 among both men and women in the country overall, and it decreased among men in Detroit over the same time period. In both years, Asians earned as much or more than their white counterparts in Detroit while earning substantially less than their white counterparts in Dallas, especially in 1989 after a decade of increasing inequality. Despite the need to look more carefully at these trends, the share of Asian workers in Detroit is quite small and their wages substantially higher than whites, so I will focus my discussion in this section and the next on black/white and Latino(a)/white inequality. However, I suspect that the reasons behind differences in racial inequality between Dallas and Detroit are largely the same for all three groups, though they may differ in degree.

Racial inequality among both men and women is greater in Dallas than in Detroit, though it should be noted that levels of racial inequality are substantially greater among men than among women (note the smaller bars on the right side of figure 3.3). We might expect racial

Figure 3.3 Racial Inequality in Dallas and Detroit, 1979 and 1989

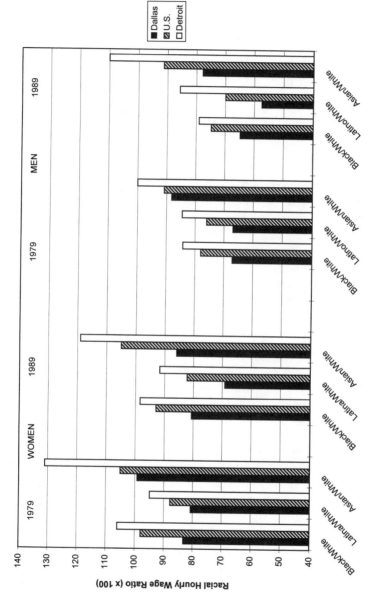

Note: See the notes to table 3.2 for data sources and definitions.

inequality and discrimination to be greater in the South, and in the case of Dallas the educational distribution of Latino/as is much less favorable as well, because of the larger share of immigrants with low levels of formal education. But, for blacks, overall educational attainment is only slightly lower, and the absolute percentage of college graduates in the black population is actually greater in Dallas (17.8 percent versus 14.4 percent), though their share relative to whites is somewhat smaller. Nevertheless, even after controlling for these differences in education by evaluating racial inequality within educational groups, all measures of racial inequality are still greater in Dallas for both men and women.[9] Given this evidence, it is reasonable to conclude that there is something distinctive about the structure of the economy as well as the composition of the labor force that perpetuates racial inequality in Dallas. Finally, it should be highlighted that racial inequality among women follows the same patterns as racial and class inequality *among men*—they are higher in Dallas and lower in Detroit. The structures of racial and class inequality among women do not overlap in these two regions, nor do they overlap with the patterns of average gender wage inequality.

These, then, are the configurations of inequality in Dallas and Detroit. Table 2.3 (in the previous chapter) summarizes the relative standing of each city on each dimension of inequality. Male wage inequality and racial wage inequality are lower in Detroit than in Dallas and lower than in the nation as a whole. More surprising was the higher average gender wage gap in Detroit, at least from the perspective of international comparative research. It is less surprising from the perspective of researchers who know that manufacturing is a predominantly male industry, though no study that I know of has ever documented greater gender inequality in industrial cities or, conversely, greater gender equality in postindustrial economies such as Dallas. Finally, class inequality was higher among women in Detroit, a finding that is also inconsistent with international comparative research. What explains these industrial and postindustrial configurations of inequality? In the next section, I consider the underlying mechanisms that produce inequality in these two very different types of economies.

EXPLAINING INDUSTRIAL/POSTINDUSTRIAL DIFFERENCES

In order to explain these configurations of inequality and to be more precise in laying out the connections between an industrial/postindustrial economy and its structure of inequality, we need to look more closely at the wage structure itself rather than wage ratios. We also need to consider alternative explanations and to rule out the charge that these are just two anomalous cases, not reflective of broader trends. After clearing much of this ground, institutional differences between

Detroit's advanced industrial regional economy and Dallas's advanced postindustrial economy emerge as the primary source of variation in the structure of inequality. This variation is generally supported by multivariate analysis (see chapters 4 to 6) and is evident in other regional economies with similar institutional and industrial histories.

THE FEMALE WAGE STRUCTURE

The average hourly wages of seven broad occupational groups, three educational groups, and all workers are presented for men and women in table 3.2. Since local cost-of-living prices make direct comparisons of wage levels unreliable, I will compare wage differences between Detroit and Dallas for the same occupation and educational groups relative to the wage difference between the cities for the average worker. That is, if the average worker makes 16 percent more in Detroit than in Dallas, and the average blue-collar worker makes 25 percent more, this means that blue-collar workers earn a wage premium and are better off in Detroit than in Dallas. Since Detroit has lost some of its regional wage advantage, the average wage difference between the two cities has declined over the decade. Among women, the Detroit/Dallas ratio of average wages declined substantially from 1.16 to 1.03, because female wages rose in Dallas while they fell in Detroit. The ratio of average wages also declined among men, from 1.23 to 1.16. Since real wage cuts occurred throughout the country for men during the 1980s, the decline in the average wage difference between the two cities resulted from greater declines in Detroit.

Looking first at female wage inequality, greater inequality in Detroit is compounded by the fact that wages were generally stagnant or falling while they stagnated or rose for most groups of women in Dallas. In Dallas, wages did fall among women in service and unskilled blue-collar occupations as well as among women with less than a high school education. This drop among less-skilled and less-educated workers in Dallas is one reason why there is less of a between-city difference in the levels of female wage inequality for the LHS/COL measure, compared to other measures. Wages also stagnated among high-school-educated workers and rose only moderately among clerical workers. At the other end, however, wages rose more substantially in Dallas for the two occupational groups with the largest share of college-educated workers (managers and professionals, and sales workers). What is remarkable is that, even amidst disproportionately strong wage growth over the 1980s for college-educated women in Dallas, which is of course a key factor in increasing inequality among women over the 1980s in Dallas, the *level* of HS/COL inequality is still substantially lower than in Detroit. What is driving such high levels of inequality among women in Detroit?

An important part of the answer lies in the significantly higher wage levels earned by college-educated women in Detroit relative to non-col-

Table 3.2 Average Hourly Wages by Occupation, Education, and Gender in Dallas and Detroit, 1979 and 1989 (1995 Dollars)

WAGE GROUPS	U.S. (METRO)		DALLAS		DETROIT	
	1979	1989	1979	1989	1979	1989
OCCUPATION						
Men						
Managers and Professionals	20.29	21.12	21.54	22.20	24.53	23.57
Technicians	17.64	17.46	18.17	17.99	21.54	19.89
Skilled Blue-Collar	15.80	14.30	15.03	13.33	21.33	17.81
Sales	16.44	16.28	18.73	17.81	18.54	17.29
Clerical	15.49	14.30	15.96	13.87	19.89	16.12
Service	10.49	9.39	10.49	8.41	13.60	10.70
Blue-Collar	14.01	12.06	12.94	10.80	18.36	16.61
Women						
Managers and Professionals	13.74	14.73	13.33	15.03	16.95	16.44
Technicians	11.82	12.94	12.18	13.60	13.74	13.60
Skilled Blue-Collar	9.97	10.18	10.38	11.02	12.81	12.81
Sales	8.85	9.30	9.68	11.47	9.39	9.30
Clerical	10.18	10.49	10.59	11.25	12.06	11.47
Service	7.54	7.39	8.08	7.46	8.94	8.25
Blue-Collar	8.85	8.25	9.12	8.58	12.18	11.36
EDUCATION						
Men						
Less than High School	13.46	11.25	12.94	10.18	18.17	15.03
High School	15.80	13.60	15.49	13.20	19.69	16.28
College	20.29	21.12	21.54	22.20	24.78	24.05
Average	16.28	15.49	16.95	15.96	20.70	18.54
Women						
Less than High School	8.17	7.69	8.58	7.85	9.68	8.85
High School	9.58	9.30	10.18	10.38	11.36	10.18
College	14.15	15.49	13.46	15.64	17.99	17.99
Average	10.28	10.80	10.70	11.82	12.43	12.18

Note: Sample includes adult working population, ages 25–64, with hourly wages between $1.00 and $250.00. U.S. estimates are of individuals living in metropolitan areas. Dallas and Detroit estimates are of individuals working in Dallas and Wayne Counties. Analyses were run on the smoothed log wage distribution and average log hourly wages were reconverted to dollars. Major occupation categories were grouped as follows: service workers includes all service workers except protective; skilled blue-collar workers includes protective service, precision production, craft, and transportation workers; and blue-collar workers includes operators and laborers.

Less than High School (LHS) equals less than 12 years of schooling; High School (HS) equals 12 years; College (COL) equals 16 or more years.

Data taken from the 1980 and 1990 5 % Public Use Microdata Sample of the Census of Population.

lege-educated women in Detroit and relative to college-educated women in Dallas. Whereas the Detroit/Dallas ratio of hourly wages for the average worker is 1.03, the ratio for the college-educated is 1.15—wages are 3 percent higher in Detroit for the average female worker, and they are 15 percent higher for the average college-educated female worker. And the variation between what one earns in one city as compared to the other is greater among workers with a college degree or more than it is among those without a college degree. Similarly, female managers and professionals in Detroit earn 9 percent more than their counterparts in Dallas, down from a whopping 27 percent more in 1979. These comparisons reveal a more compressed female occupational wage structure in Dallas in both 1979 and 1989, at least between the middle and the top, even though it widened over the course of the 1980s with genuine upgrading among highly educated and skilled women. These women were doing well in postindustrial Dallas in terms of wage growth, but their absolute wage levels were still lower than in Detroit.

THE SUPPLY-SIDE EXPLANATION

Since the position of college-educated women and the occupations they fill are critical to understanding the sources of female wage inequality and wage inequality between college-educated men and women, we need to find out why wages were so much higher for college-educated women in Detroit as compared to Dallas. One of the explanations for rising college wage premiums in the 1980s is a slowdown in the rate of growth of college-educated workers in the midst of a stronger rate of growth in the demand for these workers (Katz and Murphy 1992). Since educational differentials began to rise in the 1980s across the United States, this could not explain why there were already striking differences between Detroit and Dallas in 1980, unless the slowdown occurred earlier in Detroit. Without 1970 data I cannot assess this possibility.

Regarding the 1980s, table 3.3 presents information on the college-educated as a fraction of metropolitan-area population (panel 1) and of metropolitan-area employment (panel 2). These data show that the share of employed women with college degrees grew dramatically in both cities, by roughly 45 percent. This rate far exceeded the rate of growth of college-educated women in the overall population of each city (less than 20 percent). Since the rate of growth in the population was less than in employment, there might have been unmet demand for college-educated women. For unmet demand to result in a larger college wage premium in Detroit than in Dallas, there should be a significantly larger difference between the population and employment growth rates in Detroit. But this is not the case. The rate of growth in the population was more than five times greater in Detroit than in Dallas.

Table 3.3 Population and Employment Distribution of the College-Educated in Dallas and Detroit

	DALLAS			DETROIT		
	1980	**1990**	**CHANGE 1980–1990**	**1980**	**1990**	**CHANGE 1980–1990**
1. The College-Educated as Share of Population						
Men	35.7%	31.8%	–10.9%	26.4%	25.4%	–3.8%
Women	25.5	26.4	3.5	18.8	22.3	18.6
2. The College-Educated as Share of Employment						
Men	24.3	29.4	21.0	17.8	22.2	24.7
Women	16.2	23.7	46.3	13.1	19.0	45.0

Note: Population estimates are of adult residents, ages 25–64, in metropolitan areas of Detroit and Dallas. Employment estimates are of employed residents in metropolitan areas of Dallas and Detroit.

Data taken from the 1980 and 1990 5% Public Use Microdata Sample of the Census of Population.

The role of supply-side factors may also be explored through an assessment of part-time employment. College-educated women in Detroit are far more likely to work part-time, which has contradictory implications for a supply-side explanation. In favor of the supply-side explanation, college-educated workers may bargain for higher wages despite part-time hours if they are withholding hours in a labor shortage economy. But the difference between the share of college-educated women in the population and the share in the employed workforce is the same in the two cities, not greater in Detroit, as one would expect if there was a relatively smaller pool of college-educated women in Detroit. Against the supply-side explanation, it can be argued that part-time hours as well as high unemployment suggest an excess supply of labor if at least some part-time work is viewed as an involuntary substitute for full-time work. For these reasons, then, I am skeptical that supply-side differences contribute very much to differences between these two cities in the levels of female wage inequality or gender wage inequality. Gender wage inequality among the college-educated is still lower in Detroit after controlling for industry, part-time status, and experience (results not shown).

THE MALE WAGE STRUCTURE AND UNIONS

If we look at the male wage structure, it becomes clearer that college-educated women's wages in Detroit, and those of managers and professionals, are higher there because they are pegged to the middle of a high rent-capturing male wage distribution. Astonishingly, Detroit's male, low-skilled, blue-collar workforce makes roughly the same average hourly wage as female managers and professionals ($16.61 versus

$16.44). This male "middle" is distinguished from the top, consisting of male professionals and managers, and the bottom, consisting of male service workers. Since service occupations are filled by only 4.6 percent of the male workforce in Detroit, the overwhelming majority of men earn wages near the middle zone. This helps explain three patterns. First, male wage inequality is lower as a result of higher wages earned by men in the middle. Second, gender wage inequality is lower among the college-educated because women professionals and managers (comprising 31.2 percent of the female workforce) are beneficiaries of high wage-setting institutions, even though they do not work primarily in manufacturing industries but in health and educational services. Third, because all other women fall into nonsheltered occupations and industries, gender wage inequality among the non-college-educated and female college wage gaps are substantially greater. Previous literature brings to light only the most familiar components of this configuration of inequality, that is, lower male wage inequality and (to a lesser extent) greater *average* gender wage inequality. But even attention to the latter has been eclipsed in recent years by temporal trends favoring women relative to men.

Against the backdrop of Detroit, the occupational wage structure in Dallas is substantially less bifurcated by gender. More men are in sales, clerical, and service occupations (28 versus 19.3 percent in Detroit) and correspondingly fewer are in skilled blue-collar occupations (24.7 versus 32.7 percent in Detroit). Perhaps more important, relative wages are much lower in service and blue-collar occupations than the average male wage difference between Dallas and Detroit would predict. And male wages either declined or stagnated in every broad occupational group except managers and professionals. Meanwhile, male wages in this latter group are more similar to Detroit's than they are on average and they actually *exceed* Detroit's among sales workers. Since most college graduates are employed in these two broad occupational groups, there is less dispersion between Dallas and Detroit among college-educated males than among less-educated males. The lower floor and higher ceiling in Dallas form the basis of greater wage inequality among men and less gender wage inequality among workers without a college degree. Since college-educated women in Dallas do not share in the rents that college-educated women and less-educated men garner in Detroit, they too fall further below college-educated men. Relative to Detroit, this raises gender wage inequality among the college-educated while decreasing inequality among women.

Taking these findings together, it is now possible to correct some common misconceptions about the relative merits of postindustrialism and its relationship to inequality. The age of postindustrialism has been characterized by declining real wages, increasing inequality, and, implicitly, high *levels* of inequality as well. Yet the Dallas case reveals a postindustrial configuration of inequality in which wages rose for most women, gender wage inequality is much lower among most workers, and wage inequality among women is below the national average and below one of the most industrialized regions in the United States, even after a decade of increasing dispersion. These results are explained by several distinct dynamics in Dallas—a legacy of low wages for highly educated/skilled women, a low and declining wage floor for less-skilled men, integration of men into female dominated occupations, and a high ceiling for highly educated men. These are even dynamics, one could argue, that now characterize the nation as a whole. Yet the lower level of inequality among women and between men and women is contrary to expectations derived from Blau and Kahn's cross-national research. They linked both male and female wage compression to greater gender wage equality—a scenario in which everyone benefits from a compressed male wage structure because wages are grouped closer together across a wide range of male- and female-dominated occupations. This probably never occurred anywhere in the United States. In Detroit such "solidarity" was partial, extending only to college-educated women in paraprofessional occupations. Thus for most women the route to greater equality with men appears to be in a high-growth, flexible labor-market environment.

THE RACIAL WAGE STRUCTURE

The profiles of racial wage inequality in the two cities are more straightforward than the profiles of the other forms of wage inequality because of few gender differences. The mechanisms of inequality are nevertheless still played out in gender specific terms. Among men, for instance, blacks in both Detroit and Dallas are strongly represented in skilled blue-collar occupations (the racial breakdowns are not shown in table 3.2). Nearly 50 percent of all employed black men are either in these occupations or in the professions and management. Yet black men are also overrepresented in the three lower-paying occupations (clerical, service, and unskilled blue-collar), as are black women.

Since the broad racial occupational distributions are similar in each city, the relative compensation of these occupations becomes crucial to overall levels of racial inequality. As discussed above, city differences in the hourly wages of skilled and unskilled blue-collar work are greater than for other occupations. Strong wage-supporting institutions in Detroit lift wages for blue-collar jobs well above the average wage difference between the two cities. Therefore, those black men who are employed retain relatively well-paying jobs in a more equitable labor market by 1990s standards. While racial inequality is lower, blacks carry the burden of higher unemployment that comes with a more highly institutionalized labor market. The extremely high level of black unemployment in Detroit (21.8 percent in 1990) is therefore consistent with the comparison between the United States and its unionized European counterparts, but with a racial twist. The association between unemployment and low male wage inequality is a legacy of the old industrial system in Detroit that fails to provide anything close to full employment for subordinate racial groups (or for some whites, whose unemployment rate is much lower but still above average at 7 percent).

In our two cases, patterns of male black/white inequality and male class inequality have much in common. This cannot be said about patterns of female racial inequality and female class inequality. Racial inequality for both men and women is much greater in Dallas, where class inequality among women is lower. Black women in both cities are underrepresented in the two occupational groups employing the largest share of college-educated workers (management and professions, and sales). However, the degree of underrepresentation is less in Detroit, where 27 percent of black women are employed as managers and professionals, compared to 22 percent in Dallas. Another 18 percent are employed in technical and blue-collar occupations that pay an average wage above the average wage in sales in Detroit. This extent of racially integrated occupational attainment is embedded in a more stratified female wage structure in which *dispersion among black women* is, like class wage inequality among women, greater than in Dallas (as measured by the tenth/ninetieth ratio). The more compressed female wage structure in Dallas does not advantage blacks (or Latinas, as we will see) relative to whites because they are more deeply concentrated in the lowest-paying occupations. Although some of this may be due to higher educational attainment among whites,[10] the penalties are nevertheless much greater in Dallas's low-wage, unregulated labor market.

The Latina/o workforce in Dallas is much larger and as a whole less educated than the Latina/o workforce in Detroit and is correspondingly likely to constitute a more significant share of the lowest-paying occupations. Nearly 40 percent of Latina/os are employed in unskilled blue-collar and service occupations in Dallas, as compared to 15 percent of all employees. Latino/as also have the smallest share of their workforce in the management and professions, whereas in Detroit Latinas are overrepresented in those occupations and Latinos are overrepresented in skilled blue-collar jobs. Thus occupational attainment and integration among Latina/os in Detroit is much further along than in Dallas.

Immigration must be considered one part of the explanation for such differences across the two cities. As other researchers have argued, the low wages of immigrants, especially in labor markets where they represent a substantial presence, are equally a measure of supply-and-demand factors, as the lower unemployment rate and higher employment growth rate in Dallas will attest (Mollenkopf and Castells 1991; Portes and Zhou 1992). Although immigrants are only 11 percent of the labor force (most of whom are Latino/as), this is still twice the share of immigrants in Detroit's labor market. Moreover, the immigrants in Dallas are probably younger and have been in the United States a shorter time. We also cannot discount the fact that a less regulated economy is more likely to permit discriminatory behavior among employers, especially in metropolitan areas that have attracted so many highly skilled white migrants from other parts of the country. These factors combine to create greater racial dualism in postindustrial, immigrant cities like Dallas. Even the older, Northern, postindustrial cities, such as New York City, are more predisposed to greater levels of racial inequality than are older industrial cities. Thus the distinction is not simply a regional one.

Generalizability

Having surveyed the outcomes and dynamics of inequality in these two cities, it is worth concluding with a few comments on their generalizability. Every measure of inequality presented here was modeled as a macro-level outcome that varied across local labor markets after controlling for individual or micro-level human capital characteristics in each of the local labor markets (see chapters 4 to 6; McCall 1998, 1999, 2000a, 2000b, 2001). The labor-market outcomes were modeled as a linear function of local labor-market conditions, which were measured in several different ways. The analysis measured the direction of changes in inequality relative to the average labor market associated with each measure of restructuring, after controlling for all other measures of restructuring. Hence the analysis did not account for interaction effects, which are best explored in a detailed case study such as this one. Nevertheless, it is possible to extrapolate from the multivariate findings to the present cases. First, areas with a disproportionate share of manufacturing employment tended to be associated with each component of the Detroit configuration of inequality, with the exception of the racial wage gap between whites and Latinos. Second, the measure of joblessness yielded more ambiguous findings for men depending on the presence of other variables in the equation since unemployment by itself (without strong wage-setting institutions) is not beneficial. And, third, employment in high-technology services is also more likely to evoke the results found in the Dallas case.

A survey of cities with industrial profiles similar to Dallas and Detroit and identical configurations of inequality offers a further confirmation of these results. For example, there are two other unique configurations emerging from the larger project, one associated with immigrant-rich cities and the other with high-technology manufacturing production (see chapter 2). I found that the major "global" cities studied elsewhere are a mix of postindustrial and immigrant configurations of inequality, including Silicon Valley, New York City, Los Angeles, and Miami (which is the ideal case for the immigrant configuration of inequality). As for the industrial configuration of inequality, several small Midwestern cities with concentrated manufacturing employment had similar structures of inequality (for example, Gary, Indiana). A simple bivariate correlation matrix of the gender, class, and racial outcomes also yielded results consistent with the case-study conclusions presented here.[11]

POLITICAL AND POLICY IMPLICATIONS

Some international research has suggested that, all else being equal, countries with stronger wage-setting institutions and high unemployment as a result of adjustments to the new economy should have lower male wage inequality, which in turn should be associated with lower gender wage inequality. Blau and Kahn's research further suggested that the levels of male and female wage inequality were highly correlated across OECD countries. The political significance of these findings should not be underestimated: they imply that a single set of policies or path of economic development results in lower inequality of all kinds, or at least those forms of inequality considered thus far in cross-national research (that is, not including racial inequality). An understanding of the causes of one dimension of inequality should therefore be relevant to an understanding of the causes of other dimensions of inequality. Do we see the same patterns when comparing Detroit, an old, Northern, industrial economy with strong wage-setting institutions and high unemployment, to Dallas, a new, Southern, postindustrial economy with strong service sector growth and low unemployment?

Although both cities saw gender wage inequality decline and class and racial inequality within gender groups increase over the course of the 1980s, there were striking differences between the two cities in the level and structure of inequality. High unemployment and more advanced and encompassing wage-setting institutions in Detroit were associated with less male wage inequality and less racial wage inequality, as observers familiar with the racial and industrial character of Detroit would expect and prevailing theory predicts. Surprisingly, though, these same characteristics were also associated with lower levels of gender wage inequality among the college-educated because highly educated women in the professions and management were included within the circle of occupations and industries benefiting from union-led wage premiums. However, less-educated women were not so included, and this led to higher female wage inequality (within but not between racial groups) and significantly greater gender wage inequality among the less-educated. Historically, the level of female wage inequality in Detroit was so high that Dallas's 1989 level, after a decade of widening inequality, was about the same as Detroit's level in 1979. Similarly, gender wage inequality among less-educated workers was between 20 percent and 25 percent greater in Detroit. Dallas, without wage-support institutions that significantly raise wages for less-educated men or college-educated women, shows a configuration of inequality that is the inverse of Detroit's on every dimension of wage inequality.

The scholarly and popular focus on only the most visible effects of economic restructuring, especially as portrayed in studies of change over time, has come at the cost of serious debate over the equity conflicts embedded in alternative paths of economic development. I do not mean to imply by this particular case study that unions and other wage-setting institutions *as such* are the main causes of gender inequality or are inherently detrimental to working women. In fact, it is one of the central implications of this comparative analysis that gender inequality flourished in industrial economies because the benefits of unionization were *not* extended to workers in traditionally low-wage female occupations. A case study of a city with a different and more inclusive history of unionization might bear out the benefits of unionization for less-skilled women (Las Vegas and Minneapolis have been suggested to me), but this should not paper over the historical fact that Detroit's version of industrial unionization is the more standard one, both in the United States and in the advanced industrialized world more generally.

Moreover, this historical legacy of gender-biased unionization is unfortunately propelled into the present when national concern over the new inequality obscures the dynamics of gender, class, and race once again by pitting a supposedly equitable industrial past against a supposedly unequal postindustrial present/future.

In particular, when policy discussions are driven by trends in male wage inequality, as they currently are, the array of complicating factors raised above fall by the wayside, and Detroit emerges as a clear preference over Dallas, even with the specter of continued racialized unemployment. Much of the restructuring literature, beginning with Piore and Sable's (1984) seminal *The Second Industrial Divide*, has been preoccupied with the ability of U.S. manufacturing to become more competitive, to restructure, and to reindustrialize within either older or newer industrial regions (see also Harrison 1994). Indeed, Detroit is making a spectacular comeback. In this context, gender-related divisions are central, making a gendered analysis that considers the implications for both gender wage inequality and inequality among women imperative. Only an analysis of *levels as well as temporal trends in wage inequality* captures these dynamics—a falling gender wage gap in particular obscures them—and only an analysis that breaks inequality down into its gender, racial, and class components provides the information necessary to guide political and policy debates over how to reduce inequality.

Thus, the comparison of Detroit and Dallas reveals that each city is actually embedded within its own matrix of restructuring and inequality and no single national narrative of industrial versus postindustrial development can do justice to the mechanisms involved in this process (Moore and Pinderhughes 1993; Tienda 1995). Few (if any) actually existing paths of regional economic development have naturally offered a broad-based panacea to the problem of inequality in all its complexity. Indeed, there should be unease at the suggestion of choosing *either* Dallas or Detroit, or any other regional economy, as the better, more equitable model of economic development.

As the case of Dallas demonstrates, for example, the goal of decreasing inequality among women can be achieved through multiple avenues and is often encumbered by gender discrimination in a way that makes its achievement illusory and misleading. Equality among women may be lower due to the blocked mobility of highly skilled women in a work culture dominated by elite men, a phenomenon found in many major postindustrial cities. On the other hand, it may be lower because high-school-educated women actually are filling in the middle of the wage distribution, a phenomenon also evident in postindustrial economies such as Dallas. A third possibility is that it may be low due to the blocked mobility of virtually all women, as in Midwestern industrial regions where college-educated women do not perform as well as they do in Detroit (St. Louis and several industrial suburbs of Chicago fit this description). Finally, lower female class inequality may collide with greater racial inequality among women, as in Dallas. Racial inequality within gender groups cannot be expected to follow the patterns of inequality found among either men or women, although these case studies and the multivariate research cited above suggests that there are more similarities between class and racial inequality among men (see chapters 4 to 6).

In part in contrast to the centrality of gender inequalities in industrial economies, the case of Dallas suggests that gender would become somewhat less salient among the bulk of workers without a four-year college degree. Although some feminists have argued that the economy is becoming more "feminized"—referring not only to increasing female labor-force participation but to the free fall of men into the casualized labor market—it is perhaps more accurate to conceptualize recent shifts as a challenge to femininization, as a trend toward integration in the bottom half of the labor market (Clement and Myles 1994; Larner 1996). Given the high levels of male wage inequality and racial wage inequality in postindustrial cities such as Dallas, it follows from the integrationist perspective that it would be more fruitful to focus attention on the wage structure in its combined gender, race, and class dimensions, rather than on the female composition or character of occupations as such, as is more typical in the feminist literature. If the future looks more like Dallas than Detroit or if Dallas and Detroit are becoming more similar, as some researchers have theorized about the convergence of goods and service production (Applebaum and Batt 1994), those concerned about male wage inequality should turn their attention to reducing inequality in service-dominated economies. Similarly, feminists should reorient their politics toward a more inclusive concern for the dynamics of racial inequality and for the conditions of male as well as female low-wage workers.

In sum, researchers and advocates in the United States and in other countries can look within their borders to examine the welfare implications of different institutional and economic conditions in a process similar though not identical to that carried out in cross-national comparisons. In doing so with the two cities of Dallas and Detroit, I have found that neither one city nor the other can fully represent a blueprint for an equitable future. Dallas and Detroit are each part of the national experience of restructuring and are best understood as coexisting rather than alternative or competing paths of development. As these cities have historically evolved, each has developed a mix of positive and negative elements and each therefore requires political intervention to fully attack the problem of inequality. To be effective, such intervention will have to be targeted to where it is most needed. In particular, the findings from this comparative case study caution against assimilating the dynamics of female wage inequality to the more standard and straightforward dynamics of male wage inequality. The substantive meaning of female wage inequality changes under different configurations of inequality that bind it to patterns of gender wage inequality. Differences between college- and non-college-educated workers turn out to be especially salient in understanding gendered structures of inequality. This comparative case study also cautions against assimilating the dynamics of racial inequality among women to those of class inequality.

Taken together, then, the effects of recent economic changes on wage inequality by gender, race, and class are not reducible one to the other but must be analyzed as intricately and comprehensively as transformations in the structure of production and production relations currently are. If this challenge is taken seriously, debate will center on a range of different economic development strategies associated with distinct patterns of inequality. This in turn will demand, finally, a more contextual approach to the shifting significance of gender, class, and race in strategies aimed at reducing economic inequality.

Part II

Chapter Four

BREAKING THE CONNECTION:
OCCUPATIONAL GENDER SEGREGATION AND THE
GENDER WAGE GAP

Ending occupational sex segregation has been a major feminist cause for much of this century. This cause has been fueled at least in part by a large research literature showing that "women's work" is low-waged work even after controlling for differences from "men's work" in skills and other productivity-related characteristics; that is, women earn less than men do even when working in jobs requiring the same skills. Such evidence goes a long way toward pinpointing women's segregation into separate and devalued occupations as the root source of their lower wages. Feminist policies have seized on these findings and sought to remedy the harms of occupational segregation in two ways: by bringing women's wages in line with men's when they work in jobs requiring comparable skills, and by creating opportunities for women to move into men's occupations. Thus the two main anti-inequality feminist policies—comparable worth and affirmative action—place occupational sex segregation at the center of analysis and, as a consequence, both evaluate women's wage deficits against a presumed male occupational and wage standard. For the most part, these two policies are appropriate devices to combat exactly the kind of discrimination they were meant to.

In this chapter, I consider why the current era of economic restructuring demands a rethinking of the standard assumption that occupational sex segregation leads to gender wage inequality. As in previous chapters, my basic objective is to show that the same economic conditions do not necessarily have the same consequence for all forms of inequality and therefore that each form of inequality has to be understood both on its own *and* in relation to other forms in a configuration of inequality. I do, however, approach this basic theme from a somewhat different angle than previously. On the one hand, I simplify the discussion by restricting my analysis to gender inequality. Just as the full structure of gender, class, and racial inequality varies with each of the city-based configurations discussed in chapters 2 and 3, so should the more narrow relationship between occupational segregation and wage inequality vary across labor markets of different kinds. In other words, even when looking at indicators of the same dimension of inequality—gender—it is possible to end up with divergent patterns.

On the other hand, I complicate the discussion by expanding my analysis to include a wider range of local labor-market conditions and a larger number of labor markets (more than five hundred). This allows me to investigate whether there is a *systematic* relationship between local economic conditions and gender inequality, one that goes beyond and reinforces the relationships uncovered in the case studies of Dallas, Detroit, Miami, St. Louis, and the global cities. In fact, it is these systematic analyses of just a few measures of inequality at a time that make the configurations in previous chapters not only plausible but generalizable. The central finding here—that we cannot assume that either of these two prime indicators of gender inequality is a predictor or precursor of the other—is really a fundamental building block of the full configurations of inequality presented in earlier chapters.

I begin the systematic part of the analysis in this book with this particular building block for several reasons. First, there is so little research on gender and restructuring in the United States that there is still much to be said about the impact of economic restructuring on the two most basic and commonly cited measures of gender inequality (the average gender wage gap and the average level of occupational gender segregation). Second, the relationship between occupational segregation and the gender wage gap has been such a fundamental one in U.S. research and advocacy that it is especially ripe for closer scrutiny. And finally, I knew that I would not, fortunately, have to start from scratch in my attempt to break open this somewhat "sacred" relationship. Although it may come as a surprise to some, it has actually been well established for some time that there is no reason why occupational segregation *must* result in wage inequality. International comparative research clearly shows that some countries, such as the Scandinavian countries of Sweden and Norway, have a high degree of occupational segregation accompanied by a relatively narrow wage gap. Meanwhile, countries such as Japan and the former German Democratic Republic have less occupational segregation but greater wage inequality. Rachel Rosenfeld and Arne Kalleberg's (1991) analysis of nine OECD countries even led them to conclude that there is "little evidence that countries with more segregation have a larger gender gap in earnings" (217).

I draw from research on these other countries but focus on what they imply about the impact of recent structural changes in the U.S. economy on gender inequality. I explore how some labor market characteristics offer vivid examples of rather unconventional relationships between segregation and the wage gap. In particular, I examine the conditions in which occupational segregation is not strongly or even positively correlated with wage inequality. For example, there may be places in which economic conditions produce a degree of occupational segregation that is substantially more pronounced than the degree of wage inequality. This is not too difficult to imagine in an economy producing precipitous declines in wages among low-skilled men without comparable declines among women or changes in occupational composition. As Jill Rubery and Collette Fagan (1995) argue: "to compare the *level* of segregation while failing to compare the *meaning* of segregation ignores the scope for similar levels to be associated with markedly different outcomes" (215). That is, a high level of gender occupational segregation may be interpreted as more consequential if accompanied by an equally high gender wage gap than if accompanied by a low wage gap. As I explain in detail below, this argument has been an inchoate one in comparable-worth theory in the United States and a more explicit one in international comparative research. Yet its broader applicability to the United States has been largely ignored (for an interesting exception, see Blum 1991).

To begin exploring this argument in the context of the United States, we need to theorize occupational segregation as an independent dimension of gender economic equality, one that does not necessarily result in gender wage inequality but is contingent on the broader economic context. I do this by shifting attention from the effect of occupational segregation on wage inequality to the effect of economic conditions on segregation and wage inequality separately. In contrast to virtually all research on this topic in the United States over the last twenty-five years or so, I do not assume *a priori* that occupational segregation causes wage inequality. I do not, in other words, restrict my analysis to whether and how much of an effect occupational composition has on the gender wage gap. Instead, I examine two parallel but separate models of gender occupational composition and the gender wage gap. I also introduce a "meso-" comparative dimension to what has typically been a microfocused analysis of the net differences in productivity-related (human capital) characteristics between individual men and women. Putting these two innovations together, I test whether local economic conditions have an identical effect on occupational segregation and wage inequality, after controlling for differences in individual human capital (see the Technical Appendix). If they do, we can reasonably conclude that these two dimensions of gender inequality are in fact related in the conventional way. The same conditions result in the same outcomes presumably because occupational and wage inequalities are intertwined so thoroughly.

I show, however, that a more complex conceptualization of the relationship between segregation and wage inequality emerges when we introduce structural economic conditions into the analysis. Once we take the context of local labor-market restructuring and men's as well as women's changing labor-market positions into consideration, conventional interpretations of the sources of and solutions to gender inequality must be reconsidered. In particular, given recent labor market changes that have hurt men (as well as women) at the bottom end of the labor market, the findings presented in this chapter suggest that there should be more attention to wages and wage inequality *directly* rather than to occupational segregation as the incubator of wage inequality. This does not mean that occupational segregation is unimportant, only that its significance needs to be assessed relative to other features of the configuration—levels of wage inequality, levels of men's and women's wages, and the broader economic context. A framework that accommodates unconventional as well as conventional interpretations of occupational segregation in this way will provide a more accurate conceptualization of gender inequality, a better account of the conditions that facilitate and impede gender inequality, and a wider and more effective array of tailored policy prescriptions with which to challenge it. A central question throughout the chapter, then, is whether current feminist policies such as comparable worth and affirmative action are likely to be effective and appropriate in all environments and, if not, whether there are viable alternatives.

In the following sections, I develop and then test a conceptual framework for understanding how the relationship between occupational segregation and the wage gap varies across labor markets of different kinds. The starting point is the loose framework suggested by case studies of countries with unconventional patterns of segregation and wage inequality. I use these case studies to define a set of four conventional and unconventional relationships and then discuss the conditions that might give rise to them in local labor markets. Though my emphasis is on the unconventional patterns, I also describe the environments in which we are likely to find the conventional patterns as well. After laying out the framework, I describe the extent of variation across U.S. labor markets in both the gender wage gap and occupational gender segregation and the extent to which the two measures are correlated. I then focus in the rest of the chapter on the results from the analysis of local labor-market conditions. Although not all expectations (derived from the framework) were realized in the results, the basic underlying argument—that the centrality and significance of occupational segregation varies with its relationship to the gender wage gap and local conditions—is amply supported.

INTERNATIONAL AND INTRANATIONAL COMPARISONS

Cross-national scholarship provides a number of interesting examples of unconventional relationships between occupational segregation and wage inequality. These unconventional relationships do not occur haphazardly or randomly but are formed from particular institutional contexts that are defined by state and private-sector regulation of the wage-setting process, the provision of social services such as family care, and the structure of the education and training system (Treiman and Roos 1983; Rosenfeld and Kalleberg 1990, 1991; Blau and Ferber 1992; Blau and Kahn 1992, 1994; Sorensen and Trappe 1995; Rubery and Fagan 1995). Within this body of cross-national research, the institutional context of the United States is defined in largely negative terms because it has no formal, overarching, industrial or family care policy and is relatively deregulated, decentralized, and flexible in the setting of wage rates and the provision of occupational training (DiPrete and McManus 1996). Given these institutional differences between the United States and other advanced industrial countries, there can be no simple one-to-one correspondence between the sources of international and intranational variation in gender inequality. However, a closer look at a few selected countries will help illustrate some of the mechanisms that are at the root of unconventional relationships between occupational segregation and wage inequality by gender.

I outline in table 4.1 four possible relationships between occupational gender segregation and the gender wage gap from a comparative perspective. Previous research has focused on how the feminization of an occupation reduces its average pay so that a high degree of occupational segregation is accompanied by a high degree of wage inequality (Treiman and Hartmann 1981; England 1992).[1] This relationship is represented by cell A. In its more positive guise, this relationship is also expressed in cell D where occupational integration is supposed to guarantee a lower wage gap. In contrast, the two unconventional relationships fall in cells B and C. These represent the potential for occupational segregation and wage inequality to move in opposite directions. Since the unconventional relationships reflected by these two cells are the focus of this chapter, I discuss the institutional dynamics frequently associated with such cases in the international arena and then turn to how labor market restructuring in regional labor markets in the United States could result in similar outcomes.

In cell C we can see the case in which relatively high occupational gender segregation is accompanied by a low gender wage gap. This sce-

Table 4.1 The Relationship between Occupational Gender Segregation and the Gender Wage Gap

OCCUPATIONAL GENDER SEGREGATION	GENDER WAGE GAP	
	HIGH	**LOW**
High	A: Cross-Occupational Wage Inequality	C: Cross-Occupational Wage Equality
Low	B: Within-Occupational Wage Inequality	D: Within-Occupational Wage Equality

nario is well known to comparative scholars and is illustrated by the Scandinavian countries of Sweden and Norway. Sweden, for example, extends affordable family and child care options to women as an incentive to enter the paid labor force. These policies have indirectly created a highly gendered division of labor, distributing women into public-sector service and men into private-sector production and management occupations. In fact the Swedish system is a growing source of concern precisely because women are so thoroughly segregated into what are mainly part-time jobs with little potential for advancement into powerful segments of the state or private economy. Yet, as is also well known, the negative wage effects of segregation are significantly attenuated by Sweden's egalitarian pay structure. The encompassing and centralized union movement in Sweden adopted a solidaristic and essentially gender-neutral approach to wage-setting policies, so that almost all low-wage workers benefited from a policy of equalizing wage rates across industries and occupations (Ruggie 1984; Rosenfeld and Kalleberg 1990).[2] In such an environment, occupational segregation by gender matters less in terms of its effect on women's pay because there is *cross-occupational wage equality.*

The second scenario in which occupational segregation is less focal occurs when men and women work in the same occupations but are not paid the same amount, that is, when there is *within-occupational wage inequality.* Cell B of table 4.1 defines the case in which lower occupational segregation is accompanied by higher gender wage inequality, as in Japan (Kondo 1990; Rosenfeld and Kalleberg 1991; Brinton 1993) and the former German Democratic Republic (Sorensen and Trappe 1995). In Japan, women are more likely to be employed in manufacturing and agricultural occupations than in most other advanced industrial countries, yet a dual wage structure pays women less than men whether or not they work in the same establishments or industries. This is mainly because women in these occupations tend to work less, either by working part-time or by interrupting their work experience with child rearing. This within-occupational gender inequality extends from wages and benefits to job security in the feminized "secondary" labor market and is a durable feature of Japan's employment and wage institutions.

Although the outcomes are similar in the German Democratic Republic, the mechanisms differ in that gender differences in employment training and labor-market participation were nearly abolished as a matter of state policy (Sorensen and Trappe 1995). Despite equal qualifications and nearly continuous full-time employment over their lifetime, women's wages remained well below men's. In order to explain this outcome, Sorensen and Trappe (1995) estimated the income gap between men and women using both occupational and industrial segregation as controls. They found, however, that segregation had little or no significance in explaining the income gap. In such an environment, then, within-occupation inequality is clearly a more serious form of gender discrimination than between-occupation inequality. Occupational segregation matters less because wage inequality takes place despite occupational integration.

COMPARISONS ACROSS REGIONS WITHIN THE UNITED STATES
Although we cannot neatly distinguish between labor markets within a single country as if they were entire nation-states, we can take advantage of the considerable size and diversity of the United States to explore variation in the relationship between occupational gender segregation and the gender wage gap. All four relationships in table 4.1 theoretically exist in the context of a deregulated national economy with uneven economic and industrial development across regional labor markets. In exploring the changing significance of occupational segregation in a single country, our attention necessarily shifts from differences between state policies and national institutional environments to differences between subnational labor markets in their economic, industrial, occupational, and wage structures. In keeping with the thrust of comparative research, I am not interested in merely replicating cross-national patterns. My focus extends to the more important issue of identifying the underlying causes of wage inequality and its relationship to occupational segregation. This allows us to focus on the "conditions that facilitate or impede the achievement of gender equality" (Rosenfeld and Kalleberg 1990: 102), to reconceptualize women's economic inequality, and to update feminist policy formulations to better reflect the new economic environment brought on by restructuring over the last twenty-five years.

Of the two cells representing unconventional relationships between occupational segregation and wage inequality (cells B and C), the configuration in which segregation is high but wage inequality is low (cell C) presents the greatest challenge to conventional theory. In this scenario, it cannot be said that segregation takes place at a "deeper" but unmeasured organizational level and is therefore consistent with the conventional view, as can be said of the other unconventional relationship represented by cell B. Instead, measurement problems are not an issue and there is no way around the fact that certain contextual factors sever the direct impact of segregation on pay, creating the conditions for the type of *cross-occupational wage equality* found in Sweden. We can see this process approximated in the United States in at least two ways.

First, the intended short-term goal of comparable worth is to raise pay in female jobs to the level of similarly skilled male jobs. Segregation remains intact, as many feminist critics of comparable worth have noted, as the wage gap among comparably skilled male and female workers declines. Since the policy is aimed at low-waged and middle-income sales, service, and clerical occupations, one of its virtues is that it is more likely to be beneficial to groups at the middle and bottom of the labor market, rather than those at the top. Though promising and suggestive in theory, it is unlikely that comparable worth will ever achieve the level of institutionalization required to reach the level of cross-occupational wage equality in Sweden. This is true even in those states where strong pay-equity statutes have been implemented (but see Figart and Lapidus 1996 for the large impact it would have *if* it *were* to be implemented in the private and public sectors).

A second tendency toward wage equality across segregated occupations is rooted in an aspect of economic restructuring that is creating increasingly flexible and insecure employment conditions. What I term the deinstitutionalization of the labor market refers to a whole host of recent developments that have made jobs more flexible for employers but less secure for workers. These developments include lower pay, tenure, mobility, and benefits and a diminishing number of stable full-time jobs (Standing 1995; Osterman 1999). The severe decline of institutional constraints on wages through deunionization and the declining minimum wage are also frequently mentioned. In my analysis, I focus less on these formal wage-setting institutions, which are not measurable at the local level, and instead consider other factors that are often neglected in national studies of the new inequality.

Casualization, for instance, refers to temporary work, subcontracting, involuntary part-time work, and informal self-employment and is clearly a core part of the new flexible work environment (Belous 1989). Higher levels of structural unemployment and the demand for cheaper immigrant labor also weaken bargaining relationships between workers and managers and are indicative of greater flexibility in the labor market (Blanchflower and Oswald 1994; Topel 1994). These factors have all contributed to the elimination of rents in male-dominated jobs and widespread downward wage pressure, especially among less-skilled workers. The declining wages of men's jobs and the stagnation of women's pay could result in greater wage equalization without occupational integration, particularly if men exit from the labor market or reenter other male-typed but lower-paying occupations (Frey 1995). The argument that all factors related to the rise of flexible/insecure employment conditions will depress wages more for men than for women and lower the gender wage gap is also consistent with temporal studies showing greater real wage declines among low-skilled men than among low-skilled women. This is actually the dominant view of why the gender wage gap fell over time (see chapter 5 for more on this point).

However, several caveats need to be raised at this point about the implications for gender inequality of flexible and insecure employment conditions. Given such a wide range of factors discussed in the previous paragraph, it is certainly possible that *women* rather than men will experience greater wage penalties in some regional economies, especially since they tend to be concentrated in the least-secure and lowest-paying jobs. If so, and assuming segregation is maintained, there may be greater, not less, wage inequality between men and women, as suggested by the configuration in cell C. In addition, there is also reason to question whether some regions with insecure employment conditions may not foster greater occupational integration, particularly among low-waged workers. Immigrant-rich regions, for example, are often locations where nondurable, import-sensitive, manufacturing industries employ immigrant women as assemblers or where immigrant men and women alike work in small service businesses. In such instances, wages are likely to be below average and integration greater among low-wage workers. But whether wages will be lower by a greater degree for men than for women is difficult to predict *a priori*.

The important point to grasp is that, *whatever the outcome*, it is impossible to interpret the meaning of occupational segregation and wage inequality without taking into consideration the context of insecure employment conditions. Even if occupational and wage integration go forward, such a seemingly fortuitous state of affairs must be tempered by the context of low wages and economic insecurity. Alternatively, even if occupational and wage integration is impeded, the wider economic context suggests that economic insecurity might be best attacked by non-gender-specific economic development and redistributive programs.

The second unconventional relationship between segregation and the wage gap occurs when the extent of segregation is low relative to the degree of wage inequality, as in cell B. *Within-occupational wage inequality* is often caused by men and women working in the same occupation but not in the same industry, in the same occupation and industry but not in the same establishment, or in the same occupation and establishment but not in the same job title (Bielby and Baron 1984; Groshen

1991; Petersen and Morgan 1995). These are all forms of employment segregation and they are the reason why researchers have tried to measure the total impact of segregation by looking at very detailed job-level segregation rather than broad occupation-level segregation. Because such detail is not always available, within-occupational segregation often goes unnoticed.

This problem is compounded by inherent problems in the classification system, in particular the fact that nonmanual occupations are classified in much less detail than are manual occupations. Consequently, there may be a similarly high level of job-level segregation among service workers and among manufacturing workers, but the occupational classification system would pick up a greater degree of segregation only in manufacturing. This suggests that within-occupational wage inequality would be most extensive in U.S. labor markets dominated by industries with fewer occupational classifications and higher wage variation, such as the service industries.[3] Although our assessments of the seriousness of segregation must be sensitized to the possibility of hidden levels of segregation, it should also be emphasized that integration in moderately detailed and even broad occupational categories must be considered a step toward integration in its own right (Charles and Grusky 1995).

The next two configurations are the ones most familiar to U.S. researchers (see cells A and D). In these configurations, wage inequality results from occupational segregation and wage equality from occupational integration. Looking first at cell A, *cross-occupational wage inequality* occurs when men and women work in different and unequally compensated occupations, though this configuration does not preclude wage inequality in gender-mixed occupations. In the extreme, this configuration is best represented by regional economies dominated by mining and durable-goods manufacturing—both spatially concentrated industries—in which women are excluded from production, craft, professional, and managerial jobs. Because technological innovations in manufacturing are considered paramount in the contemporary struggle to maintain global competitiveness, I focus on regions specializing in high-technology and export-oriented manufacturing. These are industries that tend to employ men as skilled production workers, engineers, and technicians, while women work on the assembly line or in the back office. As Jenson (1989), McDowell (1991), and others have argued, this model of economic development, sometimes referred to as post-Fordism or flexible specialization, will reproduce Fordist gendered segmentation in the absence of gender-targeted training and employment policies.

Turning to cell D, we know of no model country with a high standard of living and a low degree of both gender segregation and gender wage inequality; but are there certain types of labor markets that might lead to such an outcome? One possibility is the prototypical postindustrial economy, which many have argued is characterized at one end by highly skilled and technologically advanced professionals and at the other end by low-level service, clerical, and sales workers (Harrison and Bluestone 1988; Sassen 1991). As Linda McDowell (1991) argues, contrary to expectations that a large and growing service sector increases occupational segregation and therefore wage inequality between men and women, a service-dominated economy eventually ought to incorporate the vast majority of male and female workers.[4] More specifically, I would add that integration takes place by men moving into female-typed occupations among the non-college-educated and by women moving into the male-dominated professions among the college-educated. Thus rather than reinforcing gender dualism, such environments may be reinforcing dualism along every dimension but gender.

Having said that, however, we cannot rule out the possibility that occupational integration takes place at one level of occupational detail while wage inequality within occupations persists, as discussed above. This may particularly be the case at the high end of the postindustrial occupational structure, where men are likely to dominate (Brint 1991; Sokoloff 1992). Something else to consider is whether these economies foster a higher standard of living, in terms of higher relative wage levels, for all workers or only certain groups of workers. I take up this latter concern in a preliminary way here by looking at average wage levels, and then in much greater detail in chapter 5.

In discussing cells B and D, the reader may have noticed that I have focused on some of the same conditions and yet suggested different possible outcomes. I first suggested that regional economies dominated by service industries or specializing in high-end services were likely to be more occupationally integrated. As a consequence, the level of wage inequality within occupations, if higher, would be more important than occupational segregation *per se* (as in cell B), at least at the level of occupational detail examined here. In other words, integration takes place at one level and not at a deeper level between more finely defined occupational categories, which creates the conditions for a larger gender wage gap. On the other hand, I have also just suggested in my discussion of cell D that both occupational segregation and wage inequality could be lower in service and postindustrial economies because of a more thorough process of integration at all levels. These alternatives are both plausible because the actual outcome depends on something that is unobservable—the extent of dispersion within relatively detailed occupational categories. The analysis is therefore exploratory and will be useful in identifying whether postindustrial economies are characterized by a conventional or unconventional pattern of gender inequality.

To summarize, the framework laid out in this section suggests that occupational segregation should be understood as an independent dimension of gender inequality that may or may not increase gender wage inequality. The significance and impact of segregation will depend on the underlying economic conditions; it cannot be assumed *a priori*. In one possible unconventional scenario, flexible/insecure employment conditions may leave occupational segregation intact while imposing a greater penalty on men's wages and decreasing the gender wage gap. In a second scenario, also unconventional, increasing employment in the service sector may promote a certain degree of occupational integration without necessarily lowering the gender wage gap if there is within-occupational wage inequality. These possibilities, in addition to more conventional ones, must be raised in any consideration of the new structure of gender inequality in the United States. Economic restructuring is creating environments in which current theories and policies do not automatically apply. Without abandoning a concern for places where occupational segregation still significantly increases wage inequality, we need to open the way for a nonstatic and multidimensional account of economic restructuring and gender inequality.

EVIDENCE

It is useful to begin this section, as we did the last section, with an overview of variation across nation-states in the relationship between occupational gender segregation and the gender wage gap. This will serve as a basis of comparison for the study of regional variation in the United States and as an introduction to measures of gender wage and occupational inequality. After establishing that the degree of variation in gender occupational and wage inequality across U.S. labor markets is comparable to that across countries, the discussion will focus on the conditions that result in different relationships between these two key indicators of gender inequality.

Several studies have assembled data of comparable quality for a small sample of OECD countries in order to examine occupational segregation and/or wage inequality. Using data from various years throughout the 1980s, Rosenfeld and Kalleberg (1991: 216) calculated the ratio of female to male earnings for a sample of nine countries and found it to be lowest in Japan and highest in Australia. In Japan women earn just 35 percent of men's earnings, whereas they earn 70 percent in Australia. They also calculated a measure of segregation (the dissimilarity index) in which perfect integration is marked by a score of 0.00 and perfect segregation by a score of 1.00. (Note that higher values of the segregation measure represent higher levels of inequality, whereas higher values of the female/male wage ratio represent lower levels of inequality.) The segregation measure ranged from a low of 0.28 in

Japan to a high of 0.51 in Norway. This range is very similar to another presented by Blau and Ferber (1992: 309) using International Labor Organization data for a sample of twenty-four advanced industrialized nations. Finally, the range in segregation measures in a study of eleven European countries by Rubery and Fagan (1995) using 1990 data revealed a somewhat smaller range, between 0.43 and 0.59, but Japan was excluded from the sample. Japan's unconventional mix of low segregation and high wage inequality is clear from these studies, as is the considerable degree of variation across nation-states in the level of overall gender inequality.

DOES GENDER INEQUALITY VARY ACROSS LABOR MARKETS IN THE UNITED STATES?

It probably comes as no surprise that such a large sample of labor markets also contains a lot of variation in levels of gender inequality, at least as much as there is in the sample of a dozen or so OECD countries. But variation is not only a consequence of sample size. The findings point to a degree of variation that cannot be attributed solely to less measurement or sampling error. In figure 4.1 the average gender wage gap is expressed as the ratio of female to male hourly wages and ranges from 58 percent to 86 percent with a mean of 69.5 and a standard deviation of 4.1 percent. As described in the Technical Appendix, I use a slightly different measure of segregation, the Theil Entropy Index, and a larger number of detailed occupational categories than are used in international research. But like other segregation indices, mine ranges between 0.00, indicating perfect integration, and 1.00, indicating perfect segregation. In my sample of U.S. labor markets, this measure ranges from 0.18 to 0.52 with a mean of 0.35 and a standard deviation of 0.05. I have also provided another measure of segregation in figure 4.1 (the Ratio Index) that controls for differences in women's labor-force participation and the occupational structure across labor markets (Charles 1992). It has a different scale but it too demonstrates a wide range of variation across U.S. labor markets. The extent of variation across these labor markets compares favorably not only to variation across nations but to variation over time in the United States, which went for decades until the 1970s without making a significant dent in the level of occupational segregation and wage inequality.[5]

DO SEGREGATED LABOR MARKETS HAVE HIGHER GENDER WAGE GAPS?

With variation of this magnitude, we can now look at the more interesting question of whether the underlying causes of occupational segregation are the same as those of wage inequality; that is, whether places with high occupational segregation also have high gender wage gaps. As

Figure 4.1 Spatial Variation in Raw Occupational Gender Segregation Indices and Female/Male Hourly Wage Ratios, 1989

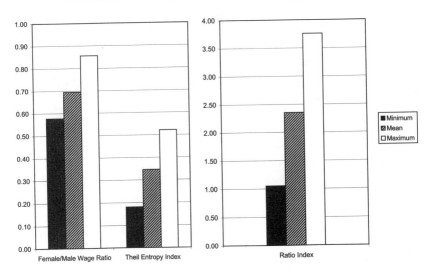

Note: See the notes to table 4.2 for data sources and definitions.

Table 4.2 Correlation between Occupational Gender Segregation and the Gender Wage Gap across Labor Markets, 1989

OCCUPATIONAL SEGREGATION INDICES	FEMALE/MALE WAGE RATIO	RATIO INDEX
Ratio Index	−0.175	
Entropy Index	−0.294	0.764

Note: Correlations across 554 U.S. labor markets. The sample includes U.S. nonfarm and non-self-employed adults, ages 25–64, with hourly wages between $1.00 and $250.00, and working in one of the selected 554 local labor markets. Both the Entropy Index and the Ratio Index are occupational segregation indices. Larger values represent higher levels of segregation, whereas larger values of the female/male hourly wage ratio represent lower levels of gender wage inequality.

See Technical Appendix for details on how the segregation indices were calculated and on the sample of 554 labor markets. Data taken from the 1990 5% Public Use Microdata Sample of the Census of Population.

presented in table 4.2, the correlation between the wage gap and my measure of segregation is –0.29. The correlation is an even lower –0.17 between the wage gap and the Ratio Index. The negative sign means that there is some tendency for the female/male wage ratio, and thus the tendency for gender equality, to decrease as occupational segregation increases. This is what we would expect. But the low absolute value of the correlations (much closer to 0.0 than to 1.0) means that highly segregated labor markets are not always the same as those with high levels of wage inequality. These weak correlations leave plenty of room to explore the two unconventional relationships between the two key indicators of women's economic status.

This can be done in a preliminary way by comparing two sets of correlations in table 4.3: 1) those between occupational segregation and measures of economic structure, and 2) those between the gender wage gap and the same measures of economic structure.[6] The correlations support both conventional and unconventional relationships between segregation and the wage gap. Recall that high values of the female/male wage ratio correspond to low levels of inequality, while high values of the segregation index correspond to high levels of segregation. That is why the correlations between the female/male wage ratio and the segregation indices in table 4.2 are negative. Therefore, if a labor market characteristic is associated with one of the conventional relationships between segregation and the wage gap (if it falls in cells A or D of table 4.1), its correlation with one of the two outcomes should be positive and its correlation with the other should be negative. This is a simple and visual way of discerning whether the causes of occupational segregation and wage inequality are the same.

A substantial number of these labor market characteristics are in fact consistent in their effects on wage inequality and occupational segregation, increasing or decreasing both at the same time. Using conventional levels of significance, six of the ten labor market variables have significant and positive associations with one outcome and significant and negative associations with the other outcome. For example, areas with a disproportionate share of service relative to manufacturing employment are more likely to be occupationally integrated and to have a lower average gender wage gap. This is also true of areas with manufacturing, FIRE (finance, insurance, and real estate), or service-industry employment growth over the 1980s. The correlation coefficients between these variables and the female/male wage ratio are all relatively weak (at roughly 0.10), though, whereas the correlations between segregation and service and FIRE growth are moderately stronger (at roughly –0.35). These results provide tentative support for the role of service dominance and growth in promoting greater integration and wage equality rather than further female "ghettoization" as some have

Table 4.3 Correlations between Occupational Gender Segregation, the Gender Wage Gap, and Labor-Market Structure, 1989

	Percent Immigrants	Percent Unemployed	Percent High-Tech Services Employment	Percent High-Tech Manufacturing Establishments	Ratio Manufacturing to Services Employment
GENDER INEQUALITY					
Female/Male Wage Ratio	0.356	0.044[a]	0.018[a]	-0.137	-0.100
Entropy Index	-0.474	0.301	-0.548	-0.318	0.197

	Percent Casualized Workers	Employment Growth in Services, 1979-1989	Employment Growth in Manufacturing, 1979-1989	Employment Growth in FIRE, 1979-1989	Percent Import-Sensitive Manufacturing Establishments
GENDER INEQUALITY					
Female/Male Wage Ratio	-0.024[a]	0.104	0.102	0.133	0.106
Entropy Index	0.366	-0.357	-0.142	-0.342	-0.173

Note: Correlations across 554 U.S. regional labor markets. The sample includes U.S. nonfarm and non-self-employed adults, ages 25-64, with hourly wages between $1.00 and $250.00, and working in one of the selected 554 labor markets. Both the Entropy Index and the Ratio Index are occupational segregation indices. Larger values represent higher levels of segregation, whereas larger values of the female/male hourly wage ratio represent lower levels of gender wage inequality.

Gender inequality data taken from the 1990 5% Public Use Microdata Sample of the Census of Population. Labor market structure data taken from sources listed in Appendix table A.1.

[a] Insignificant ($p > 0.05$).

feared. It should also be noted that the inverse of these variables results in greater segregation and wage inequality, as in cell A. For example, areas dominated by manufacturing employment are likely to foster greater gender inequality of both types.

The remaining four labor market variables are examples of unconventional relationships between segregation and wage inequality. The two high-technology variables, one representing a disproportionate share of high-technology service employment and the other a disproportionate share of high-technology manufacturing establishments, are both associated with significantly *lower* levels of occupational segregation.[7] In contrast, the average gender wage gap tends to be *greater* (though the correlation is weak) in high-technology manufacturing economies, and it tends to be average in high-technology service economies (the correlation is insignificant). These correlations are a sign that a substantial degree of integration takes place in postindustrial labor markets without a corresponding decline in the gender wage gap. Together these two high-tech variables provide instances of places where a more tempered assessment of occupational segregation's significance is warranted.

The effect of the last two labor market variables is to intensify occupational segregation without having a significant effect on the average gender wage gap. Both variables identify labor markets with insecure employment conditions, and the expectation was that occupational segregation would persist as men's wages underwent greater relative declines than women's. The correlations do indeed suggest that the level of occupational segregation increases in labor markets with high rates of joblessness (0.30) and casualization (0.37), but there is no corresponding effect on the wage gap. These results point to the new pattern of inequality discussed above, in which neither comparable worth nor affirmative action would be very effective if men's jobs and wages were being downgraded. Rather, a policy focused directly on shoring up the bottom half of the wage structure, for both men and women, would appear to be a more appropriate response. Because these two variables are perhaps the most critical in our exploration of unconventional relationships between occupational segregation and wage inequality, the next section will focus first on them, then on those that may be implicated in the second unconventional relationship, and finally on those associated with more conventional outcomes.

What Explains Regional Variation in Configurations of Gender Inequality?

Do these alternative configurations of gender inequality persist even after controlling for other relevant factors in multivariate models? If so, what are the economic conditions that underlie each configuration? To answer these questions, I analyzed the effect of each labor-market variable on three different outcome variables. The first outcome estimates the average level of occupational segregation after controlling for a standard set of human capital, demographic, industry (10), and gender interaction terms. The second and third outcomes are estimates of the average level of male hourly wages and female hourly wages, respectively. These are derived from equations run separately for men and women and are also adjusted for a standard set of human capital, industry, and demographic variables (see the Technical Appendix for further details). Having separate equations for male and female wages adds a new layer to the discussion by casting changes in the gender wage gap in terms of changes in wage levels for men and women—whether they are lower, higher, or stay the same relative to the average labor market. Each labor-market variable, then, is discussed in terms of its association with the average male hourly wage, female hourly wage, occupational segregation index, and the gender wage gap, all elements making up the configuration of inequality associated with that labor market variable.

Figure 4.2 Effects of Labor-Market Structure on the Adjusted Average Occupational Gender Segregation Index, 1989

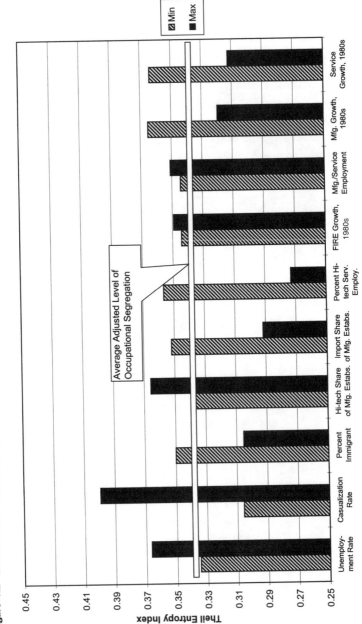

Note: See the notes to table 4.3 for data sources and definitions. See Appendix table A.1 for labor-market definitions and sources.

Figure 4.3 Effects of Labor-Market Structure on the Adjusted Average Female/Male Hourly Wage Ratio, 1989

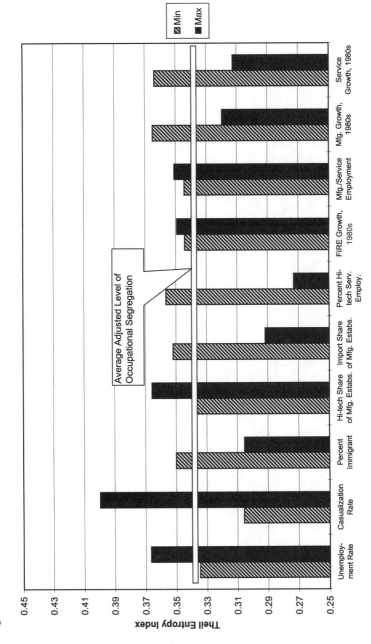

Note: See the notes to table 4.3 for data sources and definitions. See Appendix table A.1 for labor-market definitions and sources.

Figures 4.2 and 4.3 present the estimated effects of labor-market conditions on occupational segregation and wage inequality, respectively. For any particular measure of local economic conditions, the adjusted segregation index and adjusted gender wage gap will vary across labor markets as those economic conditions vary. For example, the adjusted level of segregation will be different in highly casualized versus noncasualized labor markets. The question is: How different? How much of an effect does casualization have on the level of segregation and wage inequality? To put such variation in perspective, the horizontal line cutting across figures 4.2 and 4.3 represents the estimated *average* adjusted occupational segregation index (0.346) and adjusted female/male wage ratio (0.692). Since the female/male wage ratio increases as gender inequality declines, bars *above* the horizontal line in figure 4.3 represent *lower* gender inequality. Since the occupational segregation index increases as gender inequality increases, bars *below* the horizontal line in figure 4.2 represent *lower* gender inequality. This difference between the two graphs shows again that these two measures of gender inequality are typically negatively correlated. If the bars move in the *same* direction for any particular labor-market variable, this is a sign that there is an unconventional relationship between segregation and wage inequality in those types of labor markets.

Let us look at the effect of casualization on occupational segregation as an example. Since the casualization rate varies across the 554 labor markets from a low of 16.5 to a high of 44.6 percent, the estimated level of segregation ranges from a low of 0.306 in the labor market with the lowest casualization rate to a high of 0.400 in the labor market with the highest casualization rate. This is a roughly 30 percent swing as a result of regional variation in the degree of labor-market casualization. These segregation indices for low- and high-casualization labor markets are displayed on the far left side of figure 4.2. The dark, solid vertical bar that is well above the horizontal line (the average segregation index) represents the higher-than-average level of segregation in the labor market with the highest casualization. The hash vertical bar below the horizontal line represents the lower-than-average level of segregation in the labor market with the lowest casualization. It is these maximum (solid bars) and minimum (hash bars) values that are shown in figures 4.2 and 4.3 for each labor market variable of interest. Even under the stringent controls introduced in the full multilevel model, in which all labor market variables are entered, the estimated values of occupational segregation across all explanatory variables range from 0.274 to 0.391 and the estimated values of the gender wage gap range from 0.180 to 0.434. These adjusted ranges are comparable or even greater than the ranges of "raw" unadjusted measures across advanced industrial countries.

Finally, I will also refer to a table in chapter 5 (table 5.3) that summarizes the findings on average wage levels for men and women in each type of labor market *relative to the average labor market*. The table entries of "higher," "lower," and "average" refer to the signs on the coefficients in the wage equations run separately for men and women. These signs indicate how labor markets with different economic conditions perform, again, relative to the average labor market. Positive signs indicate that wages are significantly "higher" than average and are referred to in the discussion as wage *premiums*. Negative signs indicate that wages are significantly "lower" than average and are referred to as wage *penalties*. When the coefficients were insignificant, I concluded that wage levels were "average." This information will be incorporated into the discussion below but is more fully developed in the next chapter.

In keeping with the discussion above, the presentation of results will follow the layout of table 4.1. Four configurations of occupational segregation and wage inequality are discussed: areas where occupational gender segregation and the gender wage gap are both higher (lower) relative to the average labor market, and areas where the wage gap is inversely related to occupational segregation. The discussion follows the earlier one, moving from cases exhibiting the most unconventional relationships between segregation and wage inequality (cells B and C) to those exhibiting the most conventional (cells A and D).

Unconventional Configurations of Segregation and Wage Inequality
I have argued that flexible and insecure labor market conditions will create the conditions for wage equality between men and women in a low-wage environment without necessarily promoting occupational integration (cell C). The three variables to the far left of figures 4.2 and 4.3 with dark solid bars represent three different dimensions of flexibility and insecurity. In some preliminary analyses, the effect of casualization was exactly as expected. It intensified segregation, lowered wages for both men and women, and reduced the gender wage gap by decreasing wages more for men than for women.[8] However, only some of these patterns remained in the final multilevel models presented in figures 4.2 and 4.3. While segregation still increases significantly in highly casualized regions, the wage penalties turn slightly greater for women than for men, so the gender wage gap increases along with the segregation index.

What explains these results and why do I still include them as examples of unconventional configurations? First, two key aspects of an unconventional configuration as I have defined it are consistently present in casualized labor markets—segregation is higher, but the broader environment is unfavorable to both low-skilled men and women, since wages are lower for both groups. Segregation actually reaches its highest level in the labor market with the highest casualization rate (see figure 4.2), while at the same time wages are significantly lower for the college- and non-college-educated alike. Second, a number of exploratory models reveal that the effect of casualization on men's and women's *net relative* wage penalties, and thus on the gender wage gap, is not nearly as stable as the robust negative effect on wage levels and the robust positive effect on occupational gender segregation. The net effect of men's and women's wage penalties forms the gender wage gap, and this net effect fluctuates according to the presence or absence of other labor market conditions in these other models.

More specifically, the effect of casualization on the gender wage gap is mediated by two variables that measure a labor market's broad industrial composition and change over the 1980s. The ratio of manufacturing to service industry employment and manufacturing-industry employment growth over the 1980s have a marked effect on the wage outcome of the casualization variable.[9] It seems that the spread of casualized employment significantly diminishes all workers' wages but affects men more severely than women when services dominate and manufacturing is in a growth cycle, factors that must provide some relative lift to women's wage levels. In contrast, women are worse off in heavily deindustrialized regions where manufacturing predominates. What is unconventional about casualized labor markets, then, is that segregation is higher and overall wage levels are lower regardless of extenuating circumstances, while the net gender wage gap is mediated by the broader industrial context. *It is not the level of occupational segregation that matters in determining the level of wage inequality between men and women, but different underlying economic conditions that determine whether wage penalties are worse for men or worse for women.*

The other two indicators of insecure employment conditions—high joblessness and immigrant employment—do not strictly conform to the unconventional pattern either. I mention them here (and in the section on conventional configurations as well) because they are exceptions that in some ways prove the rule of the importance of context in evaluating the significance of segregation and the sources of and solutions to gender wage inequality. Like casualization, unemployment is strongly associated with higher levels of occupational segregation regardless of the presence or absence of other labor-market variables. It is also linked to labor markets in which wage levels are below average for both men and women. Moreover, the wage penalties are actually greater for women than for men. Despite this conventional relationship between occupational segregation and wage inequality, however, I would argue that what is striking here is that the context of low relative wages for both men and women changes the significance and implications of occupational segregation. Policies inspired by the need to achieve occupational integration seem misguided against the backdrop of endemic economic distress brought on by high joblessness and casualization, in which average wages are significantly lower for *men* as well as women.

The broader economic context is also pivotal in interpreting the causes and consequences of gender inequality in immigrant-rich labor markets. As I discuss in more detail below, immigrant-rich areas have among the lowest estimated levels of gender segregation and wage inequality. This is a rather surprising outcome when placed alongside the predominant view that immigrant-rich cities are "dual" or "polarized" cities consisting of low-wage immigrant-dominated segments of both the service and manufacturing industries (Sassen 1991). Apparently, men and women work together in the same occupations, but they do so in low-end personal and retail service shops and in dead-end assembly sweatshops and factories. With this portrait in mind, these are not economies that necessarily warrant admiration for their gender equality, as they might if they held out a virtuous combination of high-tech sophistication, high wages, and greater equality among all workers. Advocating gender-based comparable-worth and affirmative action would also appear almost anachronistic since, strictly speaking, gender equality tends to be relatively advanced. Yet putting these policies to use against racial inequality, which is relatively higher in these regions *within* female-dominated, male-dominated, and mixed-gender occupations alike, may be more along the lines of what is needed (for a related discussion, see chapters 2 and 6).

One other factor was found to resemble the unconventional configuration in which wage inequality declines without a corresponding decline in occupational segregation (cell C). Employment growth over the 1980s in the advanced producer service industries of finance, real estate, and insurance is associated with higher average hourly wages and a wage premium that favors women over men. While the wage gap declines in these areas, there is no effect on the degree of occupational segregation. Regions experiencing growth in these advanced-producer services are relatively high-waged ones, and though they may exhibit a dual structure of low-wage clerical and high-wage professional occupations (Baran and Teegarden 1987; Bagchi-Sen 1995), women's wage premiums are higher relative to female wages in the average labor market and to male wages in the same labor markets. Rather than focusing on men's jobs, then, the best strategy for raising women's financial well-being may be to further shore up the quality and security of *women's existing* jobs, through employee associations, the development of career ladders, and portable benefits, for example.

In the second unconventional configuration described in cell B of table 4.1, occupational segregation tends to be lower without a comparable decline in wage inequality. This pattern is found in labor markets with a disproportionate share of employment in high-technology service industries. Occupational segregation is significantly lower and wage inequality is significantly higher. In fact, the labor market with the largest share of employment in high-tech services is the most occupationally integrated (see figure 4.2). The results are not as robust for service-industry growth, but occupational gender segregation is also significantly lower, while the wage gap is only about average. These two measures of service activity, broad service-industry growth and high-tech service employment share, are the only factors that were persistently linked to occupationally integrated labor markets and yet failed to make a major dent in the gender wage gap. This within-occupational wage inequality may derive from a number of sources—occupational segregation across industries, establishments, or job titles—or it may simply be more difficult to measure detailed occupational segregation in service-dominated economies. Still, alternative specifications with greater occupational detail delivered the same results.[10] *Thus it is fairly clear that occupational integration at a relatively detailed level of disaggregation can take place without having an impact on the degree of wage inequality.*

The last dimension of labor markets I discuss in this section offers partial support for both unconventional relationships. It was expected that as the manufacturing share of service-industry employment declines and services become a larger share of the workforce, segregation would decline if services increasingly incorporate both male and female workers (see the discussion of cells B and D above). However, the results show that segregation is basically unaffected by shifts in broad industrial composition. In contrast, wage inequality declines dramatically when employment swings decisively in favor of services. Such an outcome is due entirely to changes in women's average wages since men's wages respond hardly at all. Thus the sensitivity of women's wages, not men's wages, to shifts in broad industrial composition is governing the movement of the gender wage gap across labor markets, ranging from an estimated 0.643 in manufacturing-dominant regional economies to 0.704 in service-dominant regional economies. *Once again, it is not the level of occupational segregation that matters in determining the level of wage inequality between men and women, but different underlying economic conditions.*

In sum, there is little evidence of a conventional relationship between segregation and wage inequality in labor markets characterized by either dominance or growth in any of the service industries. The relative size and dominance of broad service-industry employment and FIRE employment growth have little effect on occupational segregation yet they significantly reduce the gender wage gap. On the other hand, broad service-industry growth and a concentration of high-end services promote occupational integration while intensifying wage inequality in one case and having no effect in the other. The main conclusion I draw from this evidence is that the shift toward services has been responsible for lower (or at least average) levels of occupational segregation, and the corresponding effect on wage inequality is essentially *unpredictable*. A decline in wage inequality, or even an average level of wage inequality, is definitely not guaranteed.

Conventional Configurations of Segregation and Wage Inequality
Evidence both strong and weak of unconventional outcomes does not mean, however, that occupational segregation never matters for the reasons it has in the past. To the contrary, it applies to perhaps the most commonly cited path to high-wage growth through investment in high-technology or technology-intensive manufacturing. Although I found that areas with a disproportionate share of high-technology manufacturing plants are likely to foster wage inequality with or without other labor market controls, occupational segregation is significantly greater only when controlling for related factors. In particular, these factors include the share of import-sensitive manufacturing establishments and immigrant workers in the local labor market, both of which are associated with greater female employment in manufacturing. In the full model, then, both occupational segregation and wage inequality are significantly higher than average. In fact, the labor market with the largest share of high-technology manufacturing establishments has one of the lowest female/male wage ratios (0.648 compared to the low of 0.643 in manufacturing dominant labor markets). Although these results were expected given the association between technology, manufacturing, and male-dominated occupations, there has been no other direct empirical evidence of greater relative gender inequality in labor markets specializing in these sectors, especially with controls for many other dimensions of restructuring. In theory, high-tech manufacturing development has many advantages explored in detail elsewhere (e.g., Piore and Sabel 1984), but fostering gender equality is currently not one of them.

Two other measures of economic structure are related to higher levels of gender inequality, but, unlike high-technology manufacturing, neither is currently considered an aspect of a progressive economic development strategy. Put side by side, the two factors of deindustrialization and unemployment result in similar outcomes, yet the significance of occupational segregation still differs because of differences in the underlying economic environment. Manufacturing employment decline—a sign of deindustrialization—and unemployment are both associated with significantly higher degrees of occupational segregation and wage inequality. Although relative wages are higher in deindustrialized regions for men and women, and relative wages are lower in slack labor markets, changes in men's and women's wages tend to favor men in each case. To those familiar with Blanchflower and Oswald's (1994) landmark study of joblessness and wage levels, these are striking findings. The disadvantages of high unemployment have previously been shown to fall disproportionately on low-skilled men, not low-skilled women (because the effect on low-skilled women was not tested). As important as this shift is in our understanding of the consequences of high joblessness, however, I maintain that the depressed nature of the local economy, including lower wages for both low-skilled men and low-skilled women, should warn against gender-based affirmative action or comparable worth strategies. In contrast, deindustrialized regions represent the ideal type of a Fordist economy and, to the extent that these regions rebound, they are precisely the ones requiring Fordist-era antidiscrimination remedies. *Thus two different environments with the same outcomes—higher occupational segregation and wage inequality between men and women—nevertheless suggest different remedies for the problem of gender inequality.*

Finally, there are several key measures that result in lower levels of both segregation and wage inequality (cell D). Among these, only labor markets with a higher-than-average percentage of immigrant workers result in significantly higher average wages for both men and women (primarily because cities with high costs of living are the very cities with the largest immigrant communities). Although labor markets with concentrations of immigrant workers may reflect a demand for cheaper labor and a trend toward polarization, as most of the literature has suggested, my analysis points to a different story when considering gender inequality. Relative wage inequalities were significantly lower because women's wage premiums were substantially greater than men's relative to the average labor market. Since immigrant-rich labor markets are positively correlated with high-technology manufacturing and services, import manufacturing, broad service sector growth, and population size, they have extremely complex industrial structures and a combination of industry segments that seem to raise female/male wage ratios for a range of different groups of workers. Within the highly unequal overall structure of these areas, then, there is more gender mixing of occupations and less "horizontal" wage inequality between men and women of the same educational background (see chapters 2 and 5). Although gender is undoubtedly considered in employers' hiring decisions, and immigrant women are channeled into some of the worst jobs, the overall structure of immigrant-rich economies is characterized more by class and racial inequality than it is by gender inequality (see chapters 2 and 6 and McCall 2001 on this point).

Two other variables also resulted in greater overall integration and wage equality by gender but they did so within the context of lower wages among men and thus in a manner more akin to casualization (cell C). Wages are lower on average and so is the gender wage gap in areas with a disproportionate share of import-sensitive manufacturing establishments and manufacturing growth over the 1980s. This is a result of wages falling more for men than for women as compared to the average labor market, a pattern found under certain conditions in casualized labor markets. Unlike casualized areas, however, segregation is significantly lower as well. Since women have increased their share of employment in manufacturing over the 1980s and they are more likely to work in nondurable import-sensitive industries, integration is most likely a result of integration at the level of production and assembly. But it must be stressed again that greater gender equality is accompanied by lower overall wages, especially among men. As with immigration, these are not necessarily regions that can serve as unequivocal models of gender equality, nor would affirmative-action or comparable-worth policies necessarily be appropriate in such a low-wage environment for men.

CONCLUSION

I began this chapter with the proposition that the relationship between occupational gender segregation and the gender wage gap can take on more than one theoretical form. I wanted to test this proposition by determining whether the same degree of cross-national variation in the segregation/wage gap relationship was also present across labor markets in the United States. If so, I also wanted to identify the local economic conditions that fostered unconventional relationships—places where segregation was high but the wage gap was low, and vice versa—and then consider the implications for anti-inequality theory and policy. I found that the relationship between these two central indicators of women's economic inequality does indeed vary considerably and systematically across regions in the United States, though not all of my expectations about how this relationship varies were confirmed.

On the one hand, some labor-market conditions had the same effect on the level of occupational segregation and the gender wage gap relative to the average labor market. These results confirmed the conventional relationship where occupational segregation (integration) is considered a major cause of wage inequality (equality). Areas with a disproportionate share of high-technology manufacturing establishments, high joblessness, and manufacturing decline were likely to have greater segregation and wage inequality. Particularly troubling are the findings for high-tech manufacturing regions, because these areas have the most potential to raise wages to a level that can maintain working-class families. As we see, though, the benefits of high-technology development are significantly skewed toward men, and therefore this is precisely the type of environment that demands gender-based affirmative-action policies. As for the conditions that create occupational integration and wage equality, the news is not much better. Areas with concentrations of immigrant workers, a disproportionate share of import-sensitive manufacturing plants, and high manufacturing growth promote gender equality, but they do so at least in part through integration and lower wages (for men and women) at the bottom end of the labor market. These conditions suggest the need for broader economic development and redistributive strategies to attack the problem of inequality in its gender as well as nongender forms.

The multivariate results also pointed to several unconventional configurations that alter the significance of occupational segregation and of the anti-inequality policies based on it. There were areas where occupational segregation was significantly lower without similar effects on wage inequality; areas where the wage gap was significantly lower without similar effects on occupational segregation; and areas where the effects on occupational segregation and wage inequality ran in opposite directions. These results are interesting for both theoretical and practical reasons. The dynamics of restructuring are creating dynamics of inequality that do not always conform to our previous understandings of how gender inequality is structured in the labor market. Segregation at a fairly disaggregated level may decline, as in service growth and high-technology service areas, while wage inequality stays the same or even intensifies. Of perhaps equal concern, wage inequality may decline despite occupational segregation and in an environment of lower overall wage levels (as in some casualized areas). In the former case men's wage premiums exceed women's, and in the latter, men's wage penalties exceed women's, with the dynamics of occupational segregation playing a less central role than those of wage determination. The segregation of occupations creates an inequality in and of itself, but the research and policy interest in this form of inequality is driven by its projected effect on wage inequality. The research in this chapter shows, however, that this might be a misguided approach. *Occupational integration does not appear to be a sufficient or even necessary condition for closing the gender wage gap.*

These results provide strong support for the conclusion that it would be appropriate to focus policies concerned with reducing gender economic inequality on the changing structure of wage inequality and wage levels rather than the gender composition of occupations as such, as in pay equity and affirmative-action schemes. Bolstering wage-setting institutions such as the minimum wage and unions would be one such policy response that has broad appeal for all low-wage workers, male and female alike. But, more generally, researchers and policy-makers would be better served by a multidimensional understanding of the relationship between restructuring and gender inequality, so that our conceptual frameworks offer a better interpretation of a changing environment and policies are refined enough to be appropriate to the tasks at hand. Clearly occupational gender segregation remains an important expression of social inequality, but as its significance changes, so should its centrality in anti-inequality theory and policy.

Chapter Five

THE DIFFERENCE CLASS MAKES: THE GENDER WAGE GAP AMONG THE COLLEGE- AND NON-COLLEGE-EDUCATED

I argued in the previous chapter that occupational gender segregation is not always the best barometer of gender wage inequality and that we should therefore focus more directly on wages and wage inequality. In this chapter I take the discussion of gender wage inequality yet another controversial step further and argue that the overwhelming focus on the *average* gender wage gap is inadequate and frequently misleading. In order to show this, I return to the college/noncollege divide that emerged as a prominent feature of configurations of inequality in earlier chapters and ask whether the distinction between the college- and non-college-educated is relevant for only a few cities or is more pervasive and systematic. This chapter focuses squarely on this question in considering whether restructuring varies in its implications for the wage gap between men and women of different class backgrounds. The basic issue is whether gender inequality is unevenly distributed among different groups of workers, so that the average gender wage gap masks low levels of gender inequality among some groups and high levels among other groups. If so, I make explicit which groups of women stand to improve their relative positions vis-à-vis men and which do not in any given labor market environment.

In order to be consistent with previous research on the importance of educational skills in the new economy, I address the issue of class differences by comparing groups of workers with different educational backgrounds (see chapters 2 and 6 for more on this point). To ensure differences in class background, I discuss only two educational groups: those with a college degree and those with less than twelve years of formal schooling. If the relative position of men and women with a college degree is the same as those without a high school degree, class differences would seem to be of little consequence, at least empirically. The impact of local economic conditions on the gender wage gap are likely to be evenly distributed among high- and low-skilled workers alike. However, if any indicator of restructuring results in higher (lower) inequality among the college-educated and lower (higher) inequality among the non-college-educated, the average gender wage gap would not provide an accurate reflection of inequality for all groups of workers. We would need to examine further the distribution and concentration of gender inequality, that is, exactly how restructuring benefits one group of women and disadvantages another, each relative to men of their same educational status. Because the average gender wage gap is perhaps the most commonly used measure of women's economic status and frequently regarded as a fair indicator of the status of *all* women and not just the average woman (Cotter et al. 1997), these questions go to the heart of how gender equality is measured and what it really means.

I examine these questions, as in previous chapters, in the context of local economic conditions in regional labor markets. In this chapter, though, I am centrally concerned with wage levels as a critical part of the economic context of gender inequality. Beyond my more general interest in the structural conditions of inequality, and the obvious importance of wage levels in defining those structural conditions, I focus on wage trends here because they have been integral to recent discussions of the declining gender wage gap. The centrality of wage trends stems, of course, from the frequently asserted claim that the declining wages of low-skilled men were the foremost factor in closing the gender wage gap over the 1980s. As this claim suggests, wage trends are an especially important part of the discussion of the gender wage gap among low-skilled workers. Therefore any examination of the "causes" of the gender wage gap, and especially one that is concerned with differences among skill groups, should investigate wage trends as a part of the mix.

In order to examine the role of wages in a spatial analysis of the gender wage gap, I need to rely on the concept of a "low-wage" or "high-wage" labor market. Although previous research has found differences in wage levels among regions to be substantial, it has not established whether the pattern of wage variation is different for men and women.[1] Hence we first need to determine whether labor markets are high-wage or low-wage separately for women and for men. Then we need to investigate whether gender wage inequality is more likely to be associated with high-wage or low-wage labor markets. In particular, we want to know whether gender wage inequality is lower only in those labor markets where men's wages are lower than average, as suggested by temporal trends; or, whether there are environments, especially for the non-college-educated, where women suffer worse wage penalties than men and thus greater wage gaps with men. Since the decline in the gender wage gap is too often reduced to men's falling wages, my spatial analysis pays as much attention to changes in women's wages as to changes in men's wages and shows that women's wages are as sensitive as men's to changes in local economic structure. I also show that the emphasis on men's wages is not a fully accurate portrayal of over-time trends either.

To give a flavor of how I blend together the three strands of economic restructuring, wage levels, and wage inequality, it might be helpful to walk step by step through the reasoning. To start, let us say that low-skilled men and low-skilled women each have an average wage in the average labor market. In any given labor market, say a high-unemployment labor market, average wage levels for both men and women are either higher than in the average labor market, lower than in the average labor market, or simply the same as in the average labor market. For instance, if wages are lower for both men and women, the labor market is considered a low-wage labor market. From this point, the gender wage gap is determined by whether women's wage penalty is less than men's wage penalty, in which case the wage gap between them would be lower as well. On the other hand, if women's wage penalty is greater than men's wage penalty, the wage gap between them would be greater. Extrapolating from this example, there are many other possible permutations of high and low wage levels, and relative wage *premiums* and wage *penalties*. Each permutation results in average, above-average, or below-average wage inequality between men and women. Since we already examined average wage levels and average wage gaps in the previous chapter, this chapter focuses on the wage gaps for the two skill groups only—the college- and non-college-educated. Our interest is in whether relative wage levels and relative wage gaps are the same for the two educational groups.

In the following sections, I begin by reviewing national studies of the gender wage gap in order to describe the current state of research on and correct some misconceptions about the impact of changes in men's and women's real wages on the gender wage gap. In addition, this overview establishes the college/noncollege divide as an important feature of both temporal trends and spatial patterns. I then move on to consider structural changes in the economy as an alternative to human capital explanations of gender inequality, providing an overview of two opposing positions on the topic. Although my interest is primarily with wage inequality, I incorporate insights from studies of occupational gender segregation that are also concerned with broad economic change. In the second section, I turn from the national level to the subnational level and focus on the dynamics of regional wage variations and their implications for gender differences in wage levels and gender wage inequality across regions for the two educational groups. The empirical results are presented in the third section, where I begin with the "high-wage" and "low-wage" status of labor markets of different kinds. I then use this information to examine the relationship between labor market restructuring and a human-capital adjusted gender wage gap for college- and non-college-educated workers.

RESTRUCTURING AND GENDER WAGE INEQUALITY: THE NATIONAL PICTURE

Over the past twenty-five years of economic restructuring, the gender wage gap has fallen at the same time that inequality of every other kind has risen. Despite the obvious coincidence of economic restructuring and decreasing gender inequality, the relationship between the two has proven difficult to conceptualize. On the one hand, the standard approach to studying changes in the gender wage gap is to parse out how much is because of improvements in women's human capital (e.g., education, experience, work attachment, and so forth) and how much is left unexplained and attributed to discrimination. Focused as they are on individuals, such approaches are unlikely to feature explanations having to do with structural economic change. Moreover, such approaches tend to focus on only the *average* gender wage gap after "controlling" for a range of individual characteristics, such as educational background. On the other hand, the connection between restructuring and inequality has been formulated mainly in terms of the causes of declining wages and rising wage inequality. This overshadows the anomalous cases of rising average female wages and declining gender inequality.

In order to have a more complete picture of both gender inequality and economic restructuring, the divide between human-capital studies of gender inequality and macrostructural studies of inequality among men needs to be bridged. I begin to bridge this divide in this section in two ways. First, I retell the popular story of the temporal decline in the gender wage gap in order to establish the importance of skill differences and the precise contribution of wages trends. This also provides an opportunity to trace the inadequacies of microexplanations of the gender wage gap. I then turn to two seemingly inconsistent perspectives on the effect of structural changes on gender inequality. These will help identify the conditions that foster gender wage inequality for the college-educated on the one hand and for the non-college-educated on the other.

THE ROLE OF SKILL DIFFERENCES AND WAGE TRENDS

As is well known, the gender wage gap declined during the 1980s more than it did at any other time in this century (Goldin 1990). What is perhaps less well known is that scholars have found that at least half of the decline in gender wage inequality cannot be explained by improvements in women's qualifications.[2] Blau and Kahn (1994, 1997) have sought an explanation for these findings in the greater declines in the gender wage gap at the bottom end of the wage distribution than at the top end. They argue that the demand for women's "unobservable" skills (the unexplained part) favored women "at lower levels of labor-market skills but favored men relative to women at higher levels" (Blau and Kahn 1994: 28; see also Katz and Murphy 1992; Bernhardt et al. 1995). Though Blau and Kahn are unusual in their attention to differences between trends at the top and at the bottom of the wage distribution, they and others have still been unable to come up with a satisfactory explanation of those differences within the human capital framework.

The need to look more closely at how and why gender wage inequality varies across skill groups is further evident in the descriptive statistics presented in table 5.1 and figure 5.1. Three patterns that are often overlooked deserve attention. First, the percentage decline from 1979 to 1989 in the gender wage gap (as measured by the female/male wage ratio) was lowest for college-educated workers (7.2 percent) and highest for non-college-educated workers (13.9 percent and 15.0 percent). This seems consistent with Blau and Kahn's conclusions about greater declines in the gender wage gap at the bottom and with the broader literature's emphasis on men's wage declines at the bottom. Second, a simple breakdown reveals that the majority of the decline in the *college* gender wage gap was due to changes in *women's* wages (77 percent), not men's wages as is true for the three other educational groups. This stems from the fact that real average wages rose more for college-educated women than for college-educated men. In contrast, real wages fell more for less-educated men than for less-educated women (see figure 5.1). Thus even though the wage gap closed more among the less-educated, college-educated women were the only group to make substantial wage gains in absolute terms. Third, the level of gender wage inequality is lowest among the college-educated in both 1979 and 1989. All three patterns strongly suggest that the closing of the gender wage gap has been mediated by educational background. Despite a falling gender wage gap for all groups, a sharp distinction between the college- and non-college-educated appears warranted in any explanation of changes in the gender wage gap, even at the national level.

While this brief survey of temporal trends points to clear differences by education, spatial trends dispel any notion that the average gender wage gap fairly represents how gender inequality is distributed among different skill groups. The range of variation in the female/male wage ratio across labor markets is exhibited in figure 5.2. These ranges are greater than over time (see chapter 4), and this holds for each educa-

Table 5.1 Female/Male Median Hourly Wage Ratios by Education, 1979 and 1989

	1979 F/M RATIO (x 100)	1989 F/M RATIO (x 100)	Δ 1979-1989 (%) (PERCENTAGE POINT CHANGE)		Δ DUE TO MEN (%)	WOMEN (%)
Less Than High School	56.0	63.8	13.9	(7.8)	72.0	28.0
High School	56.0	64.4	15.0	(8.4)	82.0	18.0
Some College	63.1	69.1	9.5	(6.0)	78.0	22.0
College	70.5	75.6	7.2	(5.1)	23.0	77.0
Average	58.8	69.8	18.7	(11.0)	71.0	29.0

Note: Sample includes nonfarm and non-self-employed adults, ages 25–64, at work, with hourly wages between $1 and $250.

Less than High School (LHS) equals less than 12 years of schooling; High School (HS) equals 12 years; Some College (SC) equals 13-15 years; College (COL) equals 16 or more years.

Data taken from the 1980 and 1990 5% Public Use Microdata Sample of the Census of Population.

Figure 5.1 Median Hourly Wages by Education and Gender, 1979-1989 (1995 Dollars)

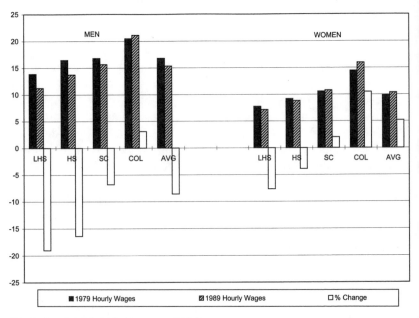

Note: See the notes to table 5.1 for data sources and definitions.

tional group. Our main interest, though, is in whether the distribution of gender wage inequality across educational groups varies across labor markets as well. In other words, in contrast to the breakdown of the nation as a whole, it is conceivable that in some labor markets the gender wage gap is lower among the non-college-educated than it is among the college-educated. If so, spatial profiles of gender wage inequality would offer much more variety than a single time series to explore the underlying causes of gender inequality for different skill groups.

This intuition is affirmed by the correlations between the gender wage gap for the college-educated and the gender wage gap for the non-college-educated across more than five hundred labor markets. These correlations are presented in table 5.2. Moderate correlations (a score of 1.0 is a perfect correlation and 0.0 indicates no correlation) among the three groups without a college degree (in the first two rows of data) stand in sharp contrast to the *absence of any significant correlation between the college gender wage gap and any of the other noncollege gender wage gaps across the 554 labor markets* (in the third row). There is even a hint (just a hint, though) of an inverse correlation between the gender wage gap for high-school-educated workers and that for college-educated workers. Based on this preliminary evidence, labor markets fostering greater equity between men and women without a college degree, the vast majority of workers, are not typically the same labor markets that promote greater equity between college-educated men and women. In other words, the distribution of the gender wage gap is uneven and not well represented by the average gap.

THE ROLE OF ECONOMIC RESTRUCTURING: TWO VIEWS

Since a good deal of changes in the gender wage gap have not been explained by previous micro-oriented scholarship, and skill differences have been largely overlooked, I turn to research on economic restructuring to develop an alternative explanation of these trends. What are the structural sources of the gender wage gap and do they differ in their impact on college- and non-college-educated workers? In order to answer this question, we need to engage the existing scholarship on economic restructuring, which has taken many different forms. Some writers have offered proscriptive visions of a new post-Fordist/postindustrial order, while others have detailed the breakdown of the old Fordist/industrial accord between capital, labor, and the welfare state. Although no single research program can be exhaustive, we lack even a synthesis of the various—and frequently inconsistent—invocations of gender and gender inequality in this broad literature. At the risk of oversimplification, I have derived two basic positions from the literature on post-Fordism, postindustrialism, deindustrialization, and feminist investigations of all three.[3]

Figure 5.2 Spatial Variation in the Female/Male Hourly Wage Ratio by Education, 1989

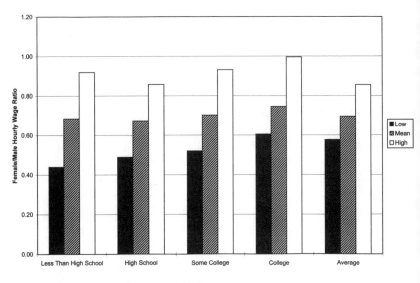

Note: See the notes to table 5.2 for data sources and definitions.

Table 5.2 Correlations between Female/Male Hourly Wage Ratios by Education, 1989

	LESS THAN HIGH SCHOOL	HIGH SCHOOL	SOME COLLEGE
High School	0.47384 (0.0001)		
Some College	0.31457 (0.0001)	0.55148 (0.0001)	
College	0.01501 (0.7245)	−0.08114 (0.0563)	0.00955 (0.8225)

Notes: Correlations across 554 U.S. regional labor markets. The sample includes U.S. nonfarm and non-self-employed adults, ages 25–64, with hourly wages between $1.00 and $250.00, and working in one of the selected 554 labor markets. Significance levels are in parentheses.

Less than High School = < 12 years of schooling; High School = 12 years; Some College = 13–15 years; College = 16 or more years.

Data taken from the 1990 5 % Public Use Microdata Sample of the Census of Population.

The first view considers economic restructuring to have been a major factor in the reduction of the gender wage gap. In accordance with basic over-time trends, one common line of argument begins with the reasons for falling wages among men, such as the shift from manufacturing to services, deunionization and casualization within both goods and service industries, automation, and increasing international competition. Mainly through their effect on men's wages, these factors have emerged as key explanations of the falling gender wage gap, especially among non-college-educated workers. In the Canadian context, Pat Armstrong (1996) refers to this process as "harmonizing downward." It invites the conclusion that inequality on the basis of gender is giving way to deeper divisions by class and race (see also Larner, 1996). In contrast are those who approach the beneficial effect of restructuring on the gender gap from the perspective of women's gains. There are now many studies of occupational and educational shifts documenting an overall upgrading in women's experience and skills in absolute terms and relative to men. This has resulted in the upward mobility of many women from the bottom to the middle of the wage distribution, increased representation of women in the professions and management, and greater employment opportunities in the burgeoning service sector.[4] Many of these studies document slow but steady progress.

In the second view, various reasons are given for a more alarming assessment of the effect of restructuring on working women. First, many feminists criticize proscriptive post-Fordist and postindustrial theories for hailing and promoting the growth of male-dominated occupations in high-technology, technology-intensive, and advanced postindustrial industries (Jenson 1989; McDowell 1991). They argue that women are excluded from the best technical jobs at all skill levels and are admitted only to those male-dominated jobs deskilled by technology (Reskin and Roos 1990). Second, many scholars have seized on the image of immigrant women working in high-tech low-wage shops, in sweatshops, and in low-wage personal and retail services, and have collapsed gender together with race and national origin to argue that gender and racial segmentation and dualism are intensifying (Harvey 1989; Leborgne and Lipietz 1992; Harrison 1994). The more general trend toward casualization and numerical flexibility, including part-time, temporary service, homework, and informal self-employment, also encompasses work that has traditionally and overwhelmingly been done by women (Cobble 1993). Finally, and related, there are those who see the persistence of gender inequality in the increasing size of the female working class in pink-collar occupations, which has been ignored by the literature's focus on men in blue-collar occupations (Clement and Myles 1994).

At a minimum, these positions consider the decline in gender inequality to be less than what it should have been, given gains in women's relative qualifications (Albelda 1986; Tienda et al. 1987). The concern is unambiguously with levels of gender inequality that are still unacceptably high. And the focus is also on women who are considered to be among the most vulnerable members of the new economy (Amott 1993). In fact, in a view of gender inequality that is sensitive to intersections with class, it could be argued that gender inequality has actually risen over time if we compare the wages of non-college-educated women, which have fallen, to those of college-educated men, which have risen slightly (see figure 5.1). But because this cannot be generalized to women and men as a whole, we need to avoid unidimensional interpretations of what is essentially a much more complex set of changes in the structure of inequality.

RESTRUCTURING AND GENDER WAGE INEQUALITY: THE REGIONAL PICTURE

The notion that women are worse off as a result of restructuring flies in the face of widespread declines in gender wage inequality over time, but it is not inconsistent with variation in the impact of economic change on different groups of workers, including those located in different regional economies and in different skill groups. It is also not inconsistent with the possibility that *some* groups of women are better off, as the first view claims. Thus we need to consider how these two contradictory outcomes can be best explored and illuminated in a spatial analysis of regional economies.

Although several spatially oriented feminist studies have already explored a range of issues related to women's economic well-being,[5] none that I know of have provided a direct analysis of gender, wages, and wage inequality. What research there is on regional wage levels and inequality has focused mainly on men or combined samples of men and women, or have ignored gender differences in separate samples. Yet we might find women relatively better off in some places and worse off in others, regardless of men's relative position. Moreover, being better or worse off may not be so easy to gauge. Wages may be higher for both men and women, but so might inequality. Since some of these issues were covered in the previous chapter and are taken up again in greater detail in the next chapter, I provide only a brief summary here. I focus on how I expect the findings on the average gender wage gap from the previous chapter to be altered when looking separately at the college- and non-college-educated. I organize the discussion around the alternative structural causes of rising "overall" inequality, which I group into the three categories of high-technology, high-flexibility, and broad industrial shifts.

HIGH-TECHNOLOGY LABOR MARKETS

There are really two opposing views on the impact of new technology on wage inequality that are relevant to a study of gender inequality. The first offers a vision of an equitable, sustainable, high-tech, production-based utopia that will supercede the industrial regime of mass production (Piore and Sabel 1984). In contrast, the second view is based on *actually existing* postindustrialism, which many observers claim is responsible for growing polarization by class, race, and gender (Harrison and Bluestone 1988; Harvey 1989; Mollenkopf and Castells 1991; Sassen 1991; Harrison 1994). Neither view expects gender relations necessarily to improve as a result of technological advances. Indeed, the average gender wage gap was significantly greater in high-tech service and high-tech manufacturing regions and occupational segregation was significantly greater in the latter (chapter 4). But in a closer reading of the second, more pessimistic view, one can decode polarization as meaning that elite white men are at the top and everyone else, including white working-class men, are at the bottom. Such an interpretation would suggest that gender inequality might be lower among the less-educated except in labor markets where unionized and male-dominated high-tech industries are concentrated, such as aerospace and defense (see the case study of St. Louis in chapter 2).

When considering the relative position of college-educated women, on the other hand, recall that high-technology industries tend to be concentrated in regions with high average wages. This is mainly due to proximity to major urban areas that have high costs of living and to an occupational structure that is top-heavy with professionals, managers, and highly skilled technicians. Although women's as well as men's wages are likely to be higher than average, especially among the more highly skilled, the top echelon of leading-sector industries are known to be dominated by white, well-educated men (Brint 1991; Sokoloff 1992; Clement and Myles 1994; Larner 1996; Armstrong 1996). Blau and Kahn (1997) have also argued that men's acquisition of unmeasured technical skills outpaced women's at the top of the wage distribution. These conditions should lead to greater gender inequality at the top, as feminist and other critics of the rosy scenario of technological advancement have long argued in theory. *In sum, gender inequality is likely to be higher at the top and lower at the bottom in high-tech regions.*

HIGH-FLEXIBILITY LABOR MARKETS

In some quarters, the "dark side" of flexibility is nearly synonymous with feminized employment: part-time, temporary, low-wage, informal, and without benefits (Harrison 1994). And the association with feminized employment has meant an association with greater gender inequality. But this portrayal needs to be qualified in at least two respects. First, a more nuanced reading of casualized employment recognizes its dual and diverse character. While much of contingent and nonstandard employment falls far short of an ideal full-time job with benefits, it can also include high-waged part-time and subcontracted employment to more highly educated women and men, respectively (Tilly 1996). Therefore low-skilled women are probably more vulnerable to the dark side of flexibility and may indeed be worse off relative to low-skilled men in highly casualized labor markets. On average, though, casualized regions tended to have significantly lower wages among both men and women and only average wage gaps between them. In this environment, college-educated women may substitute for college-educated men, driving down wages among the college-educated overall but reducing gender wage inequality among the college-educated in the process.

Second, there are other characteristics that I consider part of flexible and insecure labor markets, such as joblessness and immigration, that are not generally associated with feminized employment. These characteristics tend to be studied alongside other aspects of restructuring that have caused low-skilled men's wages to decline. Low-skilled men are thought to be hardest hit because low-skilled workers in general have traditionally been less mobile and therefore less likely to exit labor markets with an oversupply of labor, though in recent years these groups have become more mobile in response to declining economic opportunities (Borjas and Freeman 1992; Frey 1995). The question for a regional analysis is whether the consequences are more severe for low-skilled men than for low-skilled women, who are probably even less mobile than low-skilled men, in labor markets with these characteristics. On average, the gender wage gap is greater in slack labor markets and lower in immigrant-rich ones, suggesting that the relative position of low-skilled men and women in high-flexibility labor markets, is neither clear-cut nor consistent. *In sum, gender inequality is likely to be greater at the bottom and lower at the top in casualized labor markets but the outcome under other flexible and insecure employment conditions is unpredictable.*

INDUSTRIAL AND SERVICE ECONOMIES

According to the earliest labor market studies, the root of local prosperity and relative equity in the Golden Age of twentieth century industrial capitalism was manufacturing. High union density in the Midwestern manufacturing centers of the United States was perhaps the main cause of differences in wage and income levels across broad regions during the 1950s and 1960s. Regional wage differentials have since diminished with the decline of unions and manufacturing, though intermetropolitan variation in wage levels may have increased within some regions (Angel and Mitchell 1991). Although higher wages for non-college-educated workers in locally dominant, unionized industries may have spilled over into non-unionized sectors of the local private economy, contributing to lower overall levels of income inequality, gender inequality was one form of inequality that was probably higher all along, especially among the non-college-educated.

I expect measures of deindustrialization to identify regions that were centers of manufacturing in the Fordist era and as such should be associated with higher levels of gender inequality for all groups, but especially for low-skilled women. High-skilled paraprofessional women in partially unionized industries may, in contrast, have benefited from the spillover effects of Fordism (see the case study of Detroit in Chapter 3). Whether service-industry growth and service-sector dominance, the flip side of deindustrialization, are associated with greater gender inequality at the bottom, as the view of the service sector as a low-wage female ghetto would have it, or less gender inequality, as the harmonizing downward position would have it, is an open question. *In sum, gender inequality is expected to be greater at the bottom and lower at the top in industrialized regions and, by default, I expect the opposite outcomes in service-oriented regions.*

EVIDENCE

The foregoing discussion of the relationship between economic restructuring and the gender wage gap pointed to several aspects of restructuring that may reduce the gap, other aspects that may intensify it, and, more often, others that might have a different effect for different skill groups. Since my interest is in identifying "spatial routes" to gender wage (in)equality that are sensitive to men's as well as women's relative wage levels, and thus move beyond the singular focus on men's declining wages as the cause of the declining gender wage gap, I begin with a description of relative wage levels across labor markets of different kinds for the four gender/education groups. Relative wage levels are really the building blocks of relative wage gaps across labor markets, so I incorporate the findings on "high-wage" and "low-wage" labor markets in the discussion of the gender wage gaps as well. The objective, then, will be to construct configurations from information on wage levels, wage gaps, and economic conditions for each of the two educational groups (referred to below as LHS for less-than-high-school-educated workers and COL for college-educated workers).

ARE LABOR MARKETS HIGH-WAGE OR LOW-WAGE FOR ALL WORKERS?

With remarkable consistency, wage levels generally move in the same direction for men and women and for the two educational groups. A low-wage labor market for men is generally a low-wage labor market for women too. Table 5.3 summarizes these results for the four groups of workers and for the ten main labor market variables. Although not all coefficients are significant, the coefficients associated with each of the labor-market and controls variables have the same signs for men and women. These findings indicate that regional characteristics associated

Table 5.3 Relative Estimated Wage Levels across Labor Markets by Gender and Education, 1989

LABOR MARKET FEATURES	ALL MEN/WOMEN	LESS THAN HIGH SCHOOL MEN/WOMEN	COLLEGE OR MORE MEN/WOMEN
Immigration	Higher/Higher	Higher/Higher	Higher/Higher
Casualization	Lower/Lower	Lower/Lower	Lower/Lower
Unemployment	Lower/Lower	Average/Lower	Average/Higher
High-Tech Manufacturing	Higher/Higher	Higher/Higher	Higher/Higher
High-Tech Services	Higher/Higher	Higher/Higher	Higher/Higher
Import-Sensitive Manufacturing	Lower/Average	Lower/Average	Average/Average
FIRE Growth	Higher/Higher	Higher/Higher	Higher/Higher
Manufacturing Growth	Lower/Lower	Lower/Average	Lower/Lower
Services Growth	Average/Average	Average/Average	Average/Average
Manufacturing/Services	Average/Lower	Higher/Average	Higher/Higher

Note: Values of Higher, Lower, and Average indicate that hourly wages were significantly higher, significantly lower, or nonsignificant, respectively, relative to wage levels in the average labor market and after controlling for all other labor market conditions. See McCall (1998) for coefficients.

Less than High School = < 12 years of schooling; College or More = 16 or more years of schooling.

with above- (below-) average wages for men also tend to be associated with above- (below-) average wages for women. In some cases, the coefficients are not significant for men or for women, or are significant only for one or the other. But none of the variables have significant but opposite effects on men's and women's wage levels. Moreover, there is only one labor-market variable for which the effect on wage levels varies by education. Thus, for each type of labor market except one, the direction of wage changes relative to the average labor market is similar for men and women and for the college- and non-college-educated alike. So, yes, labor markets are either high-wage or low-wage for all workers.

Although I stress this unusual level of consistency in the overall direction of relative wage levels, the case where wage levels do vary by education and gender bears emphasis. This exceptional case occurs in labor markets with high joblessness. Compared to the average labor market, areas with high joblessness offer significantly higher wages to female COL workers and significantly lower wages to female LHS workers. These results only partly follow the pattern found by Blanchflower and Oswald (1994) in their landmark study of the inverse relationship between joblessness and wage levels across metropolitan areas and states. Using a larger sample of labor markets and workers, and differentiating between education and gender groups, I find that this pattern does not apply to college-educated workers. In addition, the wage premium is evident only among COL *women*, and the wage penalty only among LHS *women*. *Hence, women's wages are actually more sensitive than men's wages to local unemployment levels.* To jump ahead a bit, this means that low-wage labor markets are not necessarily the place where the gender wage gap is lower because of lower wages among *men*, as might be extrapolated from over-time trends.

Before elaborating further on the importance of gender and class differences in the findings, there is one general point that should be made about the relationship between economic restructuring and regional wage levels. One may notice in table 5.3 that most of the significant effects are in the direction of raising wages. This does not necessarily mean that restructuring has a net positive effect on the wages of the majority of U.S. workers. Some factors that result in significantly lower wages, such as casualization, may have wide geographical reach and in reality affect a far larger number of workers than the combination of two or three other factors with positive effects. Moreover, my methodological approach gauges the independent effects of each factor after controlling for other factors. Therefore there are likely to be interactions among variables within regional labor markets that alter wage levels as well.

WHAT EXPLAINS REGIONAL DIFFERENCES IN THE GENDER WAGE GAP?

Now that we know wage levels are generally higher or lower for both men and women in any given labor market, it is much easier to explain how local male and female wage levels alter local levels of the gender wage gap. A higher gender wage gap can now result from only two sources: higher wages among men in high-wage regions or lower wages among women in low-wage regions. The former is represented by a higher wage premium for men as compared to women, and the latter by a higher wage penalty for women as compared to men.

The effects of the ten labor market variables on the adjusted female/male hourly wage ratio are presented in figure 5.3 for LHS workers and figure 5.4 for COL workers. For any particular measure of local economic conditions, the adjusted female/male wage ratio will vary across labor markets as those economic conditions vary. For example, the adjusted female/male wage ratio will be different in high and low unemployment labor markets. The question is: How different? How much of an effect does joblessness have on the gender wage gap for COL and LHS workers? To put such variation in perspective, the horizontal line cutting across figures 5.3 and 5.4 represents the estimated adjusted *average* wage ratio for that skill group. These ratios are: 0.71 for LHS workers and 0.72 for COL workers. That is, LHS and COL women make about 71 percent to 72 percent of men's hourly wages after controlling for individual human capital characteristics and local economic conditions. Since the ratio increases the more women make relative to men, inequality is lower than average when any vertical bar falls above the horizontal line and higher than average when it falls below it.

For example, the estimated female/male wage ratio among LHS workers ranges from 69.2 to 79.5 in percentage terms for the variable measuring the immigrant share of local employment. The 69.2 percent is taken from the estimated ratio in the labor market with the lowest share of immigrants (0.40 percent immigrant). In figure 5.3, it is represented by the column with hash bars falling under the horizontal line, because the wage ratio is below average in this case. The 79.5 percent figure is taken from the estimated female/male wage ratio for the labor market with the highest share of immigrants (52.0 percent immigrant). It is represented by the dark column reaching high above the horizontal line, because the wage ratio is above average in this case.

The difference between the two bars is substantial considering the extensive set of controls in the model. It is comparable to the range of variation in the unadjusted wage gap over the 1980s, the decade with the largest percentage increase of this century (Goldin 1990). The range of variation across all labor market variables is even greater, from a low of 64.8 percent in the labor market with the greatest manufacturing employment decline over the 1980s (-8.6 percent average annual rate decline) to a high of 86.5 percent in the labor market with the greatest number of import-sensitive manufacturing establishments as a share of all local manufacturing establishments (84.5 percent). The overall range is of similar scale among college-educated workers (64.8 to 86.3 percent). But, as we will see in more detail momentarily, the labor market conditions associated with these extremes are quite different.

Low Wages and the Gender Wage Gap
Areas with high joblessness were the only ones to have opposite effects on wage levels for different educational groups, but I discuss them in this section on low-wage labor markets because previous research has shown that average wages tend to be lower in these areas. As I described in the above example, women's wages turn out to be more sensitive than men's wages to changes in the unemployment rate. The wage penalty in high unemployment areas is much greater for LHS women than for LHS men, whose coefficient is insignificant. As a result, the gender wage gap is greater among the low-skilled workers. Although less pronounced, this same process occurs in regions with highly casualized

Figure 5.3 Effects of Labor-Market Structure on the Adjusted Female/Male Wage Ratio for the Less-than-High-School-Educated, 1989

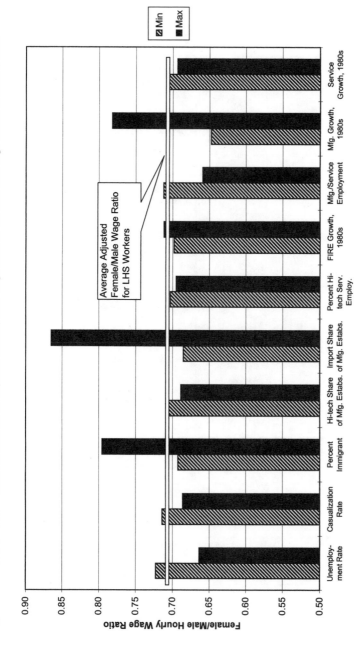

Note: See the notes to table 5.1 for data sources and definitions. See Appendix table A.1 for labor-market variable definitions and sources.

Figure 5.4 Effects of Labor-Market Structure on the Adjusted Female/Male Wage Ratio for the College-Educated, 1989

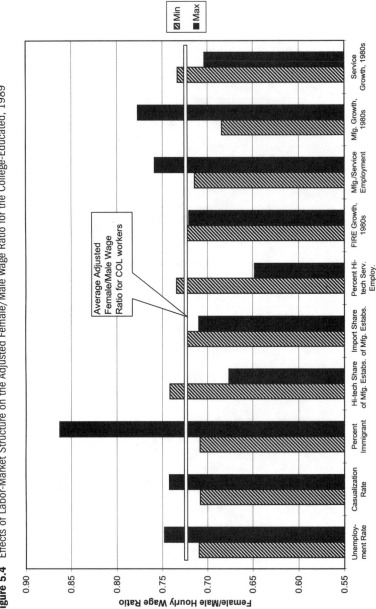

Note: See the notes to table 5.1 for data sources and definitions. See Appendix table A.1 for labor-market variable definitions and sources.

labor forces. Statistically, there are significant wage penalties for both men and women, but the female wage penalty is slightly larger. Consequently, gender inequality tends to increase among the least-educated in casualized labor markets as well as in labor markets with high joblessness. This is illustrated in figure 5.3 by the short, solid dark bars for these two characteristics (falling below the average ratio represented by the horizontal line). In contrast, the wage penalty is greater among COL men than among COL women, and this reduces the COL gender wage gap. Moreover, none of the other low-wage labor markets reduce wages more for COL women than for COL men, either. *It is only among the low-skilled that women's wage levels are negatively affected by factors more typically associated with lower wages among men, and the penalties for women actually exceed those for men.* These findings buttress the assertion that low-skilled women in particular are among the most vulnerable to new and deepening forms of flexibility and insecurity.

Under other local conditions, low wages among men in low-wage labor markets do lead to less gender inequality. As the estimated female/male wage ratios in figures 5.3 and 5.4 demonstrate, the labor market with the highest manufacturing employment growth has one of the lowest predicted levels of gender wage inequality for LHS workers (a female/male ratio of 0.782) and COL workers (0.777). While manufacturing declined nationally over the 1980s, it grew in primarily low-wage labor markets. Here the gender wage gap is lower for both LHS and COL workers as a result of greater estimated wage penalties for men. Wages are lower than average especially for LHS men, but COL men are by no means immune from the depressive wage effects of the local economy in these areas. Among women, the penalty for the college-educated is much smaller, while the LHS coefficient is insignificant. A similar pattern for LHS workers appears in low-wage areas with a disproportionate share of import-sensitive manufacturing plants, where the estimated female/male wage ratio reaches its high of 86.5 in percentage terms.

These key indicators of restructuring in the manufacturing industry show that 1980s-style manufacturing growth and import competition exact a price on male wages, especially among LHS men, and consequently contribute to lower gender wage inequality. Deindustrialization theory might have predicted that manufacturing *decline* would have resulted in lower male wage levels and foster greater gender equality. However, areas that were centers of manufacturing employment in the Fordist era and were therefore likely to have experienced negative manufacturing growth over the decade of the 1980s still (in 1990) exhibit high absolute wage levels and high levels of gender wage inequality, especially among the less-educated. On the other hand, if we think of areas specializing in import-sensitive manufacturing industries and areas with manufacturing growth as regions that are either the hardest hit by wage concessions or the least likely to be unionized in the first place, both features of deindustrialization broadly speaking, there is certainly support for the greater sensitivity of men's wages to these aspects of recent economic restructuring.

Considering low-wage labor markets as a whole, some important consequences of restructuring are clearly shared by COL and LHS women relative to men, while others separate them. In terms of similarities, wages are lower for COL and LHS women as a result of several important and widespread features of contemporary labor markets. These same labor markets lower male wages more than women's and as a consequence produce the conditions for lower levels of gender wage inequality. Among the college-educated, this occurs in regions with high rates of casualization and manufacturing growth; among the non-college-educated, this occurs in areas with import-sensitive manufacturing, manufacturing growth, and relative service industry dominance—as measured by the inverse of the manufacturing share of service employment variable, which is discussed in the next section. As has been argued elsewhere by McDowell (1991) in the case of England, Armstrong (1996) in Canada, and Larner (1996) in Australia, this route to lower gender wage inequality cannot be understood in any clearly positive way. But this argument is made less often for COL women, who are typically understood to be doing well as a result of their absolute gains.

Despite these similarities between the college- and non-college-educated, significant differences between COL and LHS women remain quantitatively and qualitatively important. In areas with highly insecure employment conditions, as measured by unemployment and casualization rates, LHS women face a harsher labor market environment than either COL women or LHS men. The negative wage penalty relative to the average labor market is as great or greater for LHS women as it is for LHS men. As a result, the LHS gender wage gap is greater in these areas, whereas in no low-wage labor market is the gender gap greater for COL workers. The greater LHS wage gap should not hide the fact, however, that these labor markets are associated with lower wages among both LHS men and LHS women and at times among the college educated as well. The relatively better position of college-educated women in particular may only be an indication of the tendency to substitute cheaper female for more costly male labor in low-wage regions.

High Wages and the Gender Wage Gap
Six of the ten main local indicators of labor market restructuring are associated with higher wages for all four groups. Yet in only one case is gender wage inequality substantially lower for both LHS and COL workers. In a second case, gender wage inequality is substantially lower only

for COL workers (and is greater among LHS workers). In a third case, wage premiums are significant for all four groups but in equivalent measure, limiting the effect on the gender wage gap. Two conclusions can be drawn rather quickly from this summary of the results. *First, higher-waged labor markets in 1990 as a general rule do not foster greater opportunities for women relative to men. Second, if women benefit at all, it is COL women who are slightly more likely to reap the benefits of high-wage labor markets by closing the gap with COL men.* Despite this seeming advantage, though, the areas in which gender wage inequality is substantially greater for the college-educated are extremely important, namely, regions specializing in high-technology manufacturing and high-technology services. I order the discussion according to whether regions are more likely to foster greater equality between men and women.

Surprisingly, immigrant-rich areas are the only ones in which wages are significantly higher and gender wage inequality substantially lower for both COL and LHS workers.[6] Wage premiums among women substantially exceed those among men in these labor markets. As indicated by the tall dark bars in figures 5.3 and 5.4, the gender wage gap drops to its lowest estimated value among COL workers (with a female/male wage ratio of 0.863) and to its second lowest value among LHS workers (0.795). Whether these results are driven by greater equality among immigrants, which is the likely explanation, or between immigrants and natives, or between natives, is unclear from this analysis but an interesting question for further research. I discussed the determinants of lower gender inequality in my case study of Miami in chapter 2, where I argued that at least part of the explanation lies in the industrial complexity and dynamism of many labor markets drawing on both low-skilled and high-skilled immigrants, as detailed in many case studies of Los Angeles, Silicon Valley, Miami, and New York City (for an overview, see Waldinger 1996). But, controlling for high-technology manufacturing and services, these findings also pertain to smaller, less balanced local economies. Unfortunately, few areas are rich with immigrants and so few areas have the twin characteristics of high wages and low across-the-board gender wage inequality.

In comparison to immigrant-rich regions, areas with substantial growth in the advanced producer services of finance, insurance, and real estate (FIRE) significantly raise wage levels but have little effect on gender wage inequality. These advanced-producer industries, especially finance industries, along with the high-technology service industries to be discussed below, are the most specialized measures of postindustrial service employment used in this and other studies. These high-end services are expected to produce a bipolar structure of primary and secondary jobs overlaid by gender differentiation (Baran and Teegarden 1987; Bagchi-Sen 1995).[7] However, I find that the effects on wages of

FIRE growth are positive and do not appear to favor men relative to similarly educated women. But it is also the only one of the high-tech group measuring *growth* rather than share of employment. This may bias the measure toward areas with smaller initial levels of employment in the advanced-producer services and away from major centers of business and financial services.

Nestled between those factors associated with lower gender wage inequality for LHS and COL workers and those associated with greater inequality for both groups is one that is mixed in its effects on the two educational groups. The variable that measures manufacturing as a share of service employment has a significant positive effect on male COL wages but has even a stronger positive effect on female COL wages, which results in lower gender wage inequality among the college-educated (as in the case study of Detroit described in chapter 3). In contrast, the female LHS coefficient is insignificant, while the male LHS is significant at the $p=0.07$ level (and is more significant for high-school-educated men), which results in slightly greater gender wage inequality among LHS workers. Thus the expectation of greater gender inequality in manufacturing-dominant labor markets is very weak but is evident among less-educated workers. Both groups of men benefit at least a little from economies oriented toward manufacturing, as do COL women. LHS women are alone in not experiencing these wage increases. Because manufacturing growth is controlled, this variable is capturing older as well as newer industrial sites. Newer sites, therefore, are reproducing the old pattern of gender wage inequality among less-educated workers and these areas (old and new) are quite widespread throughout the Eastern part of the United States (McCall 1998).

Along with the advanced-producer services of FIRE, three other variables are included to measure key dimensions of post-Fordism and postindustrialism: high-technology manufacturing, high-technology services, and service-industry growth. Not one of the three was shown to foster an environment of greater equality between men and women, though significantly higher wages are associated with the two high-technology variables. Since the effects of service-industry growth were insignificant for all four groups, I focus my comments in this section on the impact of high-tech industries. A local specialization in either high-tech manufacturing or services has a greater effect on gender wage inequality among the college-educated than among the non-college-educated. The estimated female/male wage ratio reaches its lowest (64.8 percent) and second-lowest levels (67.6 percent) among COL workers, due to the larger wage premiums garnered by COL men in high-tech labor markets. However, among LHS workers, the small difference in the female and male coefficients produces little change in the gender wage gap across these regions.

These findings associated with high-tech regions are interesting for a number of reasons. On the one hand, as predicted by the more pessimistic readings of post-Fordism and postindustrialism and certainly by temporal trends, the highest wage premiums in high-tech economies are bestowed upon the most well-educated men, whether because of the greater tendency for men to be trained in technical fields, or because of the inside networks that favor men in cutting-edge sectors, a sort of glass-ceiling effect, or a combination of both. These premiums contribute to higher levels of inequality between COL men and the three other groups. For the present, however, high-technology manufacturing or services are concentrated in relatively few areas, though it is by no means a trivial number. On the other hand, a more optimistic reading would emphasize that wages are significantly higher for all four groups and in comparable measure for LHS men and LHS women. In fact the wage premiums are larger for them than for COL women. There is reason to conclude, therefore, that upgrading is taking place at the bottom of the skill hierarchy in high-tech labor markets. It should be kept in mind, however, that less-skilled women are not relatively better placed than similarly skilled men, so the gender wage gap is still no better than average.

CONCLUSION

Given the growing importance of skill differences in today's economy and, despite this, the nearly exclusive focus on the *average* gender wage gap in scholarly studies, the central question considered in this chapter was whether gender inequality is distributed evenly among low-skilled and high-skilled workers. If not, what are the spatial routes to a lower gender wage gap for low-skilled workers, and what are they for high-skilled workers? Are women's wage levels an important factor, and are they as sensitive as men's to local economic conditions? Are the routes to lower gender inequality through low-wage or high-wage labor markets, and how does this alter interpretations of the declining gender wage gap? Finding answers to these basic questions was facilitated by the wide variation in economic conditions, wage levels, and levels of gender wage inequality across regional labor markets. Several compelling "spatial routes" to gender wage inequality emerged that move beyond the emphasis on men's declining wages and break the hold that temporal studies have had on discussions of economic restructuring, skill differentials, wages, and gender inequality. I discuss how the interpretation of gender inequality is dependent on wage levels, skill levels, and economic restructuring in turn, though there is some unavoidable overlap throughout.

Declining real wages are such an important feature of economic restructuring and inequality that they must be part of any discussion of gender wage inequality, the only form of inequality to have declined over the last few decades. In a reflection of trends over time, one might expect gender inequality to be lower in low-wage labor markets, where men suffer the deepest wage penalties relative to the average labor market. However, this is not what I found. Low-wage and high-wage labor markets were generally the same for men and women and for high-skill and low-skill workers alike. Indeed, women's wages were as sensitive as men's to local economic conditions, and sometimes more so. Moreover, higher levels of gender inequality were found in low-wage as well as high-wage labor markets. For example, labor markets with high joblessness depressed wage levels more for LHS women than for LHS men, while high-tech labor markets boosted wage levels more for COL men than for COL women. Therefore gender wage inequality was elevated in both high- and low-wage environments and despite differences in the contribution of men's wage increases or decreases. Factors associated with less gender inequality are also evident in both low- and high-wage labor markets. These spatial routes to changing gender wage inequality suggest processes much more varied than the singular emphasis on men's declining real wages in many temporal studies (e.g., Mishel and Bernstein 1994; Gordon 1996).

The results also clearly show that gender wage inequality is unevenly distributed among skill groups: spatial routes to gender wage inequality are not the same for low-skilled and high-skilled workers. First, at the national level, absolute wage gains over time are the norm only for college-educated women. Second, at the regional level, less than half the labor-market variables benefited LHS women relative to LHS men, while more than half benefited COL women relative to COL men. Third, and most remarkably, *there was absolutely no correlation between those local economies that had lower (higher) gender gaps among the college-educated and those that had lower (higher) gaps among the non-college-educated.*

For example, the scenario in which women's wages suffer a greater penalty than men's wages in low-wage labor markets is only evident among LHS workers. Under insecure employment conditions in particular—areas with high joblessness and casualization—LHS women face a harsher labor market relative to COL women and to LHS men (not to mention COL men). Meanwhile, in these same areas, gender wage inequality among the college-educated is actually significantly *lower.* This is perhaps the most instructive illustration of why class differences must be central to any discussion of equity and restructuring policies. Some economic conditions may promote less gender inequality for some groups but are still unworthy of support, because they either increase inequality for other groups or are associated with economic decline rather than with economic progress. Even the fact that college-educated women benefited mainly in such areas must give us pause, especially considering that, in stark contrast, COL women bore the brunt of inequality in the cutting-edge labor markets of the future, those that are high-wage and high-tech. Consequently, despite important class differences in the distribution and experience of gender inequality, there was really no rosy scenario to point to for college-educated women. Finally, do these breakdowns by gender and education force a revision of current theories of economic restructuring? There were several important substantive findings that support some previous research and challenge others. First, as theoretically based feminist critiques of post-Fordism and postindustrialism suggest, actually existing transformations of the economy based on technological advances in manufacturing and services are biased toward well-educated male workers, even though women as well as men receive wage premiums relative to the average labor market. Regions specializing in high-tech manufacturing and services are associated with higher absolute levels of gender wage inequality, especially among the college educated, a finding consistent with temporal trends that show smaller declines over time in the gender wage gap for college-educated workers (Blau and Kahn 1992, 1994). Also consistent with educational differences in the rate of decline in the gender wage gap, I found virtually no effect from any of these (technology) variables on the gender wage gap among the least-educated workers. Thus there is some degree of upgrading at the bottom of the labor market for both men and women, directing attention to the joint gender and class inequality generated from relatively higher wage premiums accruing to the most educated men (as in the case study of Dallas discussed in chapter 2).

Second, effects of the broad industrial composition of the local labor market offered some support for both "optimistic" and "pessimistic" views on whether and under what conditions restructuring reduces gender inequality, and here I focus on LHS workers. On the optimistic side, two measures of Fordist regions, those with manufacturing decline and a disproportionate share of manufacturing to service employment—whose influence and presence ought to be on the wane—resulted in wage premiums for LHS men and substantially higher levels of gender wage inequality among LHS workers. This is positive in the sense that these environments of inequality are less prevalent today and these results should be used to temper nostalgia about the beneficial effects of manufacturing on wages and the full structure of inequality (Milkman 1997). It is, however, a mixed blessing that service dominance, the inverse of manufacturing's share of service employment, offers lower gender wage inequality at the cost of lower male LHS wages. Moreover, the same dynamics are at work in those low-wage regions that experienced manufacturing growth over the 1980s and had a disproportionate share of import-sensitive manufacturing plants.

These are both characteristics of the broader process of deindustrialization and, not surprisingly, are therefore consistent with the focus on men's wage declines as a source of lower gender inequality.

Lastly, and perhaps most surprisingly, the only factor associated with high wages to substantially decrease COL and LHS gender wage inequality was the high share of immigrant workers. Though relatively minor in territorial coverage, these areas are dense population centers and clearly promote greater equality between men and women, across the educational hierarchy, even though they are often cited as partially responsible for the recent temporal (that is national) trend in increasing inequality. Once again, what these and other divergent findings point out is that summary measures of "income" inequality—referring typically to a combined sample of men and women, or only men, or only family units—conceal important differences by gender, class, and race. Even though I have shown that levels of gender wage inequality are lower across educational groups in immigrant-rich regions, this does not imply anything about the structure of racial and class inequality within gender groups. Despite relative equality between men and women, other forms of inequality may be more extreme and therefore of greater concern, as I have already shown in chapter 2 and will again in chapter 6. It is therefore vital in such circumstances that we conceptualize gender, as well as race and class, as only one dimension of several in any configuration of inequality.

Chapter Six

THE DIFFERENCE GENDER MAKES: WAGE INEQUALITY AMONG WOMEN AND AMONG MEN

As scholars across the social sciences have become interested again in the problem of inequality, research on the issue has become increasingly wide-ranging. At first the primary concern was with income inequality, which declined in the first few decades of strong economic growth following World War II and then reversed course in the late 1960s, to nearly everyone's surprise. Then economists—and it has been primarily economists working on the issue of rising inequality—tried to understand this new trend through the lens of another startling trend: the decline in wages among non-college-educated men that was fueling the dramatic increase in male wage inequality. Since racial disparities also began to rise after nearly two decades of steady progress, race has figured prominently in discussions of the new social inequality as well. As for gender, many scholars have at least called attention to the recent and significant closing of the gender wage gap, which stemmed in part from men's deteriorating wages.[1]

Given this relatively wide-ranging interest in new patterns of inequality, it is remarkable that there has been virtually no attention to rising inequality among women. As with most studies of women's economic status, the last two chapters have been concerned with inequality between men and women, but this chapter reconsiders the relationship between restructuring and inequality in terms of inequality among women.[2] While I do not want to deny the continuing importance of gender inequality, I do want to look at the four education/gender groups from a different perspective from that of the previous chapter. I want to shift attention to wage inequality *between* women: college-educated women on the one hand, who have enjoyed real economic gains and opportunities over the past few decades, and non-college-educated women on the other, who have fallen behind in both absolute and relative terms (see figure 5.1 in the previous chapter for wage trends between 1980 and 1990 for each of the gender/education groups).

Although what little research there is on earnings inequality among women has not focused specifically on the college/noncollege wage gap, a few important studies have already documented inequality among women as an issue of emerging significance. In what is still one of the few sociological analyses of growing wage inequality among women over the 1970s and 1980s, Shelley Smith argued that economic restructuring has "marginally increased the number of opportunities in high paying jobs, but also increased the already heavy concentration of women in jobs with lower earnings" (Smith 1991: 133, 122). Also alarmed by what they call a new trend toward "polarization" among women, Morris, Bernhardt, and Handcock (1994) predicted that polarization would only accelerate as some women made further advances at the top and others remained trapped in low-wage service jobs at the bottom (see also Bernhardt, Morris, and Handcock 1995). What is more, inequality among women is not only increasing in the abstract, so to speak, but in real life too: women are increasingly supervised by other women, and relationships of authority between women in the workplace are already becoming a central feature of many women's work experience (Brenner 1993; Clement and Myles 1994).

These and a few other studies have been breakthroughs in bringing much needed attention to the contemporary problem of inequality among women, but, despite a common emphasis on economic restructuring as the explanation for rising inequality, they have each stopped short of *empirically* investigating restructuring's role. They have also focused exclusively on women. In this chapter, I address the role of restructuring head-on, and I do so in a comparative way by examining the effects of restructuring on both men and women.[3]

In contrast to a singular focus on inequality among women, a comparative approach of this sort has many of the general advantages discussed in previous chapters—in particular, the ability to determine whether the same conditions result in different outcomes for different groups of workers. Whereas in the previous chapter I showed how the relationship between restructuring and gender inequality differed for the college- and non-college-educated, in this chapter I intend to show how the relationship between restructuring and the college/noncollege wage gap differs for men and for women. Whereas in the previous chapter I argued that evidence of class differences put into question the adequacy of the average gender wage gap as a summary indicator of gender inequality, in this chapter I argue that gender differences put into question the use of male wage inequality and even family income inequality as a summary indicator of overall wage inequality. What remains the same in both chapters is an attempt to move beyond men's labor market experience as the standard and to prove that gender-related differences in configurations of inequality are systematic rather than unique to the few cities analyzed in chapters 2 and 3.

It would be a mistake, though, to think that I am concerned only with proving the existence of gender differences and then leaving it at that. As in previous chapters, what matters is the *meaning* of those differences. The implications of gender differences in the sources of inequality within gender groups, if they exist, would be far-reaching on several fronts. First, gender differences are likely to play an important role in the ongoing controversy over the weight of different factors in explaining recent trends in inequality. At least one seminal study has already pointed to the greater influence of the declining real value of the minimum wage on increasing wage inequality among women, an effect that leading studies of inequality failed to notice because they analyzed only full-time samples of men (DiNardo et al. 1996).

Second, and related, gender differences are likely to disrupt the status of family income inequality as a general measure of social and economic progress and of the degree of openness and opportunity for disadvantaged groups (e.g., Nielsen and Alderson 1997; Jargowsky 1997). As labor-market-segmentation theory would also contend, a single measure of "overall" inequality assumes away the divisions that separate labor markets into their constitutive and often nonoverlapping parts. Since wages are the primary source of income, differences in the extent and sources of wage inequality among men and among women would provide evidence of multiple and potentially conflicting opportunity structures.[4] In such an environment, a single measure of family income inequality would not be able to represent fairly the social composition of inequality as is often assumed.

And finally, gender differences are likely to be a critical factor in the development of a new analytical role for gender in the study of inequality. While inequality among women is a worthy subject in its own right, a comparison with inequality among men requires us to stretch the analytical role of gender to include differences in the structures of inequality within gender groups. This new focus entails a shift in the meaning of gender differences, from direct differences *between* men and women to differences in the structure of inequality *within* gender groups. As is well known, most stratification research uses gender to refer to a direct comparison between men's and women's economic positions, as in the gap between men's and women's average wages. I argue, however, that a new analytical role for gender is necessary given women's large share of the labor force and the high levels of inequality among them. In fact, the increasing economic distance between different groups of women is at least as high as it is among men, as I showed in the case studies in chapters 2 and 3 and will show again in the larger sample of labor markets in this chapter. This is especially so when part-time workers are not excluded, as they typically are in most studies of inequality that end up concluding that inequality is greater among men. Given these new realities, the comparative study of inequality among women and inequality among men should become a mainstay of gender stratification scholarship as well as of the broader field of stratification.

As in previous chapters, I turn to regions as a way to isolate and compare the sources of different types of inequality. If economic characteristics of regional labor markets associated with high levels of inequality among men are also associated with high levels of inequality among women, we can conclude that gender differences are relatively unimportant. However, if significant gender differences are found, much recent research may be too limited, applying only to certain segments of the workforce. Note, however, that strictly speaking these conclusions apply only to the analysis of *levels* of inequality, not rising inequality, the focus of most previous research on overall earnings inequality. Because neoclassical equilibrium theory predicts that wages should be the same across labor markets, save for specific "compensating differentials,"[5] economists have not investigated the causes of either rising inequality or high levels of inequality in local/urban/regional labor markets.[6] Since my analysis is the first investigation of a wide range of competing explanations of skills-based wage inequality at the regional level, it has something to contribute to substantive debates over the causes of inequality, whether or not gender differences are found. In particular, I will be concerned with testing the two main competing explanations of inequality: technological and institutional changes.

Also, as in previous chapters, the building blocks for my measures of inequality are the wages of different gender and education groups. Although this strategy is widely adopted in the economics literature, especially in discussions of the role of technology, my use of the college/noncollege wage gap as an indicator of "class" inequality is controversial, so let me reiterate some of my thoughts on this usage here (see also chapter 2). The most obvious point in favor of using the college wage gap as an indicator of class inequality is that there has been a significant divergence in fortunes of college- and non-college-educated workers, both men and women alike. The college wage gap has risen by more than a third, beginning in 1979 and continuing through the 1980s and the 1990s.

Although other wage gaps between the top and bottom of the wage distribution also rose, much of the *public* discussion about restructuring and inequality has identified rising college wage premiums as one of the most significant new developments in our changing economy. The need to gain a proper education, and in many cases a college education, is now the most prominent policy response to the collapse of the middle class and rising inequality (Murnane and Levy 1996). This emphasis on education, I would argue, is a result of the tacit identification of education with class in U.S. society, suggesting that college wage gaps can function as a reasonable, if not perfect, indicator of class differences. Recently, Teixeira (2000: 2) has stated this point even more emphatically: "[A] Great Divide between those with a college degree and those without has emerged and widened into a yawning gulf in today's 'new economy.' Indeed, the Great Divide is now so significant that it can be used effectively to define the white working class."

I would not want to leave the impression, however, that the focus on skill-group and education-group wage gaps is purely objective or that it would have been my original choice. Rather, the more general scholarly and popular focus on the college wage gap is at least in part a vehicle to promote education as an individual-based, "supply-side" policy response to rising inequality. In fact, despite the overwhelming emphasis on college wage gaps, individuals within the same educational groups do vary among themselves too. Differences between groups defined by education, gender, race, age, and the like actually account for only 40 percent to 60 percent of the overall rise in wage inequality. The rest is attributable to increasing *within-group* inequality among individuals with the same characteristics (DiNardo et al. 1996). The implications of this are rarely raised: gaining a better education is not necessarily going to improve an individual's economic position if inequalities flourish among those with the same levels of education. Since other forms of inequality besides the gap between the college- and non-college-educated are important, I briefly consider gender differences in their sources at the end of this chapter as well.

My outline for the chapter, then, is as follows. In keeping with the econometric thrust of most previous research on the college wage gap, I begin with the dominant economic theory of why skills-based wage gaps should vary at all across labor markets. I then discuss the leading economic explanations of rising skills-based wage inequality over time, technology, and institutions, in terms of their likely effects on regional levels of skills-based wage inequality, and I do so with an eye to whether and how the effects should vary by gender. Following this, evidence on the patterns and sources of high college wage gaps among men and among women is presented, beginning with descriptive statistics comparing the level and regional distribution of inequality among women and among men. With substantial regional variation established, the rest of the chapter considers differences in the sources of wage inequality for men and women. The concluding section returns to the implications of those differences.

THE DETERMINANTS OF REGIONAL WAGE INEQUALITY

The central insight that undergirds any interregional research on skills-based wage inequality is that inequality varies across regions when the same skills are rewarded differently under different economic and social conditions. Spatial variation in "returns" to skills occurs when there is an under- or oversupply of workers with certain skills as compared to the available jobs requiring such skills in the local labor market (Wilson 1987; Bound and Holzer 1993). For any particular skill group, an undersupply of workers tends to result in relative wage premiums, while an oversupply results in wage penalties and/or unemployment. Such spatial-skill mismatches, broadly speaking, are not due simply to lost unionized manufacturing jobs in selected central cities. They reflect economywide transformations taking place within and across most industries (Murphy and Welch 1993) and spanning the urban-suburban boundaries of regional labor markets (Kasarda 1995; Jargowsky 1997). They also reflect entrenched racial and gender queues that vary across regions with different histories of industrial specialization, racial composition, and occupational segregation (Reskin and Roos 1990; Waldinger 1996). Regional labor markets capture the net effect of the matching process between jobs and workers, demand and supply, that takes place in local firms and labor markets (Wilson 1987; Granovetter and Tilly 1988; Sassen 1995; see also geographers Peck 1989; Hanson and Pratt 1995).[7]

With this reasoning in mind, it is relatively straightforward to connect the two leading explanations of rising skills-based wage inequality over time to variation in levels of skills-based wage inequality over space. The first and most prominent explanation is that employers have shifted their demand toward a more highly educated workforce. Most economists believe that this shift in labor demand was brought about by technological changes and by greater international trade and competition (Bound and Johnson 1992; Krueger 1993; Rodrik 1997). Because the dynamics of technology and trade are interrelated and technological explanations tend to have more clout, I call this the *high-technology* explanation. The second explanation points to changes in labor-market institutions that have resulted in greater flexibility for employers and greater insecurity for workers, especially for low-skilled workers. These changes include deunionization, deregulation, underemployment, the decline of the minimum wage and welfare benefits (in inflation-adjusted dollars), and the growth of alternative work arrangements (for instance part-time, temporary, independent contracting, informal self-employment, and so forth) (DiNardo et al. 1996; Kalleberg et al. 1997). I call this the *high-flexibility* explanation. Both high-technology and high-flexibility explanations have the appeal of identifying mechanisms that affect wage levels for broad groups of workers that cut across most industries. Thus both types of change should properly be thought of as properties of regional economies rather than of select industries.

Drawing from patterns in the national economy, my working assumption is that regional labor markets with more technology and flexibility should exhibit higher levels of inequality. I discuss the specific reasons why this should be so below, but first let me frame the discussion by introducing other possible outcomes besides regionally concentrated pockets of inequality. One alternative would occur if high-wage and low-wage workers were segregated into separate and nonoverlapping markets. Each labor market would have low or average local levels of inequality but when taken together the result would be high national levels of inequality. For example, Harrison (1994) argues that the full extent of inequality associated with high-technology industries is not concentrated in regions like Silicon Valley, because the worst assembly jobs are siphoned off to low-wage regions inside and outside the United States.[8] A similar outcome (high national inequality/low local inequality) would occur if supply-and-demand imbalances are corrected by rapid and perfect labor and capital mobility. All else being equal, if there is a surplus of relatively low-skilled workers, neoclassical equilibrium theory predicts that workers will move when their wages decline, creating surpluses elsewhere, where wages will decline in turn. The surplus will roll out and reduce wages at the bottom throughout the country, boosting levels of inequality everywhere (Williamson 1996; Frey 1995).

Because we have little systematic information on the spatial distribution of inequality, and the spatial concentration of inequality contradicts equilibrium theory, initially we simply want to determine whether wage inequality varies across labor markets, and, if so, to what extent and as a result of which conditions. That is, do high-tech and flexible economic conditions have any significant effect on local levels of wage inequality? This has never been established for many of the economic characteristics of labor markets discussed here. Next, and most important, for those factors that do affect local levels of inequality, our main interest is in whether the effects are different for men and women. If so, this will provide evidence of potentially competing opportunity structures in local economies. What fosters opportunity among less-educated men may in fact reduce opportunity among less-educated women, and vice versa.

HIGH-TECHNOLOGY LABOR MARKETS

There are at least two reasons why high-tech regions might be expected to exhibit high levels of skills-based wage inequality. First, regions with concentrations of high-technology industries should have greater demand for skilled technical workers and thus higher relative wages for such workers both inside and outside high-technology industries (Blau and Kahn 1994). Second, non-high-tech industries in regions with concentrations of high-tech industries should be more likely to implement technological innovations than their counterparts in other regions. These "spillover" effects are similar to those historically seen in areas with large manufacturing plants, where union wages for high-school-educated men had the effect of raising wages for other men whether or not they were production workers or covered by a union contract. The difference in outcome is that the advantage today in high-tech regions belongs to college-educated workers rather than to high-school-educated men in blue-collar jobs.

Given the variety of conditions characterizing high-technology development, whether levels of skills-based wage inequality are in fact higher in these environments may depend on additional factors. First, in regions where high-technology manufacturing plants are unionized and predominantly male—such as defense, aerospace, and chemicals— wages are likely to be relatively higher for non-college-educated men. This would actually lead to a narrowing of the college wage gap among men. In the same environment, as was shown in the previous chapter, women are excluded from premium college and noncollege jobs alike. This also results in lower inequality, but for reasons of gender discrimination (Jenson 1989; Colclough and Tolbert 1992).

Second, in regions where high-technology manufacturing industries are vulnerable to import competition, have low union density, and are female-dominated (such as electronics), inequality among men may be higher, since there is unlikely to be high-wage employment for less-educated male workers. Among women, inequality is not likely to be higher because non-college-educated women may have marginally better job opportunities in manufacturing than in low-wage services.

Third, high male wage inequality and low female wage inequality are also likely in centers of high-technology service employment, where there are service-sector jobs for both college- and non-college-educated women in professional, technical, and clerical occupations and considerable upgrading among college-educated men in the advanced producer services. At least one study has found that the effect of technology has been to fill in the middle of the female wage distribution (Mishel and Bernstein 1996), while there is no comparable upgrading expected among non-college-educated men (Brint 1991). The case studies of postindustrial Dallas and Silicon Valley in chapters 2 and 3 suggests as much as well. *In sum, high-tech regions are expected to raise levels of skills-based wage inequality among men to a greater extent than among women and may even contribute to lower levels of inequality among women.*[9]

HIGH-FLEXIBILITY LABOR MARKETS
Explanations for rising inequality in the United States that emphasize the high degree of flexibility in the U.S. labor market have focused almost entirely on deunionization and the declining minimum wage

(adjusted for inflation). It is virtually impossible to investigate these factors in local labor markets because union coverage rates are available only for states and metropolitan areas, and minimum wage laws normally cover entire states.

Rather than emphasize these formal wage-setting institutions, I emphasize other key developments associated with employers' search for greater flexibility and the erosion of bargaining power and job security among workers. Together, these developments in effect *deinstitutionalize* the local labor market and lead to greater competition and lower wages at the bottom end. Three such developments have been identified in previous research: 1) unemployment (Blanchflower and Oswald 1994; Galbraith 1998), 2) immigration (Topel 1994; Borjas et al. 1996), and 3) casualization, including temporary work, part-time work, independent contracting, and informal self-employment (Tilly 1992; Spalter-Roth and Hartmann 1995; Kalleberg et al. 1997).

Most previous research on the geographical concentration of joblessness and immigration has examined their effects on wage levels (and only those of native whites and blacks in the case of immigration's effect) and not on inequality as such. In addition, research has focused on the plight of low-skilled men to such an extent that there are literally no studies of the possible effects of immigration or unemployment on low-skilled women. Nevertheless, the available spatial research is better on these factors than on most others. Researchers generally conclude that on average 1) male wages are more adversely affected than female wages, and 2) the high-school dropout/college gap is more likely to increase than the high school/college gap (Blanchflower and Oswald 1994; Borjas et al. 1996). While the available evidence has been persuasive on the negative wage effects of unemployment, there has been some question as to the suitability of analyzing immigration as a regional phenomenon. I address such questions in the Technical Appendix.[10]

In the case of casualization, national studies tend to show that white women and people of color are concentrated in low-quality nonstandard work arrangements and white men in higher-status positions (such as independent contracting). As a result, contingent work, and part-time work in particular, is frequently considered one of the main determinants of gender inequality. Yet some research has also shown that part-time work may offer higher wages to highly skilled women even though the aggregate effect of part-time work is to lower average wages significantly among women as a whole (Ferber and Waldfogel 1996; Kalleberg et al. 1997). Because of these crucial distinctions in the distribution of different types of casualized labor, it seems plausible that this type of work serves to heighten inequality among women as well as to intensify gender inequality, though the former has received little attention in the literature on casualization.

With little previous research to draw from, then, it remains an open question as to whether high-flexibility labor markets defined by joblessness, immigration, and casualization will affect male and female wage inequality equally. On the one hand, if these factors have effectively changed the nature of employment relations for a large part of the low-skilled labor market, making them more flexible and insecure, they are likely to increase both. On the other hand, as we saw in the previous chapter, the gender wage gap among the college-educated is average or lower in labor markets with all three of these characteristics, suggesting that college-educated men do not fare so well in these areas. They too may be affected by changes in the institutional environment that have externalized employment relations and exposed workers at all levels to market forces to a greater degree than in other areas. *In sum, inequality is generally expected to be higher among men in high-flexibility labor markets. Among women, because college-educated women have made wage gains relative to college-educated men (according to spatial and over-time trends), and low-skilled women workers are concentrated in the low-wage labor market, inequality may turn out to be significantly greater for women as well. This may be true especially between the very top and very bottom of the educational hierarchy as measured here.*

INDUSTRIAL COMPOSITION AND CHANGE

I consider the role of broad industrial composition and shifts as a third group of factors of secondary substantive interest. These factors are also included in order to control for the broad industrial structure and employment growth of labor markets.[11] As an indicator of deindustrialization and structural change, the growth/decline of manufacturing employment is the measure I use to track changing conditions over the 1980s. I also use a static measure of the share of employment in manufacturing as compared to services in 1989 to identify labor markets where manufacturing still is a significant presence. What is of particular interest is whether the well-known, beneficial effects of manufacturing employment for reducing skills-based wage inequality among men still holds sway in 1989 and whether these benefits extend to women. While a large literature has regarded Fordist-era manufacturing employment in a positive light for men and their families, and its decline in an equally negative and alarming light, no study has tested the implicit assumption that these benefits were (or are) widely shared. *In line with historical trends, inequality among men is expected to be lower in heavily industrialized labor markets but may no longer be lower in heavily deindustrialized regions. Among women, the case study of industrial Detroit suggests that college- rather than non-college-educated women benefit from the high-wage environment of heavily industrialized regions; thus inequality may turn out to be higher among women in these areas.*

EVIDENCE

I begin this section with descriptive statistics on college wage gaps among women and among men. My aim is to provide some basic comparative data on the level of inequality among women and among men in order to show why inequality among women should be considered an emerging social issue of some significance. I then establish that there is considerable variation in the level of wage inequality across the five-hundred-plus labor markets in my sample, for both men and women. However, the spatial patterns of inequality for men and women do not seem to overlap to a large extent. Labor markets with higher college wage gaps among women are not typically the same ones that have higher college wage gaps among men. Having established these basic gender differences, the rest of the chapter then considers the underlying causes of inequality and which factors are most important in explaining high college wage gaps for men and for women.

How High Is the College Wage Gap among Women?

Earlier studies of income inequality tended to include part-time as well as full-time workers, and levels of inequality were often shown to be higher for women. Unfortunately, perceptions of inequality have been unduly influenced by recent studies that almost always exclude part-timers and find inequality to be higher for men (when they include women at all).[12] More recent studies using part-timers are mixed, but only one study so far using part-time as well as full-time workers has found inequality to be higher for men (DiNardo et al. 1996). This is why both Smith (1991) and Bernhardt et al. (1995) have warned that analyzing inequality among women in samples that are restricted to full-time workers could be biased against low-wage women workers. Despite differences in the data set and sample restrictions—such as using the decennial censuses and not the Current Population Survey (CPS)[13]—my estimates of college wage gaps are similar to the few CPS studies that combine part-time and full-time workers and report actual levels, rather than changes in levels, of educational wage gaps. There are some notable differences, however. To show how my sample of adult (ages 25 to 64) part-time and full-time workers differs from the standard study on full-timers, I begin with a brief presentation of the level of the college wage gap for men and for women in different age and work-status categories.

Figure 6.1 presents the national, unadjusted (raw) estimates of college wage gaps for four groups defined by age (18 to 64 and 25 to 64) and hours status (full-time and all workers). The wage gaps are displayed as ratios for ease of interpretation. For example, HS/COL is a ratio of the median hourly wage of workers with a high school degree and those with a college degree. The higher the ratio, the more high school workers make relative to college workers. The first pair of vertical bars on the left side show the median HS/COL ratio among full-time 18- to 64-year-olds, the typical sample in previous research. The estimates reveal little gender variation in levels of the college wage gap for this group. For both men and women, the high school-educated earn about 61 percent of the wages of college graduates. The LHS/COL gap is also very similar for men and women in the sample of full-time 18-to-64-year-olds. Taking the average of the male and female gaps, full-time workers without a high school degree earn about 51 percent of the hourly wages of college graduates.

In contrast, educational wage inequality is substantially higher among women for the three other (nontypical) age/hours groups. This is mainly because men's wages are especially sensitive to age restrictions. Male wage inequality declines once lower-waged young men are excluded, since they experienced large declines in real wages over the 1980s. The LHS/COL wage ratio of 47.9 percent for full-time male workers increases to 53.3 percent when 18-to-24-year-olds are dropped from the sample (an 11.3 percent increase). In comparison to men's, women's wages are still quite low at age 25, and so age restrictions do not have as much of an effect (compare the female LHS/COL ratios for all 18-to-64-year-olds and all 25-to-64-year-olds). As you can see in the fourth and eighth columns of figure 6.1, the combination of including part-time workers and excluding young workers, to eliminate the confounding effects of schooling, produces estimates of inequality that are substantially higher for adult women. The rest of the analysis and discussion pertain to this group of full-time and part-time adult workers, ages 25 to 64.[14]

Is the College Wage Gap Higher in Some Regions?
Now that we know that levels of inequality are high among women and therefore are an important feature of the overall landscape of inequality, the next set of questions explores the extent of spatial variation in levels of wage inequality. Are there places that exhibit higher levels of inequality among men and others that have higher levels among women? If so, this would suggest that the sources of wage inequality are not necessarily the same for men and women. Figure 6.2 presents the range of variation in *adjusted* college wage gaps for men and women across the 554 regional labor markets. The adjusted gaps reflect controls within each labor market for random and fixed effects and a standard set of individual-level characteristics (see Technical Appendix). These include marital status, number of children, immigrant status, full-time/part-time status, race-ethnicity, potential experience and its square, and industry of employment. The adjusted gaps reveal the difference between college and noncollege hourly wages for workers who are otherwise the same on all these productivity-related characteristics.

Figure 6.1 Noncollege/College Median Hourly Wage Ratios by Gender, 1989

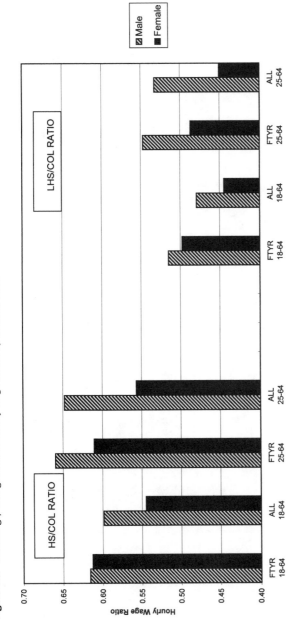

Note: The sample is not restricted to the 554 labor markets. "ALL" refers to part-time and full-time, year-round workers, and "FTYR" only to the latter. See the notes to table 6.1 for further data sources and definitions.

Figure 6.2 Spatial Variation in Adjusted Mean Noncollege/College Hourly Wage Ratio by Gender, 1989

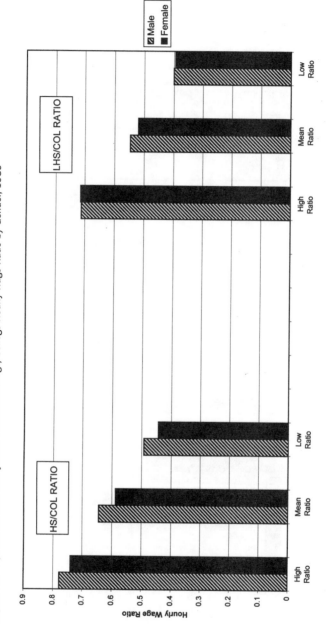

Note: See the notes to table 6.1 for data sources and definitions. Ratios adjusted for human-capital characteristics within labor markets.

Table 6.1 Correlations between Male and Female Noncollege/College Wage Gaps, 1989

	MEN			
	UNADJUSTED[a]		ADJUSTED[b]	
	HS/COL	**LHS/COL**	**HS/COL**	**LHS/COL**
Women				
Unadjusted				
HS/COL	0.023	0.013	0.121	0.154
LHS/COL	0.212	0.273	0.256	0.309
Adjusted				
HS/COL	0.031	0.031	0.184	0.243
LHS/COL	0.195	0.235	0.342	0.433

Note: Correlations across 554 U.S. regional labor markets. The sample includes U.S. nonfarm and non-self-employed adults, ages 25–64, with hourly wages between $1.00 and $250.00, and working in one of the selected 554 labor markets.

LHS = < 12 years of schooling; HS = 12 years; COL = 16 or more years.
Data taken from the Census of Population Public Use Microdata Samples from the Census of Population.

a. Calculations based on raw data.

b. Calculations are adjusted for individual characteristics in a regression of log hourly wages on marital status, number of own children, immigrant status, hours status, race, industry, potential experience and its square (see Technical Appendix for further details).

As indicated by the middle columns on the right and left sides of the figure, the mean adjusted levels of inequality remain greater for women, though the difference has narrowed from the unadjusted medians reported in figure 6.1. Figure 6.2 also shows that the range of spatial variation is substantial for both men and women. The labor market with the highest level of inequality has a noncollege/college wage ratio of 39.5 percent, and the labor market with the lowest level of inequality has a ratio nearly two times that (77.9).

While figure 6.2 shows clearly that levels of inequality vary widely across labor markets, Table 6.1 presents correlations between the male and female measures of inequality and indicates that places with high inequality among men are not typically the same as those with high inequality among women. Correlations can range from a low of zero, indicating no relationship, to 1.0, indicating a perfect relationship between two variables. Some correlations are extremely low, such as those between the female HS/COL gap and both male college/noncollege wage gaps (these correlations are higher in the full-time sample but still not strong). The female LHS/COL gap shows more of a correlation with male wage inequality but is still only weak to moderate. The highest correlations are between the male and female LHS/COL wage gaps. This suggests that there may be a general labor market effect for the lowest-skilled workers, affecting both men and women with the least amount of formal education. In other words, if the sources of inequality are in fact the same for men and women, this is more likely to be true for the LHS/COL gaps. Overall, though, inequality is distributed unevenly across regions, and there is only a weak overlap in the spatial patterns of male and female wage inequality. The question now is whether the economic conditions that foster high levels of wage inequality are also different for men and for women.

WHY ARE COLLEGE WAGE GAPS HIGHER IN SOME REGIONS?

The effects of local economic conditions on the adjusted log college wage gap are presented separately for men and women in figure 6.3 for the LHS/COL gap and in figure 6.4 for the HS/COL gap. As in previous figures, the college wage gaps are indicated by the ratio of noncollege to college wages. The meaning of the bars differs slightly from the previous two figures. For any particular measure of local economic conditions (also referred to as a labor-market variable), the adjusted college wage gap will vary across labor markets as those economic conditions vary. For example, the adjusted college wage gap will be different in high- and low-unemployment labor markets. The question is: How different? How much of an effect does joblessness have on the college wage gap? To put such variation in perspective, the horizontal line cutting across figures 6.3 and 6.4 represents the estimated *average* wage ratio. These ratios are: 1) 52.0 percent for the female LHS/COL ratio, 2) 54.7 percent for the male LHS/COL ratio, 3) 59.0 percent for the female HS/COL ratio, and 4) 64.3 percent for the male HS/COL ratio. Since the ratio increases the more non-college-educated workers earn relative to college-educated workers, inequality is lower than average when any vertical bar falls above the horizontal line and higher than average when it falls below it.

For example, since the unemployment rate varies from 2.03 to 14.0 percent in the data, the female LHS/COL wage ratio ranges from a high of 55.5 percent in the labor market with the lowest unemployment rate to a low of 46.0 percent in the labor market with the highest unemployment rate. This is a roughly 20 percent swing as a result of regional variation in unemployment rates. These wage ratios for low- and high-unemployment labor markets are displayed on the far left side of figure 6.3a. The dark, solid vertical bar that is well below the horizontal line (the mean noncollege/college wage ratio) represents a below-average wage ratio in the labor market with the highest unemployment. The hash vertical bar above the horizontal line represents an above-average wage ratio in the labor market with the lowest unemployment. It is these minimum (hash bars) and maximum (solid bars) college wage gaps that are shown in figures 6.3 and 6.4 for each labor market variable of interest.

Figure 6.3a Effects of Labor-Market Structure on the Adjusted Female LHS/COL Wage Ratio, 1989

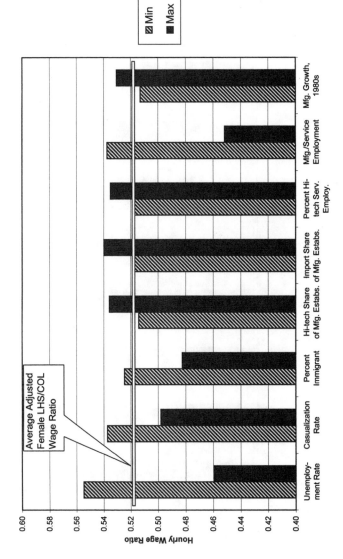

Note: See the notes to table 6.1 for data sources and definitions. See Appendix table A.1 for labor-market definitions and sources.

Figure 6.3b Effects of Labor-Market Structure on the Adjusted Male LHS/COL Wage Ratio, 1989

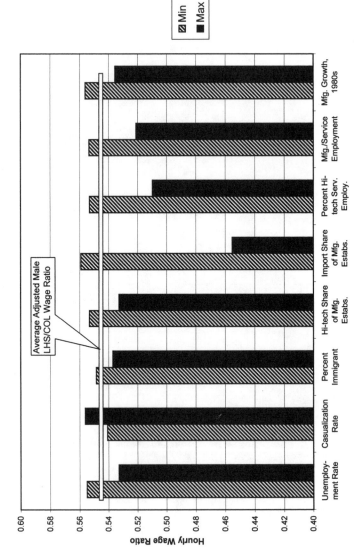

Note: See the notes to table 6.1 for data sources and definitions. See Appendix table A.1 for labor-market definitions and sources.

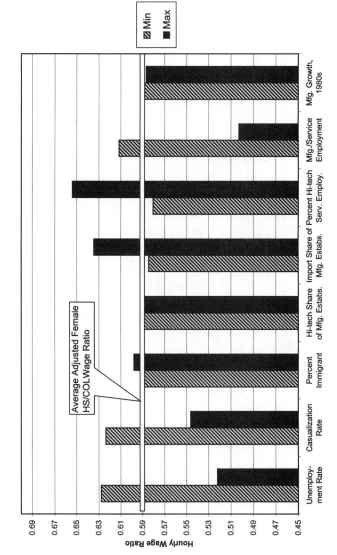

Figure 6.4a Effects of Labor-Market Structure on the Adjusted Female HS/COL Wage Ratio, 1989

Note: See the notes to table 6.1 for data sources and definitions. See Appendix table A.1 for labor-market definitions and sources.

Figure 6.4b Effects of Labor-Market Structure on the Adjusted Male HS/COL Wage Ratio, 1989

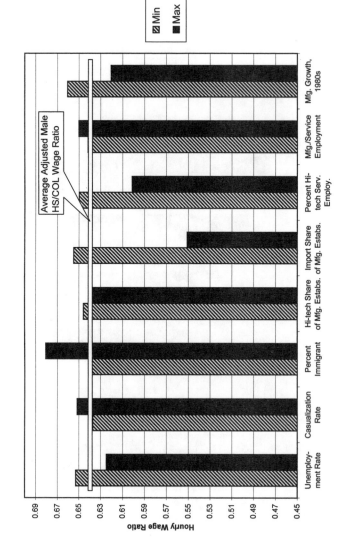

Note: See the notes to table 6.1 for data sources and definitions. See Appendix table A.1 for labor-market definitions and sources.

Figure 6.5 Spatial Variance in Noncollege/College Hourly Wage Gaps Explained by Labor-Market Type, 1989

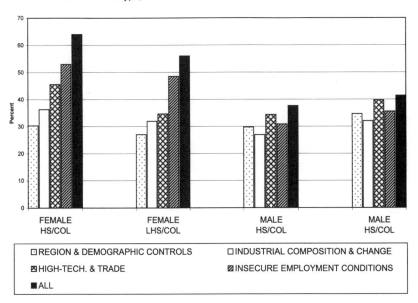

Note: See the notes to table 6.1 for data sources and definitions. See Appendix Table A.1 for labor-market definitions and sources.

In addition, because it is standard in the research literature on male inequality to determine how much each of the factors explains, I discuss how much of the variation in levels of inequality across labor markets can be explained by the three factors discussed above: high technology variables, high flexibility variables, and industrial composition and change variable. Figure 6.5 displays four groups of bars, one each for the female HS/COL, female LHS/COL, male HS/COL, and male LHS/COL wage gap. For each of these four college wage gaps, there are five bars that convey how much of the spatial variance in the college wage gap is explained by five groups of variables (from left to right): 1) the region and demographic control variables (population size, urban status, and broad region), hereafter referred to as controls, 2) industrial composition, industrial change, and the controls, 3) high-technology employment, trade-sensitive employment, and the controls; 4) flexible and insecure employment conditions and the controls; and 5) all variables.

For example, the first group of five bars on the left refers to the spatial variation in the female HS/COL wage gap. The tallest bar (in the darkest shade) is a measure of the total variation explained by all of the variables combined. A relatively high percentage (64 percent) of the spatial variation in the female HS/COL wage gap can be explained by region and demographic controls, high technology and trade, industrial composition, and insecure employment conditions. The region and demographic controls, the lowest bar (in the lightest shade), explain a little less than half of this variation (30 percent). The three bars in the middle show how much is explained when the variables in each group are combined with the region and demographic controls. Subtracting out the 30 percent associated with the controls gives the additional amount explained by the substantive variables—insecure employment conditions, high-technology and trade, or broad industrial structure. In this case, insecure employment conditions together with the controls explain 52 percent of the variation in the female HS/COL wage gap. Substracting out the 30 percent explained by the controls leaves 22 percent explained by insecure employment conditions alone. This is the largest amount explained in any of the equations by one of the three main groups of substantive variables (high flexibility, high technology, and industrial composition).

Overall Gender Differences
Recall that we first asked whether the effects of key dimensions of labor market restructuring are concentrated in specific labor markets, and, if so, whether the effects are the same for men and women. We see here that some aspects of labor markets do result in significantly higher or lower levels of inequality, for women especially. About half the coefficients for the eight labor market variables of substantive interest are statistically significant ($p < 0.05$). Up to 33 percent of the spatial variation in female college wage gaps can be explained by these variables.[15] Surprisingly, a much smaller percentage is explained in the male equations—at most 10 percent. In addition to these gender differences, there are few variables for which the coefficients are significant and in the same direction for both men and women. With these results, two broad claims about gender and the structure of labor-market inequality can be made. First, differences in the coefficients and their significance indicate that the labor-market variables generally have different effects on levels of skills-based wage inequality among women and skills-based wage inequality among men. And second, the diverse array of factors associated with restructuring in these models are better at explaining variation in levels of inequality among women. Both findings provide compelling evidence that gender matters in the debate over the causes of inequality and that we should look to regions for a better understanding of the conditions and sources of inequality for both women and men.

High-Flexibility Labor Markets Raise Inequality among Women
The group of variables describing flexible labor market conditions have the greatest impact on wage inequality among women. Labor markets

with the highest rates of joblessness, immigration, and casualization have levels of inequality which are considerably higher than average (see figure 6.3a). As can be seen in figure 6.4a, the HS/COL gap is also significantly greater in labor markets with high joblessness and casualization. For the LHS/COL gap, the coefficients on the local unemployment rate, the share of casualized workers, and the share of immigrant workers are all highly significant (p < 0.01). For the HS/COL female gap, the first two are also significant. Furthermore, the percentage of spatial variation in the college wage gap associated with these three variables is similar in the LHS/COL and HS/COL equations. At 21.5 percent to 22.7 percent, the amount explained is comparable in magnitude to the explanatory power of institutions in time-series analyses. In contrast, although high joblessness also led to significantly higher college wage gaps among men, the explanatory power of all three variables in predicting high levels of skills-based wage inequality among men is virtually nil.

High-Technology Labor Markets Raise Inequality among Men
Gender differences are apparent in the effect of technology and trade on levels of educational wage inequality as well. Technological changes have been said to be the major source of rising inequality over time, but the findings here reinforce those who have been more skeptical about this proposition. In fact, high-school-educated women appear to be doing *better* relative to college-educated women in labor markets specializing in high-technology service industries, and moderately better in labor markets with a disproportionate share of import-sensitive manufacturing establishments. The solid bars are well above the average female HS/COL ratio in figure 6.4a, indicating that the coefficients on these variables are significant and in the direction of increasing the relative wages of non-college-educated women. Moreover, the group of technology and trade variables explain a nontrivial 15.3 percent of the variation in the female HS/COL wage gap.[16] In contrast, these two indicators of trade and technology concentration result in significantly greater college wage gaps among men (see figures 6.3b and 6.4b) and explain only 5 percent of the spatial variation in the male wage gaps.

These results do not present strong evidence for the concentration of inequality in regions specializing in high technology and related sectors. However, a combination of the glass ceiling for college-educated women and modest upgrading for high-school-educated women might explain why inequality among women is significantly lower in high-tech and trade-sensitive labor markets. There is also some support for the argument that technological changes are benefiting highly educated men and at the same time hurting men with less education, which is not so surprising given the scholarly and popular focus on the deterioration of labor-market power among less-skilled men. Still, these effects are not overwhelming. If technological changes are as responsible for higher inequality as many economists predict, then the effects are not confined in any discrete way to high-tech regions.

Industrial Composition and Change Have Little Impact
The third explanation for why inequality varies across both space and time has to do with the industrial composition of employment and with the presence/absence of manufacturing in particular. Although the positive spillover effects of relatively high manufacturing wages have been documented in the past, relatively high manufacturing employment and growth do not result in greater equality among men in these 1990 data. In fact, the ratio of manufacturing to service employment results in significantly greater inequality among women for both measures (LHS/COL and HS/COL) and among men for the LHS/COL gap (but with only $p < = 0.10$). In addition, manufacturing growth resulted in greater inequality among men for the HS/COL measure. Only manufacturing *decline* fosters HS/COL equality among men, an effect that is most likely picking up the heavily deindustrialized cities of the North Central region. These areas may still provide wage supports for those men who are employed in relatively good blue-collar jobs.

Despite significant effects among men and quite strong negative effects among women, these variables have virtually no explanatory power in the male equations and only 5 percent to 6 percent in the female equations. This poor showing is consistent with the evidence that broad industrial shifts were not a major reason for the increase in wage inequality over time. Although broad industrial differences do not seem to be critical spatial determinants of levels of skills-based wage inequality overall, a strong and significant negative effect among women should still be noted. As was discussed in the case studies in chapters 2 and 3, and as suggested in the previous chapter by the lower gender wage gap among the college-educated in manufacturing-dominated areas, spillover effects have in fact benefited some groups of college-educated women. The available evidence suggests that the beneficiaries are college-educated women working as paraprofessionals in the partially unionized health, government, and education sectors.

WHAT EXPLAINS OTHER TYPES OF INEQUALITY?
Flexible and insecure employment conditions also have the most influence on within-group wage inequality (wage dispersion among workers with the same characteristics) (McCall 2000b).[18] As compared to the college wage gap, the three measures of joblessness, immigration, and casualization actually explain more of the variation of within-group wage inequality. High-flexibility labor markets account for up to 28 per-

cent of the spatial variation in the residual standard deviation among women and 17 percent among men. Once again, these factors also explained more of the variation than technology and trade or industrial shifts and composition. What differs from the spatial distribution of college wage gaps, however, is that *all three* variables exert a strong and significant effect on levels of inequality *among men as well as women*. Moreover, although there were gender differences in the descriptive data on within-group inequality (weak correlations between the spatial distribution of male and female residual inequality), the multivariate analysis revealed few gender differences in *any* of the sources of residual inequality.

However, there were notable gender differences in the *strength* of the findings that could have significant consequences for drawing conclusions about the causes of inequality. Although flexible employment conditions significantly increased levels of residual inequality for both men and women, they had the largest impact on the combined sample of part-time and full-time female workers (explaining 28 percent), and had the least impact on the sample of full-time male workers (explaining only 12 percent). The amount explained for the other groups was 22 percent for full-time women and 17 percent for all men. These differences are not trivial. They point to the ongoing importance of gender differences in the analysis of the new inequality, especially with regard to research decisions about who to include and who to exclude in the sample and which explanations to examine. These decisions in turn have consequences for policy discussions about the direction and effectiveness of anti-inequality initiatives. Including part-time women will obviously require that flexible/insecure employment conditions be given greater weight than they have had in such discussions.

In comparison to college wage gaps and within-group inequality, there were fewer gender differences in the determinants of racial wage inequality (McCall 2001). This neither supports nor contradicts previous research, which has focused little on restructuring and racial wage inequality among women (but see Browne 1999). However, my results do largely support previous research on men and can now be extended to women. The focus of previous research has been on the pivotal role of deindustrialization and deunionization in increasing black/white wage inequality and immigration in increasing Latino/white and Asian/white wage inequality (e.g., Moore and Pinderhughes 1993; Waters and Eschback 1995). These distinctions were more or less confirmed when I tested the effects of deindustrialization/deunionization and immigration on black/white, Asian/white, and Latino/white wage gaps. As in many previous studies not directly concerned with restructuring, I also found that places with large black populations resulted in greater black/white wage inequality, especially for women. Taken together, these results point to significant *racial, ethnic, and gender* differences in the sources of wage inequality with whites. The sources of racial wage inequality also diverge in many respects from the sources of other types of inequality (for example, college wage gaps and within-group wage inequality). As discussed in previous chapters, then, there is no simple overlap between the sources of gender, racial, and class inequality.

CONCLUSION

Class inequality among adult women ages 25 to 64 is not only rising, as previous research has shown, but is at least as high as it is among adult men. This is important because perceptions that inequality among women is less severe than inequality among men may be one of the reasons it has received so little attention. Another reason may be that disparities between men and women have been declining and real wages have not fallen as much for women as they have for men. Whatever the reason, stratification among women is becoming an increasingly important aspect of women's economic status. It is no less important, I would argue, than inequality between women and men. Women are frequently engaged in direct subordinate-supervisor relations of authority and power with other women, the economic fortunes of different groups of women have diverged in some of the same fundamental ways as they have for men, and anti-gender-discrimination policies have been more effective for highly educated women than for women at the bottom end of the labor market.

Given these new realities, and the fact that women constitute nearly half the nation's labor force, inequality among women must be considered an important aspect of what William Julius Wilson calls the "new social inequality," construed broadly to include all forms of inequality on the rise (Wilson 1997). The analytical role of gender in this context should be to determine whether the patterns and sources of inequality among women can be subsumed under the rubric of other measures of inequality, such as male inequality, family income inequality, or racial inequality. If there are substantive differences in the patterns and sources of within-gender inequality, they would seem to constitute a strong case for questioning the representativeness of standard measures of overall earnings inequality. The evidence of gender differences in the effects of high-flexibility and high-technology labor market conditions on skill-based wage inequality supports this alternative perspective.

Flexible labor-market conditions turned out to be the most important factor in fostering high levels of inequality between college- and non-college-educated women but not men. Disparities between the least and most educated women (the LHS/COL gap) were higher in labor markets with high rates of joblessness, casualization, and immigrant workers. The HS/COL gap was also significantly higher in two of the three cases (the exception being immigration). These factors combined to explain roughly 22 percent of regional variation in levels of inequality among women. This is more than was explained by measures of technology, trade, and broad industrial structure combined and net of regional and demographic controls. In contrast, these factors were not as important in explaining college wage gaps among men, even though areas with high unemployment also resulted in significantly higher levels of male inequality.[18]

These aspects of local economies that are associated with increased flexibility, insecurity, competition, and low wages among less-educated workers—characteristics of what I would refer to as a deinstitutionalized labor market—have received less attention in the research on rising wage inequality (McCall 2000a, 2000b). Moreover, at least two of these characteristics, casualization and immigration, have often been linked with gender inequality rather than inequality among women (Hossfeld 1990; Sassen 1991; Macdonald and Sirianni 1996). In light of these omissions in the literature, these findings have important implications for arguments about the role of increasing flexibility and insecurity in fostering inequality in the new economy. They bolster the argument that workers have less power with which to bargain for better wages and that the consequence is lower and declining wages, even in tight labor markets (with high casualization and immigration). Finding that such conditions are linked with greater inequality among women in particular suggests that their detrimental effects on women are disproportionately concentrated among less-educated women and not among women as a whole.

Thus these findings point not only to the need for a new analytical emphasis on within-gender structures of inequality but to new evidence to evaluate substantive claims about the underlying causes of inequality. Factors that have received the lion's share of attention in the literature on restructuring and rising inequality *over time*, such as technological change, turn out to be minor factors in generating high *levels* of inequality within regions, particularly among women. Not only are technology-related and trade-related factors less important than flexible and insecure employment conditions in explaining spatial variation, the female HS/COL gap is significantly *lower* in high-technology service and import-sensitive regions. At 8 percent to 15 percent, the amount of variation explained by these factors is not even trivial.

At least for women, then, inequality does not appear to concentrate within high-technology regional labor markets, though it may be diffused over larger areas. The dynamics of how inequality is structured within high-technology regions and relative to other regions is an important question to address in future case-study and macro-level research on the trends in the 1990s. In particular, it should be determined whether lower inequality among women is an effect of the glass ceiling among college-educated women or of a genuine upgrading among high-school-educated women, or both. Previous research suggests that both may be at work (Blau and Kahn 1997; McCall 1998; and chapter 5).

While I have emphasized substantive conclusions that may be drawn from the findings on women, the spatial organization of inequality among men lends some support to more conventional arguments about the role of technology and trade. Regions with an above-average share of employment in high-technology service industries had significantly higher male college wage gaps. Labor markets with a disproportionate share of manufacturing plants in import-sensitive industries tended to foster significantly higher inequality among men as well. Furthermore, these variables accounted for the largest portion of variation in the equations for men. Despite what appears to be strong evidence, however, only a small portion of the regional variance in men's inequality was explained in absolute terms (roughly 5 percent) because almost all of the explained variation was absorbed by region and demographic controls. Findings such as these offer at least some corroborating evidence for claims about the intensifying dualism of postindustrial economies (Harrison and Bluestone 1988; Sassen 1991). Still, the structure of inequality turns out to be highly variable across distinctions of gender, time, and space, and thus *generalizations* about the role of postindustrialism in creating greater inequality cannot be substantiated.

With a large body of research already on male inequality, family income inequality, racial inequality, and gender inequality, investigations into the nature of inequality among women need to be undertaken, and potential differences in the levels and sources of inequality need to be taken just as seriously. While a systematic macroanalysis such as this one can identify both similarities and differences in the sources of various types of inequality and lend credence to the case study evidence in chapters 2 and 3, additional micro-level studies are needed to determine more precisely how the broad array of multiple and potentially conflicting opportunity structures interact and overlap in concrete local labor markets.

Part III

CONCLUSION

Chapter Seven

THE HISTORY AND POLITICS OF INEQUALITY
RECONSIDERED

Gender inequality has declined in recent decades, while most forms of wage inequality have risen, and inequality among women is emerging as a key feature of women's work experience. These are just a few of the realities that make configurations of inequality necessary: different dimensions of inequality have followed different spatial and temporal trajectories and, as I have shown throughout this book, are linked to different aspects of economic restructuring and the new economy. But configurations of inequality move beyond demonstrating differences between gender, race, and class to identifying relationships—between restructuring and inequality on the one hand and among different dimensions of inequality on the other. Configurations of inequality identify distinct patterns of gender, class, and racial inequality that are associated with specific paths of economic development in regions throughout the United States. Industrial Detroit and postindustrial Dallas, for example, have configurations of inequality that are polar opposites, with gender-related cleavages taking on greater importance in the former city and class and racial cleavages in the latter.

In this final chapter, I consider whether such differences in the economic conditions and social composition of wage inequality should dictate differences in the policies and politics aimed at reducing inequality. Not surprisingly, I argue that configurations of inequality should indeed play a central role in the formulation of anti-inequality policies and in the development of an "anti-inequality" politics more generally. If we have information on the local conditions and constitution of inequality, why *not* use it in the design of context-specific anti-inequality policies and political strategies? The only reason I can foresee is a practical one—it is more likely that some other approach or set of policies appears more feasible from a political standpoint regardless of whether it pays any heed to actual social and economic conditions. I certainly consider such contingencies wherever possible, but my focus is more on the political implications—in an ideal world—of particular configurations of inequality. I use the findings from previous chapters to link specific configurations of inequality to specific policies aimed at reducing inequality and to show more generally why the local politics of inequality should be shaped by the local conditions that give rise to it.

In addition to a discussion of the political implications of local configurations of inequality, I return to the argument, introduced at the beginning of chapter 1, that the relationship between the causes of inequality and the politics of inequality is also relevant at the national level. I offer a critical reinterpretation of the politics of inequality over the course of the twentieth century and discuss the implications for national anti-inequality policies today. Not coincidentally, these implications reinforce the political implications I draw from regional configurations of inequality. Both views—national and regional—point to the relevance, indeed necessity, of a joint gender, class, and race perspective on the enduring problem of inequality. The bottom line here is *not* that context or complexity matters *as such*, or that all policies should be *either* national *or* regional, but that the politics of inequality, whether at the national or regional level, should attempt to respond fully to the social and economic conditions at hand. And those conditions reveal, in different ways and in different places, the centrality of all three dimensions of inequality.[1]

In presenting this argument, I begin with the historical angle because it provides the necessary background for discussing the contemporary politics of inequality at both the national and regional levels. Whether we are talking about so-called "universal" policies (read *class*) or "targeted" (read *gender* and *race*) policies, the frameworks we use today have their antecedents in previous historical eras of the twentieth century. The next section provides a brief historical overview of the essential features and shortcomings of these reform eras, the 1930s and 1960s. My main objective in this section is to show that the contemporary period reflects key characteristics of each era in terms of both the economic conditions and the social composition of inequality. The implication, then, is that the policies developed in each era are also relevant today. This is the positive side of the argument—current conditions suggest an urgent and ongoing need for the policies instituted during the 1930s and 1960s reform eras.

But there is also a negative side of the argument. Since each of the two policy thrusts is typically embraced on its own without regard to the need for the other, I discuss the severe limits of each one as a stand-alone solution in terms of its diagnosis and treatment of the problem of inequality. I begin in the second section with a critical assessment of 1960s-era antidiscrimination policies for overlooking the sources of inequality that are not strictly race- and gender-specific. Focusing on the gender/class nexus, I argue that the central flaw in antidiscrimination policies aimed at reducing gender inequality is that they grew out of the prosperous 1960s, when it made sense to focus on changing the composition of employment rather than its underlying structure. Structural changes since then have meant wage declines for most men as well as less-educated women, wage increases for college-educated women, and a legitimate concern for rising class inequality among *women* as well as men. This is illustrated well in several configurations of inequality with flexible and insecure economic conditions. In such environments, affirmative-action and comparable worth policies would seem less effective because they measure women's progress against a male standard which is itself problematic: highly unequal and becoming more so by the day. Antidiscrimination approaches need to be supplemented, then, with economic policies that change the underlying class structure of inequality for both men and women by raising *wages* for *all* workers at the bottom end of the labor market in predominantly male, female, and integrated jobs alike.

In the third section, I turn the tables and argue that the central flaw in policies aimed at reducing class inequality, which have enjoyed a resurgence of late, is that they bear the imprint of the 1930s in their disregard of gender and racial inequality. While broad redistributive policies address systemic economic inequalities through full employment, human-capital formation, workers associations, minimum wages, unemployment insurance, economic development initiatives, and the like, the course of postwar U.S. and European history has shown that such policies are not a sufficient remedy for unequal gender and racial divisions of labor. Moreover, with growing prosperity there should be less competition and more goodwill toward disadvantaged groups, and the resources to back it up. Given that class analysts tend to be more interested in racial than in gender inequality and a gender perspective has been all but absent from recent debates, I provide several reasons why a gender analysis especially is needed. As several configurations of inequality illustrate, gender must be recast to account for distinctive patterns of inequality among women, the gendered character of employment, and highly gendered visions of future and past economic utopias.

While my discussion is organized around the limits of gender-only and class-only perspectives, I also consider the more ambiguous role of race in the history and politics of inequality. On the one hand, race has had a more central role than gender in antidiscrimination policy formation since the 1960s. My arguments against a gender-only antidiscrimination policy for ignoring structural economic changes would therefore be relevant to similar antiracist positions as well. On the other hand, racial and class inequality among men have been rising, and both are frequently linked to economic restructuring, particularly in the influential work of William Julius Wilson. While research in this area tends to incorporate both antidiscrimination and structural economic approaches to the problem of racial inequality, it pays little attention to gender inequality or racial inequality among women. As a result, my arguments against a class-only economic policy for ignoring gender issues would also be relevant to these recent discussions of racial inequality. Finally, gender-only and class-only perspectives each fall short when they fail to incorporate explicitly a racial analysis. Because there are both similarities and differences in how racial inequality has been considered relative to gender and class, I integrate a racial analysis into both parts of my argument.

Economic Change and the Politics of Inequality: Historical Shifts

As many studies of the development of social policy in U.S. history have convincingly shown, social policies are first and foremost about redistributing resources. But social policies also serve a symbolic or formal legal function by recognizing the rights of marginalized social groups.[2] This implies that the degree of redistribution and recognition along the lines of gender, class, and race has varied across periods of social-policy formation and institutional development. While the dynamics of gender, race, and class are always present in the determination of new policies and the objectives of their framers, in the end only a *partial* definition of inequality emerges as the *target* of reform and only some social groups become the beneficiaries of the new civil and/or social rights of citizenship. Consequently, as presented in table 7.1, I characterize the 1930s and 1960s mainly in terms of their principle of redistribution (class, race, or gender) and the beneficiaries of redistribution (workers, blacks, or women). My central concern is with how these policies and the social groups they recognized were products of contemporary thinking on both the state of the economy and the proximate cause of inequality.[3]

In the 1930s, the primary objective of new state and economic institutions was to prevent working citizens from falling into poverty as a result of circumstances beyond their control. With the Depression and a new appreciation of capitalism's severe cyclical rhythms, unemployment was the most pressing problem, but dislocations due to old age, injury, and illness were also compelling. Government assistance was channeled to workers and their families, and many were given the right

Table 7.1 Typology of Anti-Inequality Reform Eras in the Twentieth-Century United States

	1930s NEW DEAL	1960s GREAT SOCIETY		1980s-PRESENT POSTINDUSTRIAL RESTRUCTURING
State of Economy	Trough of Twentieth Century	Peak of Twentieth-Century Industrial Capitalism		Structural Transition (Dislocation and Prosperity)
Cause of Inequality	Economic Change (the Depression)	Discrimination		Economic Change (Restructuring) & Discrimination
Principle of Redistribution	Class and Universal	Race	Gender	Class, Race, & Gender
Targeted Beneficiaries	Industrial Workers	Minorities	Women	Workers, Women, & Minorities
Limitations	Ignores Racial and Gender Discrimination	Ignores Class, Gender, Economic Change	Ignores Class, Race, Economic Change	Gender, Race and Class are Contigent

to organize unions, to collectively bargain with employers, and to receive a minimum wage. These social policies worked hand in hand with Keynesian macroeconomic policies of federal spending on jobs programs and infrastructure development to stimulate consumer demand. Excluded from these major industrial-era institutions, though, were the majority of workers employed in black- and female-dominated occupations, such as agriculture, domestic service, nursing, and education. Bargaining rights were even secured as bars to the inclusion of African Americans were willingly put in place. While the 1930s established strong national standards, rights, and institutions behind which all subordinated groups could rally in principle, they nevertheless must be understood as *targeted* in bestowing the most generous entitlements on members of the industrial working class. At the time, this group was disproportionately male, white, and Northern. These victories were not, and still are not, universally shared.[4]

During the Golden Age of capitalism following World War II and into the 1960s, the economy grew stronger but also more contested along different dimensions (Glyn et al. 1990). This was the period of "the great wage compression" among male workers, the fruition of wartime and postwar economic demand and the redistributive institutions of that era (Goldin and Margo 1992). The emphasis of social policy gradually shifted from one coded in the words of *security*—the demand for economic security in the insecure 1930s—to one of *opportunity* in the 1960s. According to Christopher Jencks (1992), the New Deal was "designed to prevent the nonpoor from falling into poverty" and the Great Society was "mainly concerned with helping the poor rise" (p. 3). What had changed between these two historical periods was the overall sense that there were plenty of "good" jobs to be found, particularly in the middle to late 1960s. Debate centered not on *whether* there were enough jobs but on *who* filled those jobs and the inherent unfairness of a legacy of "affirmative action" for the sons who inherited stable working-class jobs in deeply racialized and gendered industries, such as the construction trades.

The federal government took steps to remedy racial segregation at work but its initial efforts proved inadequate, and affirmative action was soon required. At first, Title VII of the Civil Rights Act (1964) and the original employment training programs of the Economic Opportunity Act (1964) were oriented toward preparing individuals for good jobs and making sure that qualified individuals were not barred from them.[5] But demands for affirmative action were sparked by the fact that qualified blacks still could not enter these jobs. Employers needed to be forced to change their hiring practices and to adopt numerical goals for the inclusion of nontraditional groups of workers.[6] The first highly publicized affirmative-action plans were launched in the late 1960s and early 1970s, but civil rights activists, and even policy-makers at the highest levels of government, had long believed that requiring employers and unions to take positive steps toward racial integration was ultimately the only way to enforce antidiscrimination law.[7]

The movement from a defensive posture of equal rights and antidiscrimination to a positive posture of affirmative action was also evident in the fight for gender equity. In 1963, the Equal Pay Act barred unequal pay between men and women working in the same job. This was a victory capping more than two decades of organizing by women's groups and unions on a range of important issues, including "increased minimum wages, equal pay, paid maternity leave, and equal employment opportunities" (Cobble 1994: 75). But even though the Civil Rights Act of 1964 was aimed principally at ending racial segregation in the South and racial inequality more generally, it turned out to be more important for women than the Equal Pay Act because its Title VII prohibited discrimination against women in *any* job.

The fair-employment regulations opened the way for requiring federally funded firms to fulfill their legal obligations by taking "affirmative action" to eliminate job discrimination due to gender.[8] The Equal Employment Opportunity Commission's initial refusal to take sex discrimination in the private sector seriously, which derived in part from Congress's lack of clear direction on sex discrimination in Title VII, was pivotal in mobilizing feminist pressure for more action on behalf of women workers. These women sought equal treatment in their access to medical and pension benefits, seniority, overtime, and male-dominated occupations (Graham 1990). Although many of these complaints were pursued through the courts, the most prominent gender-equity strategies consisted of moving women into higher-paying male-dominated occupations through affirmative action and, later, pay-equity schemes that upgraded the pay of women's occupations to that of comparable men's occupations.[9] Both strategies assumed that white men's jobs were high-wage and here to stay, an assumption that was soon to be questioned.

In comparing the overall position of workers, women, and blacks in the current period to the 1930s, then, we can easily appreciate the tremendous gains made by workers, civil rights, and women's movements. Economic forces not coinciding with major pieces of legislation, such as agricultural mechanization, World War II, and the expansion of service industries, also fostered equality in various respects up until the 1970s (Albelda and Tilly 1994). But some of these gains have been steadily eroding since 1980, creating a more mixed picture of progress toward equality.

First, most research on the fair-employment laws of the mid-to-late 1960s found them to be moderately effective in reducing average gender and racial wage gaps,[10] but these programs began to be dismantled in the 1980s and have come under especially vigorous fire in the 1990s. Second, the union wage premium, which measures the difference between wages in union and nonunion jobs, is still substantial (on the order of 20 percent), but private sector union membership is at an all-time low of only 10 percent (Mishel et al. 1997: 200). Third, poverty rates declined by half during the booming 1960s, but there has been an upward secular trend in poverty since the late 1970s, even taking into account recent reductions (Schram 1995: 146–147). Last, almost everyone agrees that employment training programs aimed at the most disadvantaged are too narrow, poorly designed, and underfunded (Weir 1992). The perception is that successful employment policies have been biased toward working- and middle-class families that provide enough of a head start for their children to take advantage of them. Despite progress of a long-term nature, then, those at the bottom are still disproportionately female and minority, while those at the top are disproportionately male and white. Meanwhile, America's famous middle class has been shrinking.

Thus inequality persists in our third and latest era, one constituted, I maintain, by a unique and volatile mix of the insecurity of the 1930s and the prosperity of the 1960s. On the one hand, the industrial institutions of the New Deal, which provided for a relatively balanced distribution of economic growth in the early postwar period, have been dismantled along with the industrial base they served. The lack of postindustrial institutions to fill their void has resulted in a radical upward redistribution of earnings and wealth (Goldin and Margo 1992; Wolff 1995; Osterman 1999). On the other hand, the U.S. economy has successfully restructured so that its brand of flexible, free-market capitalism is once again the undisputed global gold standard, after a brief period in which the so-called Asian model was emulated around the world as a more humane form of capitalism.

The fact that recent structural economic change has fostered both dynamic growth *and* widespread insecurity is something that Federal Reserve Chair Alan Greenspan frequently expresses concern over and even the optimistic *Economic Report of the President* freely admits:

> The effects of a tight labor market on wages may have been muted by the presence of widespread worker insecurity, which has been evident since the 1990–91 recession. Despite a strong job market and a high level of consumer confidence, surveys indicate that workers' fears of job loss remain high relative to the level that prevailed before the recession. Quit rates are low as well, which could reflect workers' unwillingness to leave their current jobs in the hope of "trading up" to better jobs. And strike activity is at a low ebb, although this is related at least in part to declines in unionization rates. These factors suggest that workers may be relatively unwilling to press for the wage gains that they could normally command in a labor market as tight as that of today. (U.S. Council of Economic Advisors, 1998: 61)

This state of affairs even prompted a special issue of the *New York Times Magazine* titled "Money on the Mind," a central point of which was that the "great swatch of lower- and lower-middle-class America has been untouched by the boom" (Lewis 1998: 62). Although wages at the bottom are indeed up since 1996, and a few measures of inequality have declined slightly, wages have yet to return to their previous peaks and inequality to its previous trough in the 1970s. Perhaps more important, there is no end in sight to the pursuit of maximum flexibility, and thus insecurity in the new economy.[11]

What, you might ask, underlies this new combination of insecurity and prosperity? Part of the answer is that inequality and insecurity are the result of several cracks in the edifice of today's prosperity. Even though the unemployment rate is at a thirty-year low, it is still well above the peak of the business cycle in 1969 (3.5 percent). *Average* output and productivity growth rates over the 1980s and 1990s lag far behind 1960s standards as well.[12] Meanwhile, corporate profit rates are now comparable to those of the 1960s, and the volume of and returns from financial investments are in a league all of their own. It is this more tenuous and speculative environment—in which profits and windfalls have been more unevenly distributed than in the past, and the redistribution that does occur is at the mercy of explosive and perhaps unsustainable growth (Bluestone and Harrison 2000)—that has fostered widespread insecurity and made the singular focus on gender- or race-targeting unpopular and, more important, frequently inaccurate and ineffective. Next, I explore this argument with respect to gender inequality, the only form of inequality to have declined since 1979. In the subsequent section I show why a class-only approach is equally inadequate.

THE LIMITS OF GENDER

In the 1960s, the supply of good, white, male-dominated jobs was assumed to be stable, expanding, and impeded only temporarily, if at all, by cyclical downturns. As a result, affirmative action grew out of conflicts over who filled certain privileged positions in the economy, not on questions of whether and how many of such positions there were to be filled.[13] Inequality in the white male wage and occupational structure was simply not of any significance in the 1960s and even in the 1970s, when affirmative-action and comparable-worth programs were devised and implemented. The core job structure of the economy—based on the white male standard—was taken for granted.

What separates the 1960s from today is that we can no longer assume that wage increases and job security are part and parcel of moving up the occupational ladder. This is not to deny that there has been a steady increase in the educational requirements of jobs, a key indicator of occupational upgrading (Howell and Wolff 1991), or that there are still lots of good jobs to be had in the new economy. Rather, it is a recognition of the fact that jobs throughout the bottom half of the labor market, ones that used to provide a living wage or better, have become vulnerable to a number of new economic forces: the growth of nonunionized manufacturing industries (such as electronics), the surrender to concessionary bargaining in traditionally unionized manufacturing industries, the intensification of international trade and labor competition, the automation of assembly and data-entry jobs, the deregulation and privatization of public services, the declining value of the minimum wage, and the rise of other modes of flexibility.[14] At issue, most researchers agree, is some combination of 1) technological change, the preferred explanation of neoclassical economists; 2) increased integration of world capital, goods/services, and labor markets; and 3) a whole host of institutional changes that have reduced the bargaining power of ordinary workers.

It is this shift in the economic environment since the 1950s and 1960s that has added to the difficulties of finding political support for antidiscrimination programs (though there is probably no truly auspicious time for affirmative-action and other group-oriented redistribution policies). Although things may have improved somewhat since the mid-1990s, a poll at that time reported that 60 percent of whites believed that "they have lost ground in the last ten years," and 40 percent believed that "fewer jobs or promotions for whites is a 'bigger national problem' than discrimination against minorities" (Dawson 1997: 270). Now, on the one hand, affirmative action *should* proceed regardless of changes in the underlying economic structure as long as top-paying jobs are dominated by white men and a large percentage of the racial and gender wage gaps are left explained by differences in measurable qualifications (Bergmann 1996). However, on the other hand, this does not mean that affirmative action represents the *only* principle of redistribution to embrace, particularly for the vast majority of nonsupervisory workers in the U.S. economy. Since affirmative action and comparable worth both assume that white men's jobs are higher-paying jobs, what happens when that assumption—the white male standard—is tested by years of wage stagnation and decline among working- and even middle-class men?

I would like to suggest that, had this future been known, advocates might well have shifted their attention to improving women's *wages* in a way that did not explicitly peg upgrading women's jobs to the superior but declining wages of men's jobs. Given the diversity of women's jobs and the likelihood that they would be held increasingly by men, it might have seemed as necessary to improve those jobs because they were the jobs of the future as it was to improve them because they were devalued as women's jobs. This alternative approach attacks low wages and job quality *directly*, not indirectly through comparisons to the male occupational and wage structure. Rather than focusing on moving women into men's jobs or lifting their wages to the height of men's, it now seems necessary to focus more directly on raising wages for both men and women, though still disproportionately for women.[15]

The need for an alternative cross-gender focus on lifting wages at the bottom is evident from recent national as well as regional trends. As I showed in chapter 5, at the national level men's wage declines are not the only reason for the falling gender wage gap, contrary to popular and even scholarly belief. College-educated women saw their wages rise over the course of the 1980s. That is the primary reason for the decline in the gender gap for the college-educated. Consequently, questions about how to address long-standing inequalities between men and women are complicated not only by low and declining wages among men but by absolute gains among college-educated women. In addition, at the regional level the reasons for lower gender inequality differed substantially between the college- and non-college-educated because regional wage levels differed by both gender and education. Thus there have been different avenues for closing the gender wage gap for the college- and non-college-educated, and not all of them are equivalent. In assessing the new context of gender inequality, then, we need to investigate wage levels as well as wage inequality and to do so for low-skilled as well as high-skilled workers.

My research shows that all these facets are especially important when considered together in configurations of inequality with flexible and insecure employment conditions. These configurations present stark dilemmas because they describe situations in which gender inequality is actually above average but wages are significantly below average for both men and women at the bottom end of the labor market. This occurs when several factors are present in insecure and flexible labor markets that result in less bargaining power and lower wage levels for less-educated workers. In labor markets with high joblessness, for instance, wage levels are significantly lower for workers with less than a high school education, and wage penalties are actually greatest for women in that group. Gender wage inequality is therefore above average compared to other labor markets. In contrast, college-educated women's wages are significantly higher, and consequently the gender wage gap among the college educated is lower. Highly casualized labor markets exhibit similar tendencies: wages are lower, but less-educated men and women are about equally penalized, and gender wage inequality is about average. Perhaps most important, *average gender inequality in terms of wages occurs despite significantly higher levels of occupational segregation.*

Even though the gender wage gap is actually average or above average in some cases, the confluence of economic insecurity and lower wages still challenges the wisdom of anti-inequality strategies based on women's entry into men's jobs which are assumed to be "good" jobs with "high" wages. That occupational segregation persists and men's jobs are actually relatively better paid—the gender wage gap may be about average or higher—must be weighed against the context of unemployment, casualization, and pervasively low wages at the bottom end of the labor market. Tipping the scales a notch further from a gender-only affirmative-action or comparable-worth perspective is the fact that college-educated women tend to be, strictly speaking, better off. Gender inequality among the college-educated is significantly lower, and in some cases the wages of college-educated women are significantly higher. Departing from trends in the "average" gender wage gap, and bringing the context of economic restructuring into the picture, produces a much-needed sensitivity to the joint dynamics of class and gender, which in turn produces a non-gender-centered policy approach to the problem of inequality.

If this rings true in labor markets with higher levels of gender inequality, it is even more compelling where gender inequality turns out to be lower. This is strikingly illustrated in labor markets attracting large numbers of immigrants, in which interpretations of gender inequality must become sensitized to patterns of class and racial inequality within gender groups. Of ten or so measures of key dimensions of economic restructuring, the share of immigrants in the local labor market was the only one that was significantly associated with high wage levels and lower gender inequality across the educational hierarchy. However, and perhaps less surprisingly, these areas were deeply stratified by class (among women only) and especially race (among both men and women). The degree of immigration accounted for about 20 percent to 30 percent of the spatial variation in Latino/white and Asian/white wage gaps across labor markets. In light of what we know about the prevalence of low-wage, informal, and sweatshop labor among immigrant women, we would not want to dismiss gender altogether as a key organizing principle of inequality in these labor markets (Hossfeld 1990). But featuring gender alone would be equally misleading, given greater parity among men and women on the one hand and heightened levels of racial and class inequality among women on the other. Only a joint gender, class, and race perspective captures the dynamics of inequality in such an environment.

In sum, affirmative action is imperative as long as racial and gender discrimination persist, but there are now many reasons to situate strategies of gender integration and wage equity within a broader framework of raising wages for men as well as for women at the bottom end of the labor market. First, highly educated women are the only major demographic group to have made absolute wage gains over the 1980s. There is also clear evidence that substantial "elite" *occupational* integration is taking place in the United States as compared to other advanced capitalist countries, yet *wage* integration lags behind those same countries (O'Connor, Orloff, and Shaver 1998). A "mass" strategy of equalizing wages has had the opposite effect in countries such as Sweden and Australia, where gender wage equality is greater but accompanied by less occupational integration. Perhaps a reversal of emphasis is now necessary, one in which activists in the United States are dedicated to improving wages for the bottom half of the labor market through non-gender-specific unionization, full employment, and living-wage campaigns.

Second, the context of economic restructuring makes it clear that "to be equal to an unemployed coal miner [is] just no big deal."[16] As Barbara Ellen Smith argues, the organization she participated in to facilitate women's entry into nontraditional jobs was soon called into question by the "political and economic changes of the early 1980s" (Smith 1995: 687). Barbara Reskin and Patricia Roos (1990) have likewise demonstrated that even where integration into previously male-dominated jobs took place, it came at the cost of deskilling and downgrading. Moreover, prioritizing integration into predominantly male jobs neglects the fact that a great many women's jobs are either preferable or themselves in need of upgrading (Blum 1991). Of course comparable worth was intended to take such action, but as I have argued, comparisons to a declining male standard are less justifiable in the current environment. Finally, gender-based strategies are always at least implicitly racialized and therefore must attend and at times accede to the racial context of labor market restructuring. All these reasons suggest the need to combine, not substitute, equity initiatives with broadbased economic policy aimed at raising wages and living standards in the new and expanding sectors of the economy.

THE LIMITS OF CLASS
Even though people of color and women are still much more likely to be in poverty and employed in low-wage jobs, the foregoing critique of a gender-centered perspective may explain why many scholars and politicians hearken back to New Deal themes. Highlighting structural changes and elevating the class rather than racial or gendered nature of the new inequality has definite virtues (Wilson 1987, 1996; Greenberg 1997; Kahlenberg 1998). It is not only politically expedient, with its avid popular support from the left and the right, but often makes up for its shortcomings by favoring race targeting *within* universal programs and those based on economic need (Skocpol 1991; Wilson 1999). Proponents also claim that the ends ought to justify the means. Programs targeted to the economically disadvantaged will disproportionately benefit subordinate gender and racial groups.[17] The problem is that little attention is devoted to how class, racial, and gender inequality are shaped by different dynamics and therefore might at times require different solutions. Equipped with information of this kind, we can expose the limitations and *de facto* "targeting" of universalism (read *class*) and recast the options of universalism and targeting as contingent on real configurations of inequality.

I focus on gender here because the inadequacies of a class-centered analysis are perhaps better known with regard to race. In a way that scholars of gender inequality have yet to achieve, William Julius Wilson has been almost single-handedly responsible for bringing race to the center of debates on economic restructuring, inequality, and poverty, even though he himself favors class-based and universal policies (Wilson 1987, 1996). On the subject of social policy more generally, many scholars have already demonstrated the centrality of race in social policy formation since at least the 1930s. Certainly racial equality was the primary objective of 1960s legislation (Piven and Cloward 1979; Quadagno 1994; Weir 1992, 1995b; Weir and Ganz 1997). In fact, few would disagree that racial inequality is a central American social problem, though there is intense disagreement over explanations and solutions (Winant 1997). In contrast, there has never been a comparable national recognition of the problem of gender inequality. My point is not simply about recognition: that gender-biased notions of class and race are once again eclipsing gender, though a lack of recognition is a major part of why gender can again be ignored today as it was in the early 1960s civil rights debates. Rather, my argument is that a gender analysis provides new and necessary insights into the current predicament of inequality.

In discussing the relevance of gender against a class-only approach, one has to begin by simply setting the record straight about current, and highly contradictory, perceptions of women workers and gender differences in the economy. Descriptive trends in gender inequality are quite distinct from trends in other forms of inequality and consequently are frequently misunderstood. While the 1980s brought increasing inequality within as well as between racial groups, gender inequality declined more in the 1980s than in any other decade of the twentieth century. At first, the decrease in gender inequality—the only form of inequality to decline—and the heightened visibility of managerial and professional women served to marginalize the interests of most working women and amplify the plight of working-class men, thus spawning the "angry white male" backlash and calls for class-based affirmative action. What lay below the surface of this polarizing rhetoric, however, was the fact that women were silently increasing their hours at work—even though their wages were not necessarily climbing—because their paychecks were becoming increasingly central to family survival. The contribution to family income by working mothers and wives was actually staving off declines in real median family income. And, unlike the 1930s, working women typically were not derided for stealing jobs from men (Milkman 1987). What had changed since then was the perception that women do indeed have a right to work, and indeed must work, and as a whole have made tremendous economic progress without much fanfare policy-wise.

Despite a lingering backlash against elite women, this perception of women's deserved and necessary economic progress is, I think, widely held and generally to be applauded. But what concerns me are the implications of the fact that this perception differs dramatically from perceptions of economic progress among minority racial groups. In the latter case, it is common to recognize the existence of a successful middle class *within* subordinate racial groups without assuming that the middle-class status of some members represents the social status of the *entire group*. In other words, the rise of the black middle class and the rise in inequality among blacks are each well-known and well-studied phenomena. In contrast, there is as yet little recognition of growing stratification among women.[18] Thus not only is gender inequality considered less pressing because of women's overall economic progress, but the problem of increasing class inequality among women is not on anyone's radar screen. If our goal is to diagnose and combat the new inequality, this rendering of women's economic experience and gender differences more generally is problematic for several reasons.

First, growing similarities between men and women mean, paradoxically, that a gendered analysis of the economy is perhaps more relevant now than ever. The job structure no longer privileges male jobs to the same extent it once did, particularly among the less-educated, and the working class has become increasingly feminized and majority female in service, clerical, and sales jobs (Clement and Myles 1994). This means that visions of reducing social inequality for the working class must take upgrading of women's jobs as seriously as the upgrading of men's jobs, for both men's and women's sake. Unions have increasingly recognized this and have worked in the services to organize not only women but a sector that is growing fast for both men and women (Cobble 1993; Kelley 1997). Similarly, in Europe, although policies aimed at enhancing the rights of workers in nonstandard jobs are undertaken in the name of gender equity, such policies are also meant to stave off the consequences of increasing insecurity for all workers (Ostner and Lewis 1995). But, as I argued in the previous section, if nonstandard jobs cannot be improved on the grounds of gender equity, other strategies should certainly be pursued. Paradoxically, then, even though empirically some gender barriers are clearly breaking down, a gendered analysis is needed because it is the most developed analysis of "new" forms of contingent and service employment. Those who have been concerned with gender inequality have been the most likely to recognize the strategic importance of certain kinds of "new" employment arrangements that have long been the domain of women.

Second, even though women and men are becoming more similar, gender remains important because certain remaining gender inequalities are still central to the debate on the causes of and remedies to the new inequality. The unintended effect of declining gender inequality—and the casting of women as winners against men as losers in the new economy—has been to make gender inequality appear irrelevant to policies advocated to counteract inequality. To take the most prominent example, the discussion of technology's role in causing and potentially solving the problem of inequality has had little mention of gender issues (Piore and Sabel 1984; Levy and Murnane 1992; Harrison 1994; Murnane and Levy 1996). When gender inequality itself appears to be a problem solved, it is absent from considerations of a new technological future invested with the power to level the playing field as long as everyone is properly schooled in the technological or information sciences. The perceived victims of restructuring, young non-college-educated men, are the presumed beneficiaries of a bright new technological order, without regard to the potential of reinstating gender and racial hierarchies (Jenson 1989). My research provides clear empirical evidence of greater gender and racial inequality in high-technology regions, especially high-technology manufacturing areas. While reindustrialization efforts involving technological transformations are to be applauded for delivering a new sense of hope to devastated communities, these efforts must simultaneously be construed as investments in gender and racial inequality. Economic policies must therefore be understood as organizers of multiple, and at times competing, dimensions of social inequality, especially when the implicit focus is on uplifting only particular groups of workers.

Finally, we need a new role for gender and attention to gender differences in order to distinguish between structures of inequality *within* gender groups. Attention to gender differences of this kind forces us to acknowledge that the sources of growing inequality among women may be different from those among men. As I showed in chapter 6, the sources of inequality are in fact very different for men and for women.[19] Flexible and insecure economic conditions stemming from high rates of joblessness, casualization, and immigration are associated with high local levels of skills-based wage inequality for women but, for the most part, not for men. And postindustrial service economies are more likely to exhibit higher college wage gaps for men but not for women. Moreover, contrary to the economists' emphasis on technology, labor markets specializing in high-technology industries are not as strong as insecure employment conditions at explaining regional pockets of inequality.

Since the sources of stratification do vary by gender, inequality among women is actually higher than it is among men when the part-time labor force is counted, and women comprise nearly half the working population, addressing the new social inequality with only men in mind will fail to make significant headway in reversing the new inequality. Given these gender differences, the question of whether to target based on race or gender or to universalize based on class, a *de facto* form of targeting, misses the more strategic question of *where* to target and *where* to universalize. Although inequality is rising among blacks, Latinos, and women alike, this does not necessarily imply that the reasons are the same or that the industries or regions that are less unequal for one group are less unequal for other groups.[20]

The discussion of inequality must therefore be expanded from one revolving around a unitary term—the new inequality—to one involving an open question about the overlapping and conflicting manifestations of gender, race, and class inequality. This has important implications for the study of inequality but also for related issues, such as poverty, economic development, and education. For example, while I have focused on inequality as an outcome in this book, researchers often use family income inequality as an explanation of high poverty rates and adverse health effects. In fact, relocation services have been advocated as a way to connect the unemployed to labor markets that are growing, high-waged, and less unequal (Skocpol 1991; Weir 1992). Finally, it is common for different economic development strategies to be linked to their propensity to reduce or raise inequality. All these approaches rely on a single register of inequality and consequently have the potential to misrepresent the "opportunity structure" of regional economies which may offer economic benefits to some groups but not to others.

I have tried to expose only some of the inadequacies of a single, class-centered approach to the new social inequality through an analysis of gender inequality, inequality among women, and racial inequality. Framing the discussion in this way is a response to the resurgence of class-denominated thinking about matters of recognition and redistribution, but I could have just as easily reversed the tables and challenged feminists who prominently feature gender distinctions, as I did in the previous section. My argument in either case is that the conditions and sources of inequality and the solutions put forward to halt and reverse it are not one and the same for every dimension of inequality. If the sources of inequality were universal, we would expect high-inequality regions to reflect high inequality between all groups. But I find conflicting patterns of inequality and therefore competing visions of equality. My research and that of others leads me to conclude that the new social inequality is not woven from the same cloth, except in the most general and therefore most misleading sense of the phrase. Given these realities, understanding and addressing inequality through the universalizing category of class will not suffice.

CONCLUSION

In this chapter I have used the existence of configurations of inequality to argue for a joint economic and social approach to the problem of economic inequality, one that responds to problems arising from structural economic change on the one hand and to ongoing racial and gender discrimination on the other. Surveying the two major eras of reform in the twentieth century, I have also made this argument deductively: the contemporary United States exhibits key features of both the 1930s and the 1960s and therefore should embody the principles of redistribution and recognition of both eras (see table 7.1).

This means that the insecurity brought on by recent economic restructuring must be met with new and expanded universal and need-based institutions to buffer the dislocations of an increasingly flexible and insecure labor market. Drawing upon the legacy of industrial-era reform in the 1930s, we need creative unionization campaigns in new sectors, higher minimum wages, living wages, child and health care, life-long retraining opportunities, and the like, all tailored to our postindustrial era. Yet, like the 1960s, these are also prosperous times, and gender and racial discrimination are deep and abiding features of American capitalism that can be solved only through vigorous antidiscrimination enforcement, including, most important, affirmative action. An effective anti-inequality program needs to be willing to combine the strengths of the 1930s and the 1960s in providing remedies that alter both the structure and the composition of the American economy.

It is also clear from configurations of inequality that there is no "one policy fits all" solution to the problem of economic inequality but multiple solutions depending on the state of the economy, in both temporal and spatial terms, and its unique structure of inequality. In short, the necessity of a joint gender, race, and class perspective lies in it being the best, most accurate, perspective on the contemporary problem of inequality. It is this contingent quality of configurations of inequality that some may construe as its main limitation (see table 7.1). In one configuration, gender might present the starkest divisions, while in another it might be race or class, or in yet another it might be some combination. The presence of configurations of inequality, empirically, means that the politics of any single dimension of inequality *must* be informed by the broader context of inequality and the economic conditions underlying it.

Technical Appendix

REGIONAL LABOR MARKETS

The primary unit of analysis in this study is the regional labor market. My definition of a regional labor market is derived from the 1990 Public Use Microdata Sample (5 Percent) of the Census of Population (PUMS-A). In the PUMS-A, the smallest geographical units are Public Use Microdata Areas (PUMAs). These are state planning districts composed of county parts, intact counties, and county groups with a population of 100,000 or more. Since the PUMS-A provides information on the PUMA in which an individual lives as well as the one in which he or she works, it is possible to group individuals according to their area of employment rather than the more usual area of residence. This facilitates matching with economic data from county employer reports that describe the workforce, rather than the residents, of an area. Hence, the regional labor markets are defined as places of employment, the areas where people work rather than live.

While PUMAs do not escape many of the problems endemic to drawing regional labor market boundaries, they do reflect certain preferences: they are inclusive of nonurban areas and they divide the largest metropolitan areas into smaller, more "local" units. In terms of scale, PUMAs fall somewhere between metropolitan statistical areas (MSAs) and counties, which are both commonly used in other labor market studies. Using PUMAs rather than MSAs also enhances statistical accuracy by providing a larger sample of labor-markets. A final sample of 554 PUMAs was constructed from an original 1,142 PUMAs and is described in greater detail in McCall (1998). I note here that I selected only those

PUMAs with at least two thousand individual respondents. The map in figure A.1 displays the resulting 554 PUMAs, which cover 83 percent of the original sample of individuals.

MEASURES OF ECONOMIC RESTRUCTURING

The main explanatory variables used in the analysis of wage inequality are measures of local labor-market conditions. I gathered data on several defining features of the recent period of economic restructuring at the labor market level that have yet to be measured directly (for instance, technology and casualization). I grouped these labor-market variables into three categories: flexible/insecure employment conditions, trade and technology, and broad industrial shifts. Table A.1 provides a summary of each substantive variable, how it was constructed and defined, where it came from, and other relevant information. Table A.2 provides descriptive statistics for these variables.

Not included in Table A.1 are several variables that control for basic underlying and long-term differences among labor markets. Such differences tend to be unobservable; therefore I use population size, urban status, and broad region (Northeast, Midwest, South, and West) as proxies for unobserved area effects in the multivariate analyses of chapters 4, 5, and 6. Population size and urban area control for the tendency of wages to be higher and segregation to be lower in large cities, and binary variables for the Northeast, West, and Midwest control for differences in broad regional wage levels. In some models (where significant) I added the share of manufacturing plants that employ more than five hundred workers as a control for the well-known effect of large unionized plants in lifting local wage levels. Unfortunately there are no measures of unionization rates at the county level.

MEASURES OF WAGE INEQUALITY

Measures of hourly wage inequality for each labor market (the 554 PUMAs described above) are calculated using data on annual earnings, weeks of work, and hours worked per week in 1989 from the 1990 PUMS-A. Chapters 2, 3, and 5 also report on measures of wage inequality constructed from the 1980 PUMS-A, which provides the same information for 1979. Several different samples were used throughout this study, but the primary sample was composed of 25-to-64-year-old adults who work either part-time or full-time, are not self-employed or farm industry workers, have hourly wages between $1.00 and $250.00, have a valid place-of-work code, and are white, black, Latino/a, or Asian ("other" races and ethnicities were dropped). This was the sample that was used in the multivariate analyses of chapters 4, 5, and 6. Raw descriptive measures of inequality in chapters 2 and 3, as well as in the beginning of the other substantive chapters, have less restrictive selection criteria. These are noted in each table and generally concern the inclusion of younger workers and workers who do not necessarily have a place-of-work code (since labor-market matching is not required in the nation-level or city-level descriptive statistics).

Although each of the 554 labor markets has a sample of at least two thousand individuals, the relatively small size of the labor markets (compared to a national aggregate) restricted the level of detail permitted for each measure of wage inequality. Gender wage inequality is measured for each of four educational groups: less than high school (less than twelve completed years of schooling), high school (twelve completed years of schooling), some college (thirteen to fifteen completed years of schooling), and college degree or beyond (sixteen or more completed years of schooling). These measures combine all racial-ethnic groups. Wage inequality between the college- and non-college-educated (as a proxy for class inequality) is measured for each gender group but also combines all racial-ethnic groups. Three measures of racial wage inequality were calculated (between whites and blacks, Asians, and Latina/os) for men and for women but include all educational groups. Although these restrictions are problematic in many respects, an unusual level of detail is recovered in the spatial design. Each group is cross-classified with the set of 554 regional labor markets.

The adjusted measures of wage inequality in chapters 4, 5, and 6 were calculated after controlling for other individual characteristics. For instance, college wage gaps are calculated for women after controlling for race and the other variables listed below (marital status, immigrant status, and so on). This means that each measure of inequality in the multivariate analyses is calculated for individuals with the same characteristics, and so differences in these characteristics are not an explanation of the remaining gap in wages. The precise definition of each adjusted measure of wage inequality is specified in the multivariate models and is described in that section.

MEASURE OF OCCUPATIONAL GENDER SEGREGATION
Measuring occupational segregation as an outcome is somewhat more complicated. I have selected a measure of occupational segregation that is easily adaptable to individual-unit calculations and is less likely to be dependent on female labor-force participation rates, a well-known problem with segregation indices. Theil and Finizza's (1971) relative segregation index explicitly weights occupations by size and is therefore easily translated to the individual unit. The "relative" part of the measure pertains to the gender composition of the occupation relative to the gender composition of the labor market as a whole. It is therefore less sensitive to variations in the sex ratio of the labor force (for a similar usage, see Baron et al. 1991).[1]

I calculated the following adaptation of the Theil and Finizza index H_{ij} for 110 occupations[2] from a population-weighted sample of 16-to-64-year-old workers in each labor market and then matched it by occupation and labor market to the sample of individuals selected for the analysis.

$$E_{ij} = f_{ij}\log_2(1/f_{ij}) + (1-f_{ij})\log_2(1/(1-f_{ij}))$$
where f_{ij} = proportion female in occupation i of labor market j

$$E_j = f_j\log_2(1/f_j) + (1-f_j)\log_2(1/(1-f_j))$$
where f_j = proportion female in labor market j

$$H_{ij} = (E_j - E_{ij}) / E_j$$

E_j and E_{ij} are measures of the gender "entropy" of labor market j, and of occupation i in labor market j, respectively. Entropy refers to the level of uncertainty or randomness in the gender composition of the labor market (E_j) or occupational structure (E_{ij}). If women are equally likely as not to be employed, or if they are equally likely to be employed in each occupation, then the entropy of the system is at its highest. H_{ij}, ranging from 0 to 1, is a measure of the reduction in the entropy of each occupation relative to the maximum possible entropy under the constraint of the local labor market's sex ratio. A reduction in the level of entropy translates substantively into an increase in the level of segregation.

Estimating H_{ij} requires the grouping of men and women in a single equation.[3] The average value of H_{ij}, estimated across all individuals in the labor market by the intercept, is an aggregate measure of occupational segregation for each labor market j. It should be interpreted as the average reduction in the entropy of occupations relative to the entropy of the labor market. Larger values of H_{ij} represent larger reductions in the relative entropy of the labor market and thus greater occupational segregation.

MULTIVARIATE MODELS

The relationship between economic restructuring and wage inequality in local labor markets is analyzed in a multivariate, multilevel model (Bryk and Raudenbush 1992; DiPrete and Forristal 1994). The model is multivariate in the sense that it includes multiple variables in regression equations to control for factors that might affect the results. For example, average hourly wages are calculated for women in each labor market after "adjusting" for the distribution of education and other variables that might affect average wage levels (for instance, labor markets with more college-educated workers will have higher wages; controlling for education determines whether wages are higher even among the college-educated). The model is multilevel in the sense of combining information on both individual workers and regional labor markets.

In the first level of the model, adjusted wage gaps are calculated for each regional labor market in equations with individuals as the unit of analysis. The wage gaps are estimated in a standard wage determination equation with log hourly wages as the outcome variable and a set of individual characteristics as the independent variables. The independent variables are marital status (currently married=1), number of own children, immigrant status (foreign born=1), potential experience and its square, hours worked (full-time, year-round = 1), three binary variables for race-ethnicity (black, Asian, Latina/o), three binary variables for education (less than 12 years, 12 years, 13 to 15 years, 16 or more years),[4] and nine binary variables for ten broad industries of employment. Table A.3 provides descriptive statistics for these variables.

In the second level, the effect of local economic conditions on the adjusted wage gaps is estimated in equations with labor markets as the unit of analysis. That is, the outcome variables are the adjusted wages or adjusted wage gaps, the independent variables are the measures of local economic structure, and the units of analysis are the 554 regional labor markets. The first level gives the best estimate of the wage gap before we go on to determine which labor market conditions result in wage gaps that are above and below those in the average labor market (McCall 1998, 2000a). The differencing of individual-level variables from their labor market means in the level-one equations is also a fixed-effect control for unobserved differences across labor markets that might be correlated with wages and wage gaps.

The results from the multivariate, multilevel analyses in chapters 4, 5, and 6 are variations on this basic formula. In chapter 4, average wages for men and women are estimated in separate equations for men and women (by the intercept coefficient when all of the individual-level variables are centered around their labor-market means). The gender wage gap is calculated as the difference between men's average adjusted log wages and women's average adjusted log wages. If a labor market variable significantly increases or decreases average wages for men or women (as is evident by the sign on that variable's estimated coefficient), this will change the average gender wage gap. For example, if average wages for men and women differ in the areas with the highest and lowest joblessness, as compared to their average wages in the average labor market, then the average gender wage gap would differ as well. Figure 4.3 in chapter 4 shows this estimated average gender wage gap in the labor markets with the highest and lowest values of each measure of restructuring (when all other labor-market variables are at their average levels). This same procedure is replicated in chapter 5 to determine how the average gender wage gap varies across labor markets for two different educational groups—those without a high school degree and those with a college degree. The only difference is that the educational variables are not centered and the omitted education category changes (in one model it is less-than-high-school and in the other it is college). In chapter 6, the college wage gaps are estimated more simply by the coefficients on the education-group binary variables when the college educated are the omitted category.

Most multivariate analyses use Ordinary Least Squares (OLS) to estimate equations such as these, but a more complicated estimation procedure is necessary to control for random and unobserved similarities among individuals in the same labor market and unobserved differences across labor markets (i.e., the second-level model includes random effects for each labor market). The main issue is that OLS assumes that random errors are independent and have constant variance. But it is more realistic to assume that errors are correlated among individuals in the same labor-market area and that the error variance also varies across labor markets of different sizes and compositions. Because these OLS assumptions are violated, I use iterative maximum likelihood procedures and generalized least squares to obtain unbiased and efficient estimates of the two-level model parameters (Jones 1991; Bryk and Raudenbush 1992; Xie and Hannum 1996).

Table A.1 Measures of Local Labor-Market Structure

VARIABLE	DATA SOURCE	DEFINITION
INSECURE EMPLOYMENT CONDITIONS		
Unemployment	Weighted 1990 5% Public Use Microdata Sample of the Census of Population (PUMS-A)	Unemployed as share of total civilian labor force, ages 18–64.
Casualization	Weighted 1990 PUMS-A	Share of employed workers who are either part-time, self-employed in unincorporated businesses, or in the personnel supply industry, ages 18–64.
Immigration	Weighted 1990 PUMS-A	Immigrant workers as share of total workforce, ages 18–64.
TECHNOLOGY AND TRADE		
High-Technology Manufacturing	1987 Economic Censuses Location of Manufacturing Plants[a]	Number of establishments in high-technology manufacturing industries as share of all manufacturing establishments.
		High-technology classifications from Riche et al. (1983) and Hadlock et al. (1991), based on National Science Foundation study of research and development intensity.
Import-Sensitive Manufacturing	1987 Economic Censuses Location of Manufacturing Plants[a]	Number of establishments in import-sensitive manufacturing industries as share of all manufacturing establishments.
		Import-sensitive classifications from Schoepfle (1982) and Bednarzik (1993), based on import/export ratios.
High-Technology Services	Weighted 1990 PUMS-A	Share of employed workers in high-technology service industries. See high-technology manufacturing for sources of classification.
Finance, Insurance, and Real Estate Employment Growth	Regional Economic Information System (REIS)[b] 1979–1989	Average annual employment growth.

continued on the next page

Table A.1 *Measures of Local Labor-Market Structure, continued*

VARIABLE	DATA SOURCE	DEFINITION
INDUSTRIAL COMPOSITION AND SHIFTS		
Manufacturing/ Services	REIS, 1989	Manufacturing employment as share of service employment.
Manufacturing Growth	REIS, 1979-1989	Average annual employment growth.
Services Growth	REIS, 1979-1989	Average annual employment growth.

Notes:

a. U.S. Department of Commerce (1994a).

b. U.S. Department of Commerce (1994b).

Table A.2   Descriptive Statistics for Labor-Market Variables

LABOR-MARKET VARIABLE NAME	MEAN	STANDARD DEVIATION	MINIMUM VALUE	MAXIMUM VALUE
% Immigrant	5.60	6.74	0.4	52.6
% Casualized	28.42	4.65	16.5	44.6
Unemployment Rate	6.11	2.02	2.0	14.0
High-Tech Manufacturing Establishments	11.44	4.73	1.6	36.0
Import-Sensitive Manufacturing Establishments	10.85	5.07	2.3	84.5
High-Tech Services Employment	1.84	1.75	0.0	13.9
Manufacturing/Services Employment	0.72	0.50	0.0	3.6
Manufacturing Growth	0.33	2.67	-8.6	12.3
Service Growth	4.55	1.88	-1.3	15.2
FIRE Growth	2.02	2.22	-3.2	14.9
Population (ln)	12.44	0.72	11.5	16.0
Urban	0.56	0.50	0.0	1.0
Northeast	0.20	0.40	0.0	1.0
West	0.14	0.34	0.0	1.0
Midwest	0.29	0.45	0.0	1.0

Note: Sample consists of 554 U.S. regional labor markets. For data sources, see Table A.1. ln = natural log.

Table A.3 Descriptive Statistics for Individual-Level Variables

VARIABLE NAME	FEMALE SAMPLE (N = 1,516,731)		MALE SAMPLE (N = 1,710,139)	
	MEAN	STANDARD DEVIATION	MEAN	STANDARD DEVIATION
Married	0.64	0.48	0.73	0.44
Number of Own Children	0.76	1.04	0.84	1.13
Foreign-Born	0.10	0.30	0.11	0.31
College Plus	0.25	0.43	0.28	0.45
Some College	0.32	0.46	0.28	0.45
High School	0.32	0.47	0.29	0.45
Less than High School	0.12	0.32	0.15	0.36
Experience	21.86	10.83	21.78	10.79
Full-time, Year-round	0.60	0.49	0.80	0.40
Black	0.11	0.31	0.08	0.27
Asian	0.03	0.18	0.03	0.17
Latino/a	0.07	0.25	0.08	0.27
Log Hourly Wage	2.19	0.59	2.54	0.61
Industries:				
Ag, Fishing, Forestry	0.00	0.06	0.01	0.07
Mining	0.00	0.05	0.01	0.10
Construction	0.01	0.11	0.10	0.29
Manufacturing	0.15	0.35	0.27	0.44
TCPU	0.05	0.22	0.11	0.32
Wholesale Trade	0.03	0.17	0.06	0.24
Retail Trade	0.14	0.35	0.11	0.32
FIRE	0.10	0.30	0.05	0.22
Services	0.46	0.50	0.21	0.41
Government	0.05	0.23	0.07	0.25

Notes: The sample includes U.S. nonfarm and non-self-employed adults, ages 25–64, with hourly wages between $1.00 and $250.00, and working in one of the 554 regional labor markets.

Data taken from the 1990 5% Public Use Microdata Samples of the Census of Population.

Figure A.1 Sample of 554 Public Use Microdata Areas (composed of U.S. counties and county groups)

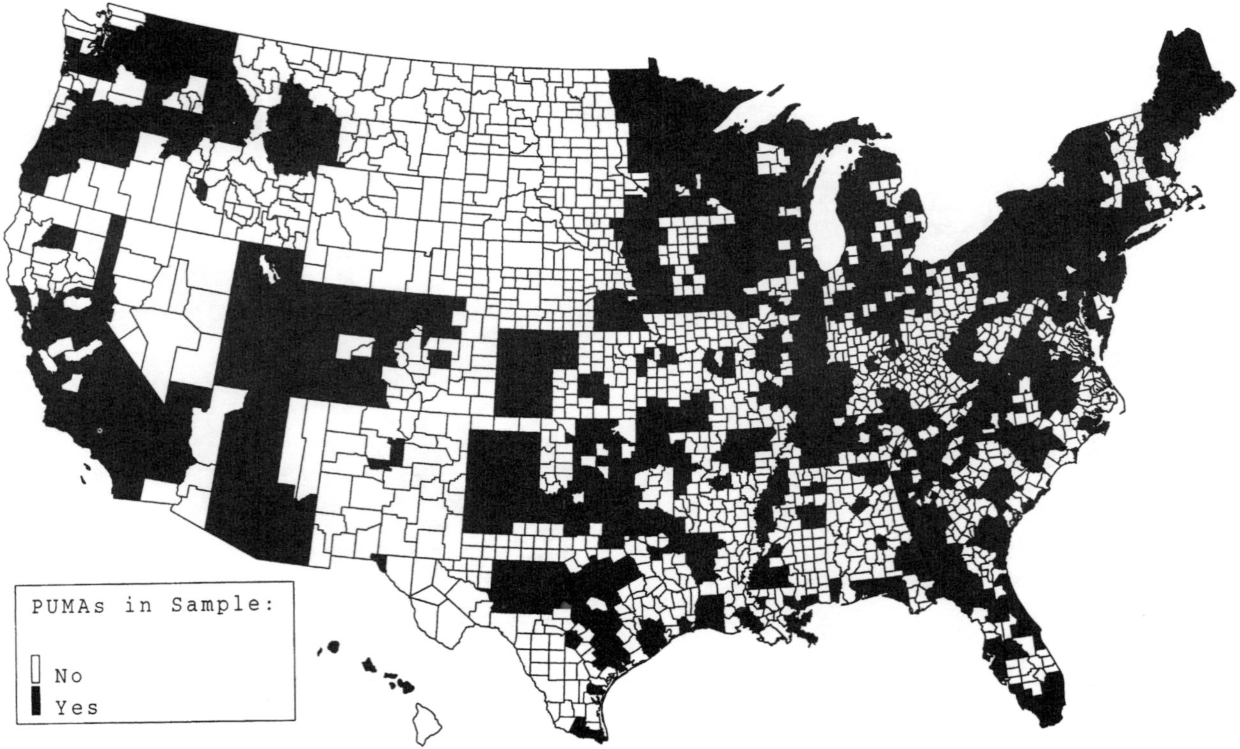

PUMAs in Sample:

No
Yes

Notes

CHAPTER ONE
RESTRUCTURING INEQUALITIES: A GENDER, CLASS, AND RACE
PERSPECTIVE

1. There is actually no consistent and reliable source of data on attitudes about inequality. However, the *New York Times* quoted a poll about the "economic boom" in which "78 percent of the respondents said that they believe the 'rich get richer and the poor get poorer'" (Kurson 1998: 62).

2. It is not my purpose to describe the "new inequality" in any detail here. Many other sources have provided an in-depth accounting of these trends (e.g., Mishel et al. 1994, 1997). For an excellent overview, see Freeman (1997). This note does, however, provide data on some of the general trends.

Depending on the sample and measures, the United States has the highest levels of income and wage inequality and one of the highest increases (along with Britain) in inequality over the 1980s among a group of eight to ten OECD countries (Mishel et al. 1997: 396ff; Atkinson et al. 1995: 40; Freeman and Katz 1994: 40). Within the United States, real average hourly and weekly earnings of production and nonsupervisory workers, who constitute 80 percent of all wage and salary earners, peaked in 1973 and have fallen ever since, especially during the 1980s (Mishel et al. 1997: 140). The declines have been most acute among men, whose 1998 median wage is 12.4 percent below its 1979 level. Low-wage (tenth percentile) women have also lost out, with 1998 wages that are 11.2 percent below their 1979 level. As a result of falling wages for the majority of workers, despite two long recoveries in the 1980s and 1990s, nearly every measure of wage and income inequality has been on a rising trajectory since at least 1979 (Levy and Murnane 1992; Karoly 1993; Mishel et al. 1997). For example, a comprehensive analysis by the Census Bureau has documented a secular rise in family income inequality beginning in 1968. Reversing the early postwar trend, the share of income accruing to the top fifth of families has increased steadily from 40.9 percent in 1968 to 47.2 percent in 1999 (Weinberg 1996; U.S. Bureau of the Census 2000: Table F-2). Poverty rates also reached their lowest level in the late 1970s (11.4 percent overall) and have risen since then for whites and Latinos. Although they have recently started to decline, poverty rates for blacks nevertheless remain very high (25 percent) (U.S. Bureau of the Census 2000: Table 760).

Since there have been some signs of improvement, especially for blacks, it is actually possible, some have argued, to see the "red-hot" productivity and output growth of the late 1990s as a foundation for a rearticulation of the high-growth/low-inequality nexus observed in the 1950s and 1960s (Bluestone and Harrison 2000). See Levy (1988) for a description of the welfare benefits of postwar economic growth, and see Blank (1997) for a discussion of the current disconnect between growth and poverty/inequality reduction.

3. I collapse universal and class-based redistribution here and throughout this book because class-based redistribution is considered of general interest to the majority of the population and never discussed as a "targeted" program, whereas gender-based and race-based redistributive programs are always discussed as "targeted programs." In other words, working-class interests are seen as general interests, whereas nonclass interests are seen as particularistic interests. I use this terminology, collapsing universal and class-based policies together, though I believe that class-based policies are also targeted policies (for more on this, see Chapter 7).

4. Proponents of the first position often challenge the contention that living standards have fallen and inequality has risen. For the second position, see Wilson (1987, 1997), Greenberg and Skocpol (1997), Kahlenberg (1998), Gordon (1996), Harrison (1994), Bluestone and Harrison (2000), and Osterman (1999). For the third position, see Bergmann (1996), Lawrence and Matsuda (1998), Reskin (1998).

5. It is necessary at this point briefly to define the terms "gender," "class," and "racial inequality" (see Chapter 2 for a more detailed definition of the inequality measures used in this study). First, although rising inequality encompasses more than divergences in wages, I restrict my analysis to wage inequality because the data on wages are better than on wealth and benefits, because previous research has also focused on wage inequalities, and because it would be beyond the scope of a single book of this type to examine employment as well as wage inequalities by gender, class, and race. Second, although a principal motivation of mine is to disaggregate measures of "overall" inequality into their component parts, I am limited by the complexity of any such endeavor and cannot examine the "full" range and intersection of inequalities (if there is such a thing). Thus in this book, I attempt to maintain as much consistency as possible with accepted measures of wage inequality in the literature. More specifically, gender inequality refers to wage and occupational differences between men and women, class inequality refers to wage differences between college- and non-college-educated workers, and race inequality refers to wage differences between whites and three other racial-ethnic groups—blacks, Asians, and Latino/as. Given these definitions, I analyze gender inequality by class (that is, within educational groups, which I also refer to as skill groups), class inequality by gender, and racial inequality by gender and race-ethnicity. Racial inequality is particularly ill served by this broader view, since racial inequality varies substantially within the broad racial-ethnic groups of blacks, Asians, and Latinos. However, differences across detailed regions do account for a good part of this variation. I try to note these differences wherever possible, but in this chapter I have chosen to simplify the discussion by grouping them together under the label of "racial inequality." For a fuller treatment of racial wage inequality, see chapters 2 and 3 and McCall (1999, 2001).

6. Feminist scholars in other rich capitalist countries have written more on the subject of gender and economic restructuring than have scholars in the United States (see Jenson 1989; McDowell 1991; Clement and Myles 1994; Bakker 1996; Larner 1996), as have scholars from less developed countries (see the summary provided by Mohanty (1997); see also Ward (1990) and Bakker (1994)). The discussion of economic restructuring in the gender stratification literature has been limited in the United States, but see Amott (1993), Morris et al. (1994), Bernhardt et al. (1995), and Bianchi (1995) for a descriptive analysis of general trends, Reskin and Roos (1990) for a detailed analysis of gendered transformations in individual occupations and industries, and the collection of papers in Browne (1999) for a primarily human-capital-oriented microanalysis of trends in racial inequality among women. The Institute for Women's Policy Research has also been a leading advocate of a wide range of policies, including unionization and a higher minimum wage, aimed at improving the economic situation of low-income women. By and large, though, there has been little sociological research on economic restructuring and inequality (Morris and Western 1999) and virtually no attention to non–racially based inequalities among women in any of the social sciences.

7. Keynesian macroeconomic policies came into favor during the 1930s as a way to correct economic crises with state spending on infrastructure and jobs programs to stimulate consumer demand, employer investments, and economic growth.

8. I use the Public Use Microdata Samples (5 %) of the Census of Population for 1980 and 1990 as my source of data on individuals. I use the Economic Censuses and Regional Economic Information System from the Bureau of Economic Analysis as my sources of data on the economic conditions of counties. For further details, see the Technical Appendix.

9. For example, New Deal–era public jobs programs were filtered through urban political machines; pockets of depression in the 1950s and 1960s were dealt with through area redevelopment block grants (which were slashed in the 1980s); federal dollars have been pumped into

selected industrial parks and high-technology incubators around the country; and strategic trade interests have allowed government bailouts and buildups of certain regionally concentrated industries such as aerospace and automobiles (Krugman 1991; Weir 1992; Tyson 1992). Moreover, the nuts and bolts of economic planning—zoning authority and taxation for infrastructural, residential, and commercial development—all fall under local jurisdiction (Weir 1995a; Katz 1999).

10. It is commonplace to criticize globalization for rising inequality between and within countries but there is never any detailed empirical evidence of the full structure of inequality in the cities, regions, or nations under study. An exception is Saskia Sassen (1991, 1998), who has placed inequality, polarization, and casualization at the center of her analyses of contemporary globalization.

11. By place-based interest formation I do not mean to disagree with Guinier's (1994) criticism of minority districting as privileging shared geography over shared political interests. My use of "place" would include the large multimember districts she imagines in a quasi-proportional representation system.

12. See, for example, Moraga and Anzaldúa (1983), Collins (1990), Janiewski (1991), Crenshaw (1991), Higgenbotham (1992).

13. See Albelda (1985, 1986), Smith (1991), Cunningham and Zalozar (1992), King (1992), Corcoran and Parrott (1992), Badgett and Williams (1994), Browne (1997, 1999).

14. Macroquantitative and microqualitative studies of gender, race, and class usually differ substantially in method. Microqualitative studies can be more flexible in defining the social position of an individual or social group. Macroquantitative studies must take the aggregate definition of a social group for granted and analyze the structural relationships among different social groups. That is, the macro-level measurement of inequality assumes that workers can be placed in discrete categories and the attributes of one category can be compared to the attributes of another. Measurement is mostly confined, therefore, to binary comparisons.

15. Geographers Susan Hanson and Geraldine Pratt (1995) have demonstrated this in extraordinary detail in their neighborhood-level analysis of occupational gender segregation in Worcester, Massachusetts. There is now considerable evidence of the local creation of niche employment for certain kinds of workers, such as white suburban housewives or immigrants, as well as the region-specific substitution of immigrant workers for native workers (Nelson 1986; Sassen 1995; Hagan 1998; Waldinger 1996). I do not strive for this level of case-study detail, however, and instead seek to compare structures of inequality *across* labor markets.

16. Some of these studies provide an in-depth analysis of one dimension of inequality, and some refer to overall levels of inequality, but none provide a description of the full structure of inequality.

17. In my study, these characteristics include high joblessness, immigration, and casualization (for example, part-time, temporary, and informal self-employment). This may be regarded as an odd grouping in the United States, but these characteristics are more frequently discussed in the European literature under the general theme of increasing flexibility and insecurity, which stems from the decline of internal labor markets, the decline of full employment macroeconomic policies, and the proliferation of contingent employment contracts (McFate 1995; Standing 1995; Bourdieu 1998; but see Galbraith (1998) on the crucial role of macroeconomic institutions in setting employment policy in the United States). U.S. researchers are more prone to measure deinstitutionalization as the decline of formal wage-setting institutions such as the minimum wage and unions (DiNardo et al. 1996). These are no doubt extremely important, but they cannot be examined at the local labor-market level and are not the only institutional factors of relevance to workers in the new economy.

CHAPTER THREE
INDUSTRIAL AND POSTINDUSTRIAL CONFIGURATIONS OF INEQUALITY: DETROIT AND DALLAS

1. Freeman and Katz (1995: 6). Whether such a trade-off is either necessary or even a correct reading of the record is still open to debate. See Abraham and Houseman (1995), Gordon (1996), Galbraith et al. (1999), Esping-Andersen (1999). Some key points of controversy are whether certain outlier countries should be included, whether and how the European countries should be broken down into separate groups rather than averaged together, and whether the Gini coefficient or some other measure should be used as the indicator of inequality. For my purposes, however, it is enough to identify characteristics that qualitatively distinguish regional economies from one another, and to do so based on what previous theory and research have shown to be potentially important factors. It should also be noted that the negative relationship between wages and unemployment found by David Blanchflower and Andrew Oswald in *The Wage Curve* (1994),

and also in my own large-scale research, is not being tested in this comparative case study because Detroit is unique in its history of strong industrial development and unions.

2. They show that the average female wage ranks higher up on the male wage distribution in the United States, but the dollar value associated with each percentile difference is greater as result of greater dispersion in the U.S. male wage structure.

3. As Ann Markusen (1996: 296) writes in her article on industrial districts, "[e]valuation of the welfare implications of each type of sticky place is a complex task and rarely undertaken. Scholars of the new industrial districts literature have generally written in a normatively favorable if implicit way about the virtues of new industrial districts as providers of good jobs and long-term stability and dynamism."

4. On manufacturing earnings by region, see Kasarda (1995). Statistics in this section are gathered from a number of sources. Nonreferenced statistics in the text and in Table 3.1 are from my analysis of county data from the Regional Economic Information System, the 1977 and 1987 Economic Censuses, County Business Patterns, and the Public Use Microdata Samples (5%) of the 1980 and 1990 Census of the Population. All statistics refer to Dallas and Wayne Counties, unless otherwise noted, but statistics from the larger metropolitan areas yielded the same conclusions.

5. On trends in immigration and migration, see Frey (1995).

6. Unless otherwise noted, I restrict my discussion to the 1990 figures. The 1980 patterns are similar.

7. The relative standing of Detroit and Dallas on measures of wage inequality among women and among men as reported here does not change when using the residual standard deviation as the measure of inequality. The residual standard deviation was calculated from a regression equation controlling for education, experience, race, immigration, family status, and hours worked.

8. For simplicity, I discuss the results for only three educational groups, although the analysis was conducted for workers with one to three years of college education as well. The patterns for this latter group are the same as for the non-college-educated groups, defined as all workers without a four-year college degree. The patterns reported here are also observed when medians are used.

9. For example, among the college-educated, the male black/white ratio is 0.664 in Dallas and 0.838 in Detroit, and the male Latino/white ratio is 0.749 in Dallas and 0.882 in Detroit; the female black/white ratio is 0.950 in Dallas and 1.06 in Detroit, and the Latina/white ratio is 0.871 in Dallas and 0.963 in Detroit. The contrasts are similar for other educational groups.

10. Black/white and Latina(o)/white inequality is still greater in Dallas within educational groups (see note 9).

11. For example, the bivariate correlations (across more than five hundred labor markets in 1990 and presented in chapters 2, 5, and 6) between female and male wage inequality and between the gender wage gap for the college-educated and for the non-college-educated are weak to nonexistent. The correlations between male wage inequality, racial wage inequality, and the average gender wage gap are actually negative and range between −0.17 and −0.34.

CHAPTER FOUR
BREAKING THE CONNECTION: OCCUPATIONAL GENDER SEGREGATION AND THE GENDER WAGE GAP

1. Although recent research using stringent longitudinal controls on work history and other detailed individual characteristics finds a much smaller negative effect of occupational gender composition on earnings (Macpherson and Hirsch 1995; Tam 1997). These studies shift attention to the gender distribution of specialized skills as the root of job segregation.

2. It is widely feared that recent efforts to scale back Sweden's generous welfare provisions, which were responsible for the large-scale transfer of women's domestic labor from their private homes to the public domain, will undermine these arrangements.

3. Although I use an intermediate occupational classification that has 110 categories (described in the Technical Appendix), the analysis undoubtedly still obscures occurrences of intraoccupational wage inequality. One could imagine, for example, significant stratification among men and women categorized by the three-digit census occupational code "financial managers" or "supervisors and proprietors of sales occupations." However, occupational segregation was also estimated using the most detailed census occupational codes cross-classified by ten one-digit census industries, and the results did not differ substantively from those presented here.

4. In contrast, many researchers have taken the position that an increase in service employment spells an increase in female ghettoization and occupational gender segregation (Tienda et al. 1987; Lorence 1992; Charles 1992). Charles (499), for example, concludes that "among countries with low segregation levels, only the United States, with its large employee class and large service sector, is *structurally* predisposed to high levels of sex segregation" (my emphasis).

5. A comparison of the unadjusted female/male wage ratios from my sample of labor markets, which range from 0.577 to 0.856, to the ratios over the period from 1973 to 1993 from Macpherson and Hirsch's (1995) study, which range from 0.528 to 0.893, shows only a slightly larger range over time. Moreover, the range over time is significantly narrower when the sample is restricted to full-time workers. Macpherson and Hirsch (466-467) do not report as large a discrepancy between the full-time and part-time samples for occupational gender segregation (using the Duncan segregation index). Both ranges (0.677 to 0.537, 0.665 to 0.530) are considerably smaller than the range across my sample of labor markets using the Theil relative segregation index (0.181 to 0.514) (see also Abrahamson and Sigelman 1987; Stafford and Fossett 1989).

6. The rationale for selecting these ten macro measures of local economic conditions is presented in the Technical Appendix. In brief, these factors fall into three categories: insecure employment conditions (unemployment, casualization, and immigration), trade and technology (import-sensitive manufacturing, high-technology manufacturing, high-technology services), and industrial shifts and composition (the ratio of manufacturing to services employment, and three measures of employment growth over the 1980s in manufacturing, services, and FIRE).

7. This was expected only in the case of services. Greater occupational integration in high-technology manufacturing regions is most likely due to the inclusion of high-technology manufacturing industries that employ female assemblers, such as electronics and computer equipment, along with those that employ unionized male production workers, such as aerospace and chemicals. These other factors will be controlled in the multivariate analysis presented below.

8. In equations with only the unemployment rate added, the casualization variable was significantly associated with higher levels of occupational segregation but had no significant effect on wage inequality. When casualization and unemployment were combined with the third measure of insecure employment conditions—the share of immigrant workers—the casualization rate conformed to expectations (these results are not shown): occupational segregation was significantly greater while both men's and women's wages were significantly lower than in the average labor market, with men's wage penalties greater than women's. As a result, the gender wage gap narrowed significantly in highly casualized and segregated labor markets.

9. When the relative share of manufacturing and service industry employment is *not* controlled, as in the above models, occupational gender segregation is significantly above average and gender wage inequality significantly below average levels. Under these conditions the gender wage gap is lower because the negative gap in men's wages relative to the average labor market is greater than women's. When controlling for the relative size of the service sector, men's wage declines equal women's, while segregation remains significantly higher. The addition of manufacturing employment growth over the 1980s to the mix produces an even stronger result: women's wage penalties exceed men's, and the gender wage gap climbs significantly above the average.

10. It was also suggested above that the bipolar structure of postindustrial localities promotes occupational integration and wage equality for different reasons at the top and the bottom of the wage/occupational structure. More detailed results (reported in Chapter 5) show that the gender wage gap is lower among high-school-educated workers but not among the most- and least-educated. Men receive higher relative wage premiums, especially among workers with a college degree.

CHAPTER FIVE
THE DIFFERENCE CLASS MAKES: THE GENDER WAGE GAP AMONG THE COLLEGE- AND NON-COLLEGE-EDUCATED

This chapter is based on McCall (1998), which reports much of the statistical detail that is left out of this chapter.

1. On the correlates of pay variation across regions, see, among others, Farber and Newman (1989), Katz and Krueger (1991), Angel and Mitchell (1991), Blanchflower and Oswald (1994), Topel (1994).

2. See Wellington (1993), Blau and Kahn (1994, 1997), Sorensen (1991), Macpherson and Hirsch (1995) for large estimates of unexplained variance.

3. These two positions share much in common with earlier summaries by Glass et al. (1988) and Lorence (1991), which focused on whether the growing service economy would on balance hurt (the differential-opportunity model) or benefit (open-opportunity model and reduced-male-opportunity model) women. My review is similar in offering a "pessimistic" and an "optimistic" view, except that I incorporate a wider array of factors associated with economic restructuring in the 1980s and examine them from the perspective of class differences in the dynamics of gender inequality.

4. There is now a large literature exploring various aspects of these trends; see especially Gittleman and Howell (1995), DiPrete and Forristal (1995).

5. Several studies have explored the spatial effects of labor market restructuring on gender differences in occupational shifts, the concentration of women's employment in specific occupations and industries, women's labor force participation, and poverty among female-headed households (Bagchi-Sen 1995; Scott 1992; Morales and Ong 1991; Jones and Rosenfeld 1989; Lorence 1992; Kodras and Padavic 1993; England 1993; Ward and Dale 1992; Jones and Kodras 1990).

6. Most research on immigration is motivated by the expectation that declining real wages and increasing wage inequality are at least partially attributable to an influx of less-skilled immigrant workers into the labor force. Some researchers argue that immigration has created an "oversupply" of less-skilled workers, or that there is an increasing "demand" for low-skilled immigrant workers to replace low-skilled native workers. In either case the result is that immigration places downward pressure on native wages. Most of the research in this area shows almost no effect of the local concentration of immigrants on the local wage level of natives (for contributions and reviews, see Borjas and Freeman 1992; Borjas et al. 1992; Topel 1994; Sassen 1995; Waldinger 1996; Borjas, Freeman, and Katz 1996). I cannot address this debate in full here, but it should be noted that I use more stringent controls for unmeasured price differentials between regions and find that wages among the less-skilled are *higher* in areas with a disproportionate share of immigrant workers. This is not inconsistent with the fact that immigrants, for other reasons, tend to concentrate in high-wage regions. The differences between my study and previous studies may be due to my use of rural and urban labor markets, the measurement of immigrant workers rather than residents in the region, and the inclusion of both high- and low-skilled immigrants in the measure.

7. Bagchi-Sen finds that states with FIRE growth over the 1980s are associated with growth in "high-order white collar jobs, but only for males. For females, however, producer services such as FIRE determine growth in low-order white and pink collar positions" (277). Bagchi-Sen controls for growth in other major industries but does not control for individual characteristics or other important macro factors, such as employment conditions and the presence of more specialized industries. Her analysis is also restricted to occupational differences. Although I cannot comment on occupational differentiation, it is important to distinguish between occupational and wage differentiation and not to assume that one necessarily prefigures the other (see chapter 4).

CHAPTER SIX
THE DIFFERENCE GENDER MAKES: WAGE INEQUALITY AMONG WOMEN
AND AMONG MEN

This chapter is based on McCall (2000a), which reports much of the statistical detail that is left out of this chapter.

1. On historical trends in earnings inequality, see Levy (1988), Harrison and Bluestone (1988), Levy and Murnane (1992), Freeman (1994), Weinberg (1996), U.S. Bureau of the Census (1998), Table F-2. On historical trends in male wage inequality, see Blackburn, Bloom, and Freeman (1990), Mincer (1991), Murphy and Welch (1992), Freeman (1993), Blau and Kahn (1996). On racial inequality and restructuring, see Wilson (1987, 1996, 1997), Juhn, Murphy, and Pierce (1991), Moss and Tilly (1991), Bound and Freeman (1992). On the relationship between male wage inequality and the gender wage gap, see Blau and Kahn (1997) and Bernhardt et al. (1995).

2. Almost all previous research on inequality among women has been concerned with racial inequality, specifically black/white inequality (e.g., Albelda 1985, 1986; Cunningham and Zalozar 1992; McCrate and Leete 1994, Badgett and Williams 1994; Browne 1997). My focus is on a form of "class" inequality between working women at the top and bottom of the educational and wage hierarchies (see below), though I briefly consider gender differences in racial wage inequality and within-group "residual" wage inequality at the end of this chapter.

3. Economists DiNardo, Fortin, and Lemieux (1996) are the only researchers who have

discussed gender differences in the sources of within-gender wage dispersion, but their approach focuses on changes over time in supply, demand, and institutional factors measured in aggregate terms at the national level.

4. Such differences in turn pose a challenge to the many studies relying on income inequality as a key independent or dependent variable. As an independent variable, family-income inequality is typically intended to represent the overall structure of labor-market inequality, but this becomes problematic if there are multiple and conflicting opportunity structures. And the use of family-income inequality as a dependent variable may very well result in misleading conclusions without parallel tests for the determinants of other types of inequality.

5. An example of a compensating differential is unemployment. If we define unemployment as a disamenity, economists argue that workers will demand higher wages to compensate for living and working in such an environment. On the other hand, workers will accept lower wages to work in an environment with amenities, such as nice weather. Statistically, it is impossible to measure or control for all possible permanent area characteristics that might affect wages and wage inequality, so it is common to control for such unobserved heterogeneity by including random and fixed effects for each labor market unit. I do so using the random-effects and fixed-effects methods (see Technical Appendix). In results reported below on within-group inequality, I also controlled for fixed state-level effects by including forty-three state dummies, and the results were unchanged.

6. The only factor that has been investigated as a cause of rising and high levels of wage inequality through extensive area analyses is immigration (Borjas, Freeman, and Katz 1996). Yet, like immigration, many dimensions of economic restructuring are geographically concentrated—such as high joblessness, deindustrialization, high-technology services and manufacturing—and should be investigated along with immigration as correlates of high local levels of wage inequality.

7. Blanchflower and Oswald (1994: 3) go so far as to say that subnational geographical units represent "mini-economies," while Sassen calls them "economic subsystems" (Sassen 1995: 115). For a more in-depth discussion of the advantages of studying inequality regionally, see Nielsen and Alderson (1997:14–15), Xie and Hannum (1996: 951–953) and chapter 1.

8. However, there has been no systematic evidence to support this contention nor the contention that inequality is concentrated in these regions.

9. This conclusion is consistent with Blau and Kahn (1994) and Katz and Murphy (1992) who argue that technical change favored women relative to men at lower skill levels and men relative to women at higher skill levels (see chapter 5).

10. This is mainly because of an increasing tendency for low-skilled/low-wage men to leave labor markets with a large influx of immigrant workers (Filer 1992; Frey 1995). If this is the case, a decline in wages among native white and/or black workers would not be discernable *within* immigrant-rich labor markets but diffused throughout the broader region or country as a whole. My analysis offers a partial test of whether these concerns are as valid for women as they appear to be for men.

11. Despite popular perceptions of the importance of deindustrialization, most temporal studies have found industrial shifts to be of relatively minor significance in the explanation of rising wage inequality (Murphy and Welch 1993).

12. A decisive shift took place sometime in the late 1980s when enough credible evidence had accumulated to convince skeptics that patterns of wage equality had indeed taken a "U-turn" for the worse (Harrison and Bluestone 1988). It was around that time that research on inequality began to shift from analyses of annual earnings among all workers to analyses of hourly wages among full-time, year-round workers. The rise in inequality was apparent in hourly wages as well as in annual earnings, suggesting that variation in hours worked was not responsible for rising inequality in annual earnings. If anything, increased work effort in the form of longer hours was working against the decline in real hourly wages, which was considered the root cause of the new inequality. Although it was necessary to restrict analyses to hourly wages in order to disentangle the effects of hours worked from hourly wages, it was not necessary to restrict the analysis of hourly wages to full-time workers only.

Most earlier studies used summary indices of inequality, such as the Gini coefficient, the Theil Entropy Index, and the coefficient of variation. Each of these measures registered higher levels of inequality among women throughout the time series even after correcting for hours worked (Levy and Murnane 1992: 1344–1345). Karoly's (1993: 90–93) careful analysis of hourly and weekly wage gaps between the top (ninetieth), middle (fiftieth), and bottom (tenth) percentiles of the wage distribution also included part-time as well as full-time workers. Some of these measures of inequality were greater for women (ninetieth/fiftieth), while others were greater for men (ninetieth/tenth, fiftieth/tenth) (see also Mishel and Bernstein 1994: 144–145). Among more recent studies of college/noncollege wage differentials, those restricted to full-time workers show higher levels of inequality among men (e.g., Katz and Murphy 1992; Gittleman 1994).

13. The advantage of using the decennial census files is that they are the largest and most accurate samples for local areas available from the U.S. Bureau of the Census. The disadvantage relative to the CPS is that hourly wages must be constructed from annual earnings and hours worked in the previous year, whereas the CPS provides hourly and/or weekly wages at the time of the survey.

14. Part-time workers were combined in the analysis with full-time workers for both substantive and statistical reasons, but the main conclusions were supported when the analyses were replicated with a sample restricted to full-time, year-round workers (see McCall 2000a).

15. This is derived in Figure 6.5 by subtracting the percentage explained by the regional and demographic controls in the female HS/COL equation (30.3 percent) from the percentage explained by all of the variables in the female HS/COL equation (64.0 percent).

16. Figure 6.5 indicates that the group of trade and technology variables explain 8.2 percent of the variation in the female LHS/COL gap as well. In the reduced equations (including region and demographic controls and trade and technology variables), both technology variables were positive and significant, presenting further evidence of lower inequality in these regions for women.

17. The residual standard deviation is used to measure within-group wage inequality. See the Technical Appendix for a detailed description of the variables included (McCall 2000b).

18. In related research, Borjas et al. (1996) concluded that the effects of immigration were spatially diffuse. Their reasoning was that the baseline cross-sectional model predicting earnings levels yielded "sufficiently different effects on female and male earnings to make us leery of interpreting these results as reflecting the effect of immigration on wages" (246). Although the results are significant only for the LHS/COL female gap, this reasoning misses the point that the effects of these factors are in fact mediated by gender.

CHAPTER SEVEN
THE HISTORY AND POLITICS OF INEQUALITY RECONSIDERED

1. In other words, my emphasis is on the connection between context and policies, not on any particular geographical scale. In practice, there are several possible ways the national/regional split could be played out. First, if national policy does not adhere to local conditions, then local policies may be necessary to counteract or complement national initiatives. Second, if local policies are possible or emergent based on local conditions, then local policies may take on greater importance than national policies. Third, if local politics/policies are successful, they could inspire similar initiatives in other regions or at the national level. Thus there is no reason to insist that the politics of inequality transpire at only one scale or another.

2. I borrow the language of recognition and redistribution from Nancy Fraser (1997). For analytical purposes, Fraser contrasts cultural struggles around gender, race, and sexuality to class struggles demanding economic redistribution. Her distinction bears an uncanny resemblance to the polarization of class versus race and gender perspectives in the policy arena. In practice, however, Fraser would agree that recognition and redistribution represent the dual symbolic and material aspects of each form of social inequality (class, race, gender, sexuality, nation, and so forth). This is how I use the terms.

3. Emphasizing the influence of economic conditions on social policy formation does not negate the fact that policies are the culmination of and bear the imprints of years of previous political action and institutional development (Skocpol 1992).

4. There is an enormous literature on and considerable controversy over interpretations of various aspects of the New Deal era, but my overview draws mainly from points of consensus (see Piven and Cloward 1979; Pearce 1990; Nelson 1990; Quadagno 1994; Mink 1995).

5. Note too that Congress passed language in the 1964 Civil Rights Act that was meant to forbid requiring quotas as a remedy (Graham 1990: 192).

6. As Biondi (1998: 66) argues: "[f]ar from articulating a special interest, or demanding 'preferential treatment', this civil rights struggle sought its eradication."

7. The legal history of affirmative action is considerably more complex than this linear narrative suggests. Graham traces the vague and unintentionally controversial language back to the Wagner Act of 1935. Parties found to be engaging in unfair labor practices were "to cease and desist from such unfair labor practice, and to take such *affirmative action*, including reinstatement of employees with or without back pay, as will effectuate the policies of this Act" (Graham

1990: 33). Similar language was incorporated into President Roosevelt's wartime executive orders to outlaw discrimination in federal employment and defense industries and also into state-level anti-discrimination laws administered by the Fair Employment Practices Commissions in the 1940s and 1950s.

In 1961, President Kennedy's Executive Order (EO) 10925 against racial discrimination in federal employment and contracts stated that "[t]he contractor will take affirmative action to ensure that applicants are employed, and that employees are treated during employment, without regard to their race, creed, color, or national origin" (Graham 1990: 28). It was not until 1965, with President Johnson's EO 11246, that this very phrase was to constitute affirmative-action law in federal employment and contracts. On the radical origins of affirmative-action policy see Sugrue (1996), Biondi (1998), Reskin (1998), Lawrence and Matsuda (1998).

8. While in 1965 EO 11246 enacted affirmative-action law on the basis of race, it took President Johnson until 1967 to issue EO 11375, an amendment to include gender as a protected category under EO 11246 (Graham 1990: 187).

9. Like affirmative action (see note 7), the idea of pay equity for comparable work has a long and interesting history. For example, Dorothy Sue Cobble shows that in the 1940s and the 1950s women unionists and their supporters "argued for fair rates for the job *irrespective* of the sex of the worker" (Cobble 1994: 64, my emphasis).

10. See Gottschalk (1990) for a survey of this literature, which draws principally from the research of Smith and Welch (1984) and Leonard (1985). See also Leonard (1989, 1990).

11. Although I have been using "insecurity" in a general sense to indicate changes in living standards, inequality, and employment, the word has an increasingly technical definition, namely, shorter durations in a single job, firm, or occupation and therefore less job stability and career development. Bernhardt et al. (1998) find a 34 percent increase in the odds of a job change for young, white, male workers in the 1980s and 1990s as compared to the late 1960s and 1970s.

12. The average annual rate of real GDP growth was 4.4 percent in the 1960s, 2.8 percent in the 1980s, and 2.3 percent in the 1990s. There is even more of a disparity in productivity growth rates, averaging 3.2 percent in the 1960s, and roughly 1.25 percent in the 1980s and 1990s (U.S. Council of Economic Advisors 1998: Tables B-4, B-42, B-50; 1999, 86). However, output and productivity growth have been growing at a fast and unexpected pace in the last few years and may yet reach long-term levels exceeding those of the 1960s. The 1996 to 1998 average productivity and output growth rates, for instance, were 1.93 and 3.7. As of this writing, however, these rates have started to slow.

13. It is important to recognize that there were dissenters on the robust state of the economy, especially among those who were aware of "pockets" of depression and growing joblessness during the early phases of automation and deindustrialization (Sugrue 1996). The 1958 and 1961 recessions also generated debate around structural interpretations of poverty and inequality. Envisioned, however, were comprehensive retraining and jobs programs for male breadwinners and youths (Pearce 1990; Weir 1992).

14. In some regions of the United States undergoing early phases of deindustrialization, these were considered important issues in the 1950s as well (Weir 1992; Sugrue 1996).

15. For related arguments and the critical role that gender-sensitive unionization campaigns would play in this alternative approach, see Blum (1991). The perspective of 1940s and 1950s women unionists is also relevant: "They argued that economic justice and fair treatment for the majority of women can be provided only through employee representation and collective power, not through individual upward mobility" (Cobble 1994: 72). They pursued this strategy through minimum wage and fair "rate for the job" campaigns, the contemporary equivalent of which would be the remarkably popular and successful living-wage campaigns launched in cities throughout the country in the last several years. Evelyn Nakano Glenn also promotes living wages as a way to compress the racial gap between "skilled" and "unskilled" women workers (for instance, between licensed nurses and nurses' aides), thus challenging the centrality of female/male comparisons in pay equity schemes (Glenn 1992: 37).

16. Quotation taken from an interview conducted by Barbara Ellen Smith (1995: 686).

17. I am grouping together those who explicitly use the language of class and those who prefer the language of universalism or economic need. These approaches share varying degrees of opposition to race- and gender-targeting as well as a belief that the language of class, universalism, and economic need is more unifying politically. It should also be noted that I am speaking principally of policy-makers and researchers, not of new theoretical work on class, which is much more critical of the term (Hall 1997). See also note 3 in chapter 1.

18. Marta Tienda (1995) makes an analogous point about Latina/os.

19. Research by DiNardo et al. (1996), for example, also has shown that the declining value of the minimum wage has been a more important factor in increasing inequality among women, whereas deunionization has been a more important factor in increasing inequality among men.

20. For example, the adverse effects of rustbelt deindustrialization on blacks and Puerto Ricans is often contrasted to the effects of sunbelt reindustrialization in low-wage manufacturing industries on Mexicans and Asians (Lamphere et al. 1993; Moore and Pinderhughes 1993; Morales and Bonilla 1993; Tienda 1995).

TECHNICAL APPENDIX

1. As a check on the suitability of the Theil and Finizza index, I calculated the index at the individual level for each labor market and compared it to the calculation of a segregation index that is computed at the occupational level and controls for variations in occupational structure and female labor force participation (but cannot be calculated at the individual level) (see Charles 1992). The two indices are highly correlated (0.76), lessening the possibility of distortions in the level of segregation due to spatial differences in the occupational structure or the female labor-force participation rate.

2. This occupational classification was constructed to be as detailed as possible, given the inclusion of labor markets with small population sizes. The Census Bureau publishes an "intermediate occupational classification" that in 1980 included 134 categories. This was the base from which I carefully collapsed categories that were missing data in at least 10 percent of the labor markets for both men and women. I also broke out occupations that should be distinctive from a wage or gender perspective, such as supervisors and sales personnel in different gender-typed industries. This procedure yielded 110 categories in total.

3. This is due to the occupational weighting of the total size of the occupation (including men and women) that occurs when the mean gender composition of occupations is estimated. A full set of interactions with gender produced the same results. The estimates and results reported here do not include the gender interactions. I have also tested these results using separate equations with different segregation measures, such as the Variance Index, and with more detailed occupations crossed-classified with ten industries. The substantive results are robust across these other specifications.

4. Which of these four education variables is omitted depends on which wage gap is being calculated.

References

Abraham, Katharine, and Susan Houseman. 1995. "Earnings Inequality in Germany." Pp. 371–404 in *Differences and Changes in Wage Structures*, ed. R. Freeman and L. Katz. Chicago: University of Chicago Press.

Abrahamson, Mark, and Lee Sigelman. 1987. "Occupational Sex Segregation in Metropolitan Areas." *American Sociological Review* 52: 588–597.

Alarcon, Norma. 1991. "The Theoretical Subjects of *This Bridge Called My Back* and Anglo-American Feminism." Pp. 356–369 in *Haciendo Caras: Making Face, Making Soul*, ed. G. Anzaldúa. San Francisco: Aunt Lute Press.

Albelda, Randy. 1985. "'Nice Work If You Can Get It': Segmentation of White and Black Women Workers in the Post-War Period." *Review of Radical Political Economics* 17(3): 72–85.

———. 1986. "Occupational Segregation by Race and Gender, 1958–1981." *Industrial Labor Relations Review* 39(3): 404–424.

Albelda, Randy, and Chris Tilly. 1994. "Towards a Broader Vision: Race, Gender, and Labor Market Segmentation in the Social Structure of Accumulation Framework." Pp. 212–230 in *Social Structures of Accumulation*, ed. D. Kotz, T. McDonough, M. Reich. New York: Cambridge University Press.

Amos, Orley. 1988. "Unbalanced Regional Growth and Regional Income Inequality in the Latter Stages of Development." *Regional Science and Urban Economics* 18: 549–566.

Amott, Teresa. 1993. *Caught in the Crisis: Women and the U.S. Economy Today*. New York: Monthly Review Press.

Angel, David, and Jeffrey Mitchell. 1991. "Intermetropolitan Wage Disparities and Industrial Change." *Economic Geography* 67: 124–135.

Appadurai, Arjun. 1995. *Modernity at Large: Cultural Dimension of Globalization*. Minneapolis: University of Minnesota Press.

Appelbaum, Eileen, and Rosemary Batt. 1994. *The New American Workplace.* Ithaca, NY: Cornell University Press.

Appelbaum, Eileen, and Ronald Schettrat. 1995. "Employment and Productivity in Industrialized Economies." *International Labour Review* 134 (4–5): 605–623.

Armstrong, Pat. 1996. "The Feminization of the Labor Force: Harmonizing Down in a Global Economy." Pp. 29–54 in *Rethinking Restructuring: Gender and Change in Canada,* ed. I. Bakker. Buffalo: University of Toronto Press.

Atkinson, Anthony, Lee Rainwater, and Timothy Smeeding. 1995. *Income Distribution in OECD Countries.* Paris: Organization for Economic Development.

Badgett, M. V. Lee, and Rhonda Williams. 1994. "The Changing Contours of Discrimination: Race, Gender, and Structural Economic Change." Pp. 313–329 in *Understanding American Economic Decline,* ed. M. Bernstein and D. Alder. New York: Cambridge University Press.

Bagchi-Sen, Sharmistha. 1995. "Structural Determinants of Occupational Shifts for Males and Females in the U.S. Labor Market." *Professional Geographer* 47(3): 268–279.

Bakker, Isabella, ed. *The Strategic Silence: Gender and Economic Policy.* Atlantic Highlands, NJ: Zed Books.

———, ed. 1994. 1996. *Rethinking Restructuring: Gender and Change in Canada.* Buffalo: University of Toronto Press.

Baran, Barbara, and Suzanne Teegarden. 1987. "Women's Labor in the Office of the Future: A Case Study of the Insurance Industry." Pp. 201–223 in *Women, Households, and the Economy,* ed. L. Beneria and C. Stimpson. New Brunswick, NJ: Rutgers University Press.

Baron, James, Brian Mittman, and Andrew Newman. 1991. "Targets of Opportunity: Organizational and Environmental Determinants of Gender Integration within the California Civil Service, 1979–1985." *American Journal of Sociology* 96: 1362–1401.

Barro, Robert, and Xavier Sala-i-Martin. 1990. "Economic Growth and Convergence across the United States." Working Paper. Cambridge, MA: National Bureau of Economic Research.

Bednarzik, Robert. 1993. "An Analysis of U.S. Industries Sensitive to Foreign Trade, 1982–1987." *Monthly Labor Review* 2: 15–31.

Belous, Richard. 1989. *The Contingent Economy.* Washington, DC: National Planning Association.

Bergmann, Barbara. 1996. *In Defense of Affirmative Action.* New York: Basic Books.

Bernard, Andrew B., and J. Bradford Jensen. 1998. "Understanding Increasing and Decreasing Wage Inequality." Working Paper no. 6571. Cambridge, MA: National Bureau of Economic Research.

Bernhardt, Annette, Martina Morris, and Mark Handcock. 1995. "Women's Gains or Men's Losses? A Closer Look at the Shrinking Gender Gap in Earnings." *American Journal of Sociology* 101: 302–328.

Bernhardt, Annette, Martina Morris, Mark Handcock, and Mark Scott. 1998. "Summary of Findings: Work and Opportunity in the Post-Industrial Labor Market." Institute for Education and the Economy, Teachers College, Columbia University.

Bianchi, Suzanne. 1995. "Changing Economic Roles of Women and Men." Pp. 107–154 in *State of the Union: America in the 1990s,* Vol. 1, ed. R. Farley. New York: Russell Sage Foundation.

Bielby, William, and James Baron. 1984. "A Woman's Place Is with Other Women: Sex Segregation within Organizations." Pp. 27–55 in *Sex Segregation in the Workplace,* ed. B. Reskin. Washington, DC: National Academy Press.

Biondi, Martha. 1998. "Grassroots Affirmative Action: Black Workers and Organized Labor in Postwar New York City." *New Labor Forum* 2: 61–66.

Blackburn, McKinley, David Bloom, and Richard Freeman. 1990. "The Declining Economic Position of Less Skilled American Men." Pp. 31–67 in *A Future of Lousy Jobs?* ed. G. Burtless. Washington, DC: Brookings Institution.

Blanchflower, David, and Andrew Oswald. 1994. *The Wage Curve.* Cambridge, MA: MIT Press.

Blank, Rebecca. 1997. *It Takes a Nation: A New Agenda for Fighting Poverty.* New York and Princteon, NJ: Russell Sage Foundation and Princeton University Press.

Blau, Francine, and Marianne Ferber. 1992. *The Economics of Women, Men, and Work,* 2nd ed. Englewood Cliffs, NJ: Prentice Hall.

Blau, Francine, and Lawrence Kahn. 1992. "The Gender Earnings Gap: Learning from International Comparisons." *American Economic Review* May: 533–537.

———. 1994. "Rising Wage Inequality and the U.S. Gender Gap." *American Economic Review* 84: 23–28.

———. 1995. "The Gender Earnings Gap: Some International Evidence." Pp. 105–144 in *Differences and Changes in Wage Structures,* ed. R. Freeman and L. Katz. Chicago: University of Chicago Press.

———. 1996. "International Differences in Male Wage Inequality: Institutions versus Market Forces." *Journal of Political Economy* 104(4): 791–837.

———. 1997. "Swimming Upstream: Trends in the Gender Wage Differential in the 1980s." *Journal of Labor Economics* 15(1): 1–42.

Bluestone, Barry, and Bennett Harrison. 2000. *Growing Prosperity.* New York: Houghton Mifflin.

Blum, Linda. 1991. *Between Feminism and Labor: The Significance of the Comparable Worth Movement.* Berkeley: University of California Press.

Borjas, George, and Richard Freeman, eds. 1992. *Immigration and the Work Force.* Chicago: University of Chicago Press.

Borjas, George, Richard Freeman, and Lawrence Katz. 1992. "On the Labor Market Effects of Immigration and Trade." Pp. 213–244 in *Immigration and the Work Force,* ed. G. Borjas and R. Freeman. Chicago: University of Chicago Press.

———. 1996. "Searching for the Effect of Immigration on the Labor Market." *American Economic Review* 86(2): 246–251.

Bound, John, and Richard Freeman. 1992. "What Went Wrong? The Erosion of Relative Earnings and Employment among Young Black Men in the 1980s." *Quarterly Journal of Economics* 107(1): 201–232.

Bound, John, and Harry Holzer. 1993. "Industrial Shifts, Skills Levels, and the Labor Market for White and Black Males." *Review of Economics and Statistics* 75(3): 387–396.

Bound, John, and George Johnson. 1992. "Changes in the Structure of Wages in the 1980's: An Evaluation of Alternative Explanations." *American Economic Review* 82: 371–392.

Bourdieu, Pierre. 1998. *Acts of Resistance: Against the Tyranny of the Market.* New York: New Press.

Brenner, Johanna. 1993. "The Best of Times, The Worst of Times: US Feminism Today." *New Left Review* 200: 101–159.

Brint, Stephen. 1991. "Upper Professional: A High Command of Commerce, Culture, and Civic Regulation." Pp. 153–204 in *Dual City: Restructuring New York,* ed. J. Mollenkopf and M. Castells. New York: Russell Sage Foundation.

Brinton, Mary. 1993. *Women and the Economic Miracle: Gender and Work in Postwar Japan.* Berkeley: University of California Press.

Browne, Irene. 1997. "Explaining the Black-White Gap in Labor Force Participation among Women Heading Households." *American Sociological Review* 62(2): 236–252.

———, ed. 1999. *Latinas and African American Women at Work: Race, Gender, and Economic Inequality.* New York: Russell Sage Foundation.

Bryk, Anthony, and Stephen Raudenbush. 1992. *Hierarchical Linear Models for Social and Behavioral Research: Applications and Data Analysis Methods.* New York: Sage Publications.

Card, David, and Alan Krueger. 1995. *Myth and Measurement: The New Economics of the Minimum Wage.* Princeton, NJ: Princeton University Press.

Charles, Maria. 1992. "Cross-National Variation in Occupational Sex Segregation." *American Sociological Review* 57: 483–502.

Charles, Maria, and David Grusky. 1995. "Models for Describing the Underlying Structure of Sex Segregation." *American Journal of Sociology* 100: 931–971.

Clement, Wallace, and John Myles. 1994. *Relations of Ruling: Class and Gender in Postindustrial Societies.* Buffalo: McGill-Queens University Press.

Cobble, Dorothy Sue, ed. 1993. *Women and Unions.* Ithaca, NY: ILR Press.

———. 1994. "Recapturing in Working-Class Feminism: Union Women in the Postwar Era." Pp. 57–83 in *Not June Cleaver: Women and Gender in Postwar America, 1945–1960,* ed. J. Meyerowitz. Philadelphia, PA: Temple University Press.

Colclough, Glenna, and Charles Tolbert. 1992. *Work in the Fast Lane.* Albany: State University of New York Press.

Collins, Patricia Hill. 1990. *Black Feminist Thought.* New York: Routledge.

Corcoran, Mary, and Sharon Parrott. 1992. "Black Women's Economic Progress." Unpublished manuscript, University of Michigan.

Cotter, David, Joann DeFiore, Joan Hermsen, Brenda Marsteller Kowalewski, and Reeve Vanneman. 1997. "All Women Benefit: The Macro-Level Effect of Occupational Integration on Gender Earnings Equality." *American Sociological Review* 62: 714–734.

Crenshaw, Kimberle. 1991. "Mapping the Margins: Intersectionality, Identity Politics, and Violence against Women of Color." *Stanford Law Review* 43(6): 1241.

Cunningham, James, and Nadja Zalozar. 1992. "The Economic Progress of Black Women, 1940–1980: Occupational Distribution and Relative Wages." *Industrial and Labor Relations Review* 45(3): 540–555.

Curme, Michael, Barry Hirsch, and David Macpherson. 1990. "Union Membership and Contract Coverage in the United States, 1983–1988." *Industrial and Labor Relations Review* 44(1): 5–33.

Dawson, Michael. 1997. "Globalization, the Racial Divide, and a New Citizenship." Pp. 264–278 in *The New Majority: Toward a Popular Progressive Politics*, ed. S. Greenberg and T. Skocpol. New Haven, CT: Yale University Press.

DiNardo, John, Nicole M. Fortin, and Thomas Lemieux. 1996. "Labor Market Institutions and the Distribution of Wages, 1973–1992: A Semiparametric Approach." *Econometrica* 64(5): 1001–1044.

DiPrete, Thomas, and Jerry Forristal. 1994. "Multilevel Models: Methods and Substantive Applications." *Annual Review of Sociology* 20: 331–357.

———. 1995. "Socioeconomic Change and Occupational Location for Successive Cohorts of American Male and Female Workers." *Social Science Research* 24: 390–438.

DiPrete, Thomas, and Patricia McManus. 1996. "Institutions, Technical Change, and Diverging Life Chances: Earnings Mobility in the United States and Germany." *American Journal of Sociology* 102(1): 34–79.

England, Kim V. L. 1993. Suburban Pink-Collar Ghettos: The Spatial Entrapment of Women? *Annals of the Association of American Geographers* 83: 225–242.

England, Paula. 1992. *Comparable Worth: Theories and Evidence.* New York: Aldine de Gruyter.

England, Paula, Karen Christopher, and Lori Reid. 1999. "Gender, Race, Ethnicity, and Wages." Pp. 139–182 in *Latinas and African American Women at Work*, ed. I. Browne. New York: Russell Sage Foundation Press.

Esping-Andersen, Gosta. 1990. *The Three Worlds of Welfare Capitalism.* Cambridge, UK: Polity Press.

———. 1999. *Social Foundations of Postindustrial Economies.* New York: Oxford University Press.

Farber, Stephen, and Robert Newman. 1989. "Regional Wage Differentials and the Spatial Convergence of Worker Characteristic Prices." *Review of Economics and Statistics* 71(2): 224–231.

Ferber, Marianne, and Jane Waldfogel. 1996. "'Contingent' Work: Good, Bad or Indifferent?" Cambridge, MA: Radcliffe Public Policy Institute.

Fernandez Kelly, M. Patricia. 1995. "Social and Cultural Capital in the Urban Ghetto: Implications for the Economic Sociology of Immigration." Pp. 213–247 in *The Economic Sociology of Immigration: Essays on Networks, Ethnicity, and Entrepreneurship*, ed. A. Portes. New York: Russell Sage Foundation.

Figart, Deborah, and June Lapidus. 1996. "The Impact of Comparable Worth on Earnings Inequality." *Work and Occupations* 23(3): 297–318.

Filer, Randall. 1992. "The Effect of Immigrant Arrivals on Migratory Patterns of Native Workers." Pp. 245–269 in *Immigration and the Work Force*, ed. G. Borjas and R. Freeman. Chicago: University of Chicago Press.

Fraser, Nancy. 1997. *Justice Interruptus*. New York: Routledge.

———. 2000. "Rethinking Recognition." *New Left Review* 3: 107–120.

Freeman, Richard. 1993. "How Much Has De-Unionization Contributed to the Rise in Male Earnings Inequality?" Pp. 133–163 in *Uneven Tides*, ed. S. Danziger and P. Gottschalk. New York: Russell Sage Foundation.

———, ed. 1994. *Working under Different Rules*. New York: Russell Sage Foundation.

———. 1997. *When Earnings Diverge: Causes, Consequences, and Cures for the New Inequality in the U.S.* Report no. 284. Washington, DC: National Planning Association.

Freeman, Richard, and Lawrence Katz. 1994. "Rising Wage Inequality: The United States versus Other Advanced Countries." Pp. 29–62 in *Working under Different Rules*, ed. R. Freeman. New York: Russell Sage Foundation.

———. 1995. "Introduction and Summary." Pp. 1–22 in *Differences and Changes in Wage Structures*, ed. R. Freeman and L. Katz. Chicago: University of Chicago Press.

Freeman, Richard, and William Rodgers III. 1999. "Area Economic Conditions and the Labor Market Outcomes of Young Men in the 1990s Expansion." Working Paper no. 7073. Cambridge, MA: National Bureau of Economic Research.

Frey, William. 1995. "The New Geography of Population Shifts." Pp. 271–336 in *State of the Union: America in the 1990s*, vol. 2, ed. R. Farley. New York: Russell Sage Foundation.

Fujita, Masahisa, Paul Krugman, and Anthony Venables. 1999. *The Spatial Economy*. Cambridge: MIT Press.

Galbraith, James K. 1998. *Created Unequal: The Crisis in American Pay*. New York: Twentieth Century Fund Book.

Galbraith, James K., Pedro Conceicao, and Pedro Ferreira. 1999. "Inequality and Unemployment in Europe: The American Cure." *New Left Review* 237: 28–51

Gittleman, Maury. 1994. "Earnings in the 1980s: An Occupational Perspective." *Monthly Labor Review* 117(7): 16–27.

Gittleman, Maury, and David Howell. 1995. "Changes in the Structure and Quality of Jobs in the United States: Effects by Race and Gender, 1973–1990." *Industrial and Labor Relations Review* 48: 420–440.

Glass, Jennifer, Marta Tienda, and Shelley Smith. 1988. "The Impact of Changing Employment Opportunity on Gender and Ethnic Earnings Inequality." *Social Science Research* 17: 252–276.

Glenn, Evelyn Nakano. 1992. "From Servitude to Service Work: Historical Continuity in the Racial Division of Paid Reproductive Labor." *Signs* 18(1): 1–43.

Glyn, Andrew, Alan Hughes, Alain Lipietz, and Ajit Singh. 1990. "The Rise and Fall of the Golden Age." Pp. 39–125 in *The Golden Age of Capitalism:*

Reinterpreting the Post-War Experience, ed. S. Marglin and J. Schor. Oxford: Clarendon Press.

Goldin, Claudia. 1990. *The Gender Gap: An Economic History of American Women.* New York: Cambridge University Press.

Goldin, Claudia, and Robert Margo. 1992. "The Great Compression: The Wage Structure in the United States at Mid-Century." *Quarterly Journal of Economics* 107 (1): 1–34.

Gordon, David. 1996. *Fat and Mean.* New York: Free Press.

Gottschalk, Peter. 1990. "Reducing Gender and Racial Inequality: The Role of Public Policy." Pp. 241–269 in *New Developments in the Labor Market,* ed. K. Abraham and R. McKersie. Cambridge: MIT Press.

Graham, Hugh. 1990. *The Civil Rights Era.* New York: Oxford University Press.

Granovetter, Mark, and Charles Tilly. 1988. "Inequality and Labor Processes." Pp. 175–219 in *The Handbook of Sociology,* ed. Neil Smelser. Newbury Park, CA: Sage Publications.

Greenberg, Stanley. 1997. "Popularizing Progressive Politics." Pp. 279–298 in *The New Majority: Toward a Popular Progressive Politics,* ed. S. Greenberg and T. Skocpol. New Haven, CT: Yale University Press.

Greenberg, Stanley, and Theda Skocpol, eds. 1997. *The New Majority: Toward a Popular Progressive Politics.* New Haven, CT: Yale University Press.

Groshen, Erica. 1991. "The Structure of the Female/Male Wage Differential: Is It Who You Are, What You Do, or Where You Work?" *Journal of Human Resources* 26: 457–472.

Guinier, Lani. 1994. *The Tyranny of the Majority.* New York: Free Press.

Hadlock, Paul, Daniel Hecker, and Joseph Gannon. 1991. "High Technology Employment: Another View." *Monthly Labor Review* 114(7): 26–30.

Hagan, Jacqueline Maria. 1998. "Social Networks, Gender, and Immigrant Incorporation: Resources and Constraints." *American Sociological Review* 63 (1): 55–67.

Hall, John, ed. 1997. *Reworking Class.* Ithaca, NY: Cornell University Press.

Hanson, Susan, and Geraldine Pratt. 1992. "Dynamic Dependencies: A Geographic Investigation of Local Labor Markets." *Economic Geography* 68: 373–405.

———. 1995. *Gender, Work, and Space.* New York: Routledge.

Harrison, Bennett. 1994. *Lean and Mean.* New York: Basic Books.

Harrison, Bennett, and Barry Bluestone. 1988. *The Great U-Turn.* New York: Basic Books.

Harvey, David. 1989. *The Condition of Postmodernity.* Cambridge, MA: Basil Blackwell.

———. 1996. *Justice, Nature, and the Geography of Difference.* Cambridge, MA: Basil Blackwell.

Higgenbotham, Evelyn Brooks. 1992. "African American Women's History and the Meta-Language of Race." *Signs* 22 (3): 649–685.

Holston, James, ed. 1999. *Cities and Citizenship.* Durham, NC: Duke University Press.

Hossfeld, Karen. 1990. "'Their Logic against Them': Contradictions in Sex, Race, and Class in Silicon Valley." Pp. 149–178 in *Women Workers and Global Restructuring,* ed. K. Ward. Ithaca, NY: Cornell University Press.

Howell, David, and Edward Wolff. 1991. "Trends in the Growth and Distribution of Skills in the U.S. Workplace, 1960–1985." *Industrial and Labor Relations Review* 44: 486–502.

Janiewski, Dolores. 1991. "Southern Honor, Southern Dishonor: Managerial Ideology and the Construction of Gender, Race, and Class Relations in Southern Industry." Pp. 70–91 in *Work Engendered*, ed. A. Baron. Ithaca, NY: Cornell University Press.

Jargowsky, Paul. 1997. *Poverty and Place: Ghettos, Barrios, and the American City.* New York: Russell Sage Foundation.

Jencks, Christopher. 1992. *Rethinking Social Policy.* Cambridge, MA: Harvard University Press.

Jenson, Jane. 1989. "The Talents of Women, the Skills of Men: Flexible Specialization and Women." Pp. 141–155 in *The Transformation of Work*, ed. S. Wood. Winchester, MA: Unwin Hyman Inc.

Jones, Jo Ann, and Rachel Rosenfeld. 1989. "Women's Occupations and Local Labor Markets: 1950 to 1980." *Social Forces* 67(3): 666–692.

Jones, John Paul, III, and Janet Kodras. 1990. "Restructured Regions and Families: The Feminization of Poverty in the U.S." *Annals of the Association of American Geographers* 80(2): 163–183.

Jones, Kelvyn. 1991. "Specifying and Estimating Multi-Level Models for Geographical Research." *Transactions of the Institute of British Geographers* 16: 148–160.

Juhn, Chinhui, Kevin Murphy, and Brooks Pierce. 1991. "Accounting for the Slowdown in Black-White Wage Convergence." Pp. 107–143 in *Workers and Their Wages*, ed. M. Kosters. Washington, DC: American Enterprise Institute.

Kahlenberg, Richard. 1998. "Class-Based Affirmative Action: A Natural for Labor." *New Labor Forum* 2: 37–43.

Kalleberg, Arne, E. Rasell, K. Hudson, D. Webster, B. Reskin, N. Cassirer, E. Appelbaum. 1997. *Nonstandard Work, Substandard Jobs: Flexible Work Arrangements in the U.S.* Washington DC: Economic Policy Institute.

Karoly, Lynn. 1993. "The Trend in Inequality among Families, Individuals, and Workers in the United States: A Twenty-Five-Year Perspective." Pp. 19–97 in *Uneven Tides: Rising Inequality in America*, eds. S. Danziger and P. Gottschalk. New York: Russell Sage Foundation.

Kasarda, John. 1995. "Industrial Restructuring and the Changing Location of Jobs." Pp. 215–268 in *State of the Union: America in the 1990s*, Vol. 1, ed. R. Farley. New York: Russell Sage Foundation.

Katz, Bruce, ed. 1999. *Reflections on Regionalism.* Washington, DC: Brookings Institution.

Katz, Lawrence, and Alan Krueger. 1991. "Changes in the Structure of Wages in the Public and Private Sectors." *Research in Labor Economics* 12: 137–172.

Katz, Lawrence, and Kevin Murphy. 1992. "Changes in Relative Wages, 1963–1987: Supply and Demand Factors." *Quarterly Journal of Economics* 107(1): 35–78.

Keck, Margaret, and Kathryn Sikkink. 1998. *Activists beyond Borders: Advocacy Networks in International Politics.* Ithaca, NY: Cornell University Press.

Keith, Michael, and Steve Pile, eds. 1993. *Place and the Politics of Identity.* New York: Routledge.

Kelley, Robin D. G. 1997. "The New Urban Working Class and Organized Labor." *New Labor Forum* (fall): 6–18.

King, Mary. 1992. "Occupational Segregation by Race and Sex, 1940–1980." *Monthly Labor Review* (April): 30–36.

Kirschenman, Joleen, and Kathryn Neckerman. 1991. "'We'd Love to Hire Them, But...': The Meaning of Race for Employers." Pp. 203–232 in *The Urban Underclass,* ed. P. Peterson and C. Jencks. Washington, DC: Brookings Institution.

Kodras, Janet, and Irene Padavic. 1993. "Economic Restructuring and Women's Sectoral Employment in the 1970s: A Spatial Investigation across 380 U.S. Labor Market Areas." *Social Science Quarterly* 74(1): 1–27.

Kondo, Dorinne. 1990. *Crafting Selves: Power, Gender, and Discourses of Identity in a Japanese Workplace.* Chicago: University of Chicago Press.

Krueger, Alan. 1993. "How Computers Have Changed the Wage Structure: Evidence from Microdata, 1984–1989." *Quarterly Journal of Economics* 108(1): 33–60.

Krugman, Paul. 1991. *Geography and Trade.* Cambridge: MIT Press.

———. 1996. *Pop Internationalism.* Cambridge: MIT Press.

Kurson, Ken. 1998. "Money on the Mind: Statistics." *New York Times Magazine* (July 6).

Lamphere, Louise, Patricia Zavella, Felipe Gonzales, and Peter Evans. 1993. *Sunbelt Working Mothers.* Ithaca, NY: Cornell University Press.

Larner, Wendy. 1996. "The 'New Boys': Restructuring in New Zealand, 1984–94." *Social Politics* 3(1): 32–56.

Lawrence, Charles, III, and Mari Matsuda. 1998. "We Won't Go Back." *New Labor Forum* 2: 51–60.

Leborgne, Daniele, and Alain Lipietz. 1992. "Conceptual Fallacies and Open Questions on Post-Fordism." Pp. 332–348 in *Pathways to Industrialization and Regional Development,* ed. M. Storper and A. Scott. New York: Routledge.

Leibfried, Steven, and Paul Pierson, eds. 1995. *European Social Policy.* Washington, DC: Brookings Institution.

Leonard, Jonathan. 1985. "Affirmative Action as Earnings Redistribution: The Targeting of Compliance Reviews." *Journal of Labor Economics* 3: 363–384.

———. 1989. "Women and Affirmative Action." *Journal of Economic Perspectives* 3 (1): 61–75.

———. 1990. "The Impact of Affirmative Action Regulation and Equal Employment Law on Black Employment." *Journal of Economic Perspectives* 4 (4): 47–63.

Levy, Frank. 1988. *Dollars and Dreams: The Changing American Income Distribution.* New York: Norton and Russell Sage Foundation.

Levy, Frank, and Richard Murnane. 1992. "U.S. Earnings Levels and Earnings Inequality: A Review of Recent Trends and Proposed Explanations." *Journal of Economic Literature* 30(3): 1333–1381.

Lewis, Michael. 1998. "All Money, All the Time." *New York Times Magazine* (July 6).

Lorence, Jon. 1991. "Growth in Service Sector Employment and MSA Gender Earnings Inequality: 1970–1980." *Social Forces* 69: 763–783.

———. 1992. "Service Sector Growth and Metropolitan Occupational Sex Segregation." *Work and Occupations* 19 (2): 128–156.

Macdonald, Cameron Lynne, and Carmen Sirianni, eds. 1996. *Working in the Service Society.* Philadelphia, PA: Temple University Press.

Macpherson, David, and Barry Hirsch. 1995. "Wages and Gender Composition: Why Do Women's Jobs Pay Less?" *Journal of Labor Economics* 13: 426–471.

Markusen, Ann. 1987. *Regions: The Economics and Politics of Territory.* Rowman & Littlefield.

———. 1996. "Sticky Places in Slippery Space: A Typology of Industrial Districts." *Economic Geography* 72(1): 293–313.

———. 1999. "Fuzzy Concepts, Scanty Evidence, Policy Distance: The Case for Rigor and Policy Relevance in Critical Regional Studies," *Regional Studies.* 33(9): 869–884.

Markusen, Ann, and Candace Howes. 1993. "Trade, Industry, and Economic Development." Pp. 1–44 in *Trading Industries, Trading Regions,* ed. H. Noponen, J. Graham, and A. Markusen. New York: Guilford Press.

Massey, Doreen. 1984. *Spatial Divisions of Labour.* London: Macmillan.

McCall, Leslie. 1998. "Spatial Routes to Gender Wage (In)equality: Regional Restructuring and Wage Differentials by Gender and Education." *Economic Geography* 74(4): 379–404.

———. 1999. "Racial-Ethnic Differences in the Sources of Wage Inequality with Whites in U.S. Labor Markets." Paper presented at the Population Association of America meetings, March, New York.

———. 2000a. "Gender and the New Inequality: Explaining the College/Non-College Wage Gap." *American Sociological Review* 65(2): 234–255.

———. 2000b. "Explaining Levels of Within-Group Wage Inequality in U.S. Labor Markets." *Demography* 37(4): 415–430.

———. 2001. "Sources of Racial Wage Inequality in Metropolitan Labor markets: Racial, Ethnic, and Gender Differences." Forthcoming, *American Sociological Review.*

McCrate, Elaine, and Laura Leete. 1994. "Black-White Differences among Young Women, 1977–1986." *Industrial Relations* 33(2): 168–183.

McDowell, Linda. 1991. "Life without Father and Ford: The New Gender Order of Post-Fordism." *Transactions of the Institute of British Geographers* 16: 400–419.

McFate, Katherine. 1995. "Introduction: Western States in the New World Order." Pp. 1–26 in *Poverty, Inequality, and the Future of Social Policy,* ed. K. McFate, R. Lawson, and W. J. Wilson. New York: Russell Sage Foundation.

Milkman, Ruth. 1987. "Women Workers and the Labor Movement in Hard Times: Comparing the 1930s with the 1980s." Pp. 111–132 in *Women, Households, and the Economy,* ed. L. Beneria and C. Stimpson. New Brunswick, NJ: Rutgers University Press.

———. 1997. *Farewell to the Factory: Auto Workers in the Late 20th Century.* Berkeley: University of California Press.

Mincer, Jacob. 1991. "Human Capital, Technology, and the Wage Structure: What Do Time Series Show?" Working Paper No. 3581. Cambridge, MA: National Bureau of Economic Research.

Mink, Gwendolyn. 1995. *The Wages of Motherhood: Inequality in the Welfare State, 1917–1942.* Ithaca, NY: Cornell University Press.

Mishel, Lawrence, and Jared Bernstein. 1994. *The State of Working America 1994–1995*. Armonk, NY: M. E. Sharpe.

———. 1996. "Technology and the Wage Structure: Has Technology's Impact Accelerated Since the 1970s?" Paper presented at the NBER Labor Studies Workshop, July.

Mishel, Lawrence, Jared Bernstein, and John Schmitt. 1997. *The State of Working America, 1996–97*. Armonk, NY: M. E. Sharpe.

Mohanty, Chandra. 1997. "Women Workers and Capitalist Scripts: Ideologies of Domination, Common Interests, and the Politics of Solidarity." Pp. 3–29 in *Feminist Genealogies, Colonial Legacies, Democratic Futures*, ed. J. Alexander and C. Mohanty. New York: Routledge.

Mollenkopf, John, and Manuel Castells, eds. 1991. *Dual City: Restructuring New York*. New York: Russell Sage Foundation.

Moore, Joan, and Raquel Pinderhughes, eds. 1993. *In the Barrios: Latinos and the Underclass Debate*. New York: Russell Sage Foundation.

Moraga, Cherríe, and Gloria Anzaldúa. 1983. *This Bridge Called My Back*. New York: Kitchen Table, Women of Color Press.

Morales, Rebecca, and Frank Bonilla, eds. 1993. *Latinos in a Changing U.S. Economy*. Thousand Oaks, CA: Sage Publications.

Morales, Rebecca, and Paul Ong. 1991. "Immigrant Women in Los Angeles." *Economic and Industrial Democracy* 12: 65–81.

Morris, Martina, Annette D. Bernhardt, and Mark S. Handcock. 1994. "Economic Inequality: New Methods for New Trends." *American Sociological Review* 59: 205–219.

Morris, Martina, and Bruce Western. 1999. "Inequality in Earnings at the Close of the Twentieth Century." *Annual Review of Sociology* 25: 623–657.

Morrison, Philip S. 1990. "Segmentation Theory Applied to Local, Regional and Spatial Labour Markets." *Progress in Human Geography* 14: 488–528.

Moss, Philip, and Chris Tilly. 1991. "Why Black Men Are Doing Worse in the Labor Market: A Review of Supply-Side and Demand-Side Explanations." New York: Social Science Research Council.

Murnane, Richard, and Frank Levy. 1996. *Teaching the New Basic Skills*. New York: Free Press.

Murphy, Kevin, and Finis Welch. 1992. "The Structure of Wages." *Quarterly Journal of Economics* 107(1): 284–326.

———. 1993. "Industrial Change and the Rising Importance of Skill." Pp. 101–132 in *Uneven Tides: Rising Inequality in America*, ed. S. Danziger and P. Gottschalk. New York: Russell Sage Foundation.

Nelson, Barbara. 1990. "The Origin of the Two-Channel Welfare State: Workmen's Compensation and Mothers' Aid." Pp. 123–151 in *Women, the State, and Welfare*, ed. L. Gordon. Madison: University of Wisconsin Press.

Nelson, Kristen. 1986. "Labor Demand, Labor Supply, and the Suburbanization of Low-Wage Office Work." pp. 149–168 in *Production, Work, and Territory*, ed. A. Scott and M. Storper. Boston: Allen & Unwin.

Nielsen, François, and Arthur S. Alderson. 1997. "Income Inequality in U.S. Counties, 1970 to 1990." *American Sociological Review* 62: 12–33.

O'Connor, Julia, Ann Shola Orloff, and Sheila Shaver. 1998. *States, Markets, Families: Gender, Liberalism and Social Policy in Australia, Canada, Great Britain and the United States.* New York: Cambridge University Press.

Orfield, Myron. 1997. *Metropolitics: A Regional Agenda for Community and Stability.* Washington, DC: Brookings Institution.

Orloff, Ann. 1993. "Gender and the Social Rights of Citizenship." *American Sociological Review* 58(3): 303–328.

Osborne, David. 1988. *Laboratories of Democracy.* Boston, MA: Harvard Business School Press.

Osterman, Paul. 1999. *Securing Prosperity.* Princeton, NJ: Princeton University Press.

Ostner, Ilona, and Jane Lewis. 1995. "Gender and the Evolution of European Social Policies." Pp. 159–193 in *European Social Policy,* ed. S. Leibfried and P. Pierson. Washington, DC: Brookings Institution.

Pearce, Diana. 1990. "Welfare Is Not for Women: Why the War on Poverty Cannot Conquer the Feminization of Poverty." Pp. 265–279 in *Women, the State, and Welfare,* ed. L. Gordon. Madison: University of Wisconsin Press.

Peck, Jamie. 1989. "Reconceptualizing the Local Labour Market: Space, Segmentation and the State." *Progress in Human Geography* 13: 42–61.

———. 1996. *Work-Place: The Social Regulation of Labor Markets.* New York: Guilford Press.

Petersen, Trond, and Laurie Morgan. 1995. "Separate and Unequal: Occupation-Establishment Sex Segregation and the Gender Wage Gap." *American Journal of Sociology* 101: 329–365.

Piore, Michael, and Charles Sabel. 1984. *The Second Industrial Divide: Possibilities for Prosperity.* New York: Basic Books.

Piven, Frances Fox, and Richard Cloward. 1979. *Poor People's Movements.* New York: Vintage Books.

Portes, Alejandro, and Alex Stepick. 1993. *City on the Edge: The Transformation of Miami.* Berkeley: University of California Press.

Portes, Alejandro, and Min Zhou. 1992. "Gaining the Upper Hand: Economic Mobility among Immigrant and Domestic Minorities." *Ethnic and Racial Studies* 15(4): 491–521.

Quadagno, Jill. 1994. *The Color of Welfare.* New York: Oxford University Press.

Quigley, John M. 1998. "Urban Diversity and Economic Growth." *Journal of Economic Perspectives* 12(2): 127–138.

Ragin, Charles. 1987. *The Comparative Method.* Berkeley: University of California Press.

Reskin, Barbara. 1998. *The Realities of Affirmative Action in Employment.* Washington, DC: American Sociological Association.

Reskin, Barbara, and Patricia Roos. 1990. *Job Queues, Gender Queues: Explaining Women's Inroads into Male Occupations.* Philadelphia: Temple University Press.

Riche, Richard, Daniel Hecker, and John Burgan. 1983. "High Technology Today and Tomorrow: A Small Slice of the Employment Pie." *Monthly Labor Review* 106(11): 50–59.

Rodrik, Dani. 1997. *Has Globalization Gone Too Far?* Washington, DC: Institute for International Economics.

Rosenfeld, Rachel, and Arne Kalleberg. 1990. "A Cross-National Comparison of the Gender Gap in Income." *American Journal of Sociology* 96: 69–106.

———. 1991. "Gender Inequality in the Labor Market." *Acta Sociologica* 34: 207–225.

Rubery, Jill, and Colette Fagan. 1995. "Gender Segregation in Societal Context." *Work, Employment and Society* 9(2): 213–240.

Ruggie, Mary. 1984. *The State and Working Women: A Comparative Study of Britain and Sweden.* Princeton, NJ: Princeton University Press.

Sandel, Michael. 1997. "The Political Economy of Citizenship." Pp. 133–148 in *The New Majority: Toward a Popular Progressive Politics,* ed. S. Greenberg and T. Skocpol. New Haven, CT: Yale University Press.

Sassen, Saskia. 1991. *The Global City.* Princeton, NJ: Princeton University Press.

———. 1995. "Immigration and Local Labor Markets." Pp. 87–127 in *The Economic Sociology of Immigration,* ed. A. Portes. New York: Russell Sage Foundation.

———. 1998. *Globalization and Its Discontents.* New York: New Press.

Sassen, Saskia, and M. Patricia Fernandez Kelly. 1991. "Recasting Women in the Global Economy: Internationalization and Changing Definition of Gender." Paper prepared for the American Sociological Meetings, Cincinnati, Ohio, August.

Savitch, H. V., and Ronald Vogel, eds. 1996. *Regional Politics: America in a Post-City Age.* Thousand Oaks, CA: Sage Publications.

Saxenian, AnnaLee. 1994. *Regional Advantage: Culture and Competition in Silicon Valley and Route 128.* Cambridge, MA: Harvard University Press.

Schoenberger, Erica. 1994. "Competition, Time, and Space in Industrial Change." Pp. 51–66 in *Commodity Chains and Global Capitalism,* ed. G. Gereffi and P. Korzeniewicz. Westport, CT: Praeger.

Schoepfle, Gregory. 1982. "Imports and Domestic Employment: Identifying Affected Industries." *Monthly Labor Review* 105(8): 13–26.

Schram, Sanford. 1995. *Words of Welfare.* Minneapolis: University of Minnesota Press.

Scott, Allan J. 1992. "Low-Wage Workers in a High-Technology Manufacturing Complex: The Southern California Electronics Assembly Industry." *Urban Studies* 29: 1231–1246.

Skocpol, Theda. 1991. "Targeting within Universalism: Politically Viable Policies to Combat Poverty in the United States." Pp. 411–436 in *The Urban Underclass,* ed. C. Jencks and P. Peterson. Washington, DC: Brookings Institution.

———. 1992. *Protecting Soldiers and Mothers: The Political Origins of Social Policy in the United States.* Cambridge, MA: Harvard University Press.

Smith, Barbara Ellen. 1995. "Crossing the Great Divides: Race, Class, and Gender in Southern Women's Organizing, 1979–1991." *Gender and Society* 9(6): 680–696.

Smith, James, and Finis Welch. 1984. "Affirmative Action and Labor Markets." *Journal of Labor Economics* 2: 269–301.

Smith, Neil. 1992. "Geography, Difference, and the Politics of Scale." Pp. in *Postmodernism and the Social Sciences,* ed. J. Doherty, E. Graham, and M. Malek. New York: St. Martin's Press.

Smith, Neil, and Cindi Katz. 1993. "Grounding Metaphor: Towards a Spatialized Politics," Pp. 67–83 in *Place and the Politics of Identity*, ed. Michael Keith and Steve Pile. New York: Routledge.

Smith, Shelley. 1991. "Sources of Earnings Inequality in the Black and White Female Labor Forces." *Sociological Quarterly* 32: 117–138.

Sokoloff, Natalie. 1992. *Black Women and White Women in the Professions.* New York: Routledge.

Sorensen, Annemette, and Heike Trappe. 1995. "The Persistence of Gender Inequality in Earnings in the German Democratic Republic." *American Sociological Review* 60: 398–406.

Sorensen, Elaine. 1991. *Gender and Racial Pay Gaps in the 1980s: Accounting for Different Trends.* Washington, DC: Urban Institute.

Spalter-Roth, Roberta, and Heidi Hartmann. 1993. "What Do Unions Do for Women?" Research Paper. Washington, DC: Institute for Women's Policy Research.

———. 1995. "Contingent Work: Its Consequences for Economic Well-Being, Gender Division of Labor, and the Welfare State." Research Paper. Washington, DC: Institute for Women's Policy Research.

Staeheli, Lynn, Janet E. Kodras, Colin Flint, eds. 1997. *State Devolution in America : Implications for a Diverse Society.* Thousand Oaks, CA: Sage Publications.

Stafford, Therese, and Mark Fossett. 1989. "Occupational Sex Inequality in the Nonmetropolitan South, 1960–1980." *Rural Sociology* 54 (2): 169–194.

Standing, Guy. 1995. "Labor Insecurity through Market Regulation: Legacy of the 1980s, Challenge for the 1990s." Pp. 153–196 in *Poverty, Inequality, and the Future of Social Policy*, ed. K. McFate, R. Lawson, and W. J. Wilson. New York: Russell Sage Foundation.

Sugrue, Thomas. 1996. *The Origins of the Urban Crisis.* Princeton, NJ: Princeton University Press.

Tam, Tony. 1997. "Sex Segregation and Occupational Gender Inequality in the United States: Devaluation or Specialized Training?" *American Sociological Review* 102: 1652–1692.

Teixeira, Ruy. 2000. "America's Forgotten Majority." Online retrieved January 16, 2000, from http://intellectualcapital.com/issues/issue326/item7424.asp.

Teixeira, Ruy, and Joel Rogers. 2000. *America's Forgotten Majority.* New York: Basic Books.

Theil, Henri, and Anthony Finizza. 1971. "A Note on the Measurement of Racial Integration of Schools by Means of Informational Concepts." *Journal of Mathematical Sociology* 1: 187–194.

Tienda, Marta. 1995. "Latinos and the American Pie: Can Latinos Achieve Economic Parity?" *Hispanic Journal of Behavioral Sciences* 17(4): 403–429.

Tienda, Marta, Shelley Smith, and Vilma Ortiz. 1987. "Industrial Restructuring, Gender Segregation, and Sex Differences in Earnings." *American Sociological Review* 52: 195–210.

Tilly, Chris. 1992. "Dualism in Part-Time Employment." *Industrial Relations* 31(2): 330–347.

———. 1996. *Half a Job: Bad and Good Part-Time Jobs in a Changing Labor Market.* Philadelphia: Temple University Press.

Topel, Robert. 1994. "Regional Labor Markets and the Determinants of Wage Inequality." *American Economic Review* 84(2): 17–22.

Treiman, Donald, and Heidi Hartmann, eds. 1981. *Women, Work, and Wages: Equal Pay for Jobs of Equal Value.* Washington, DC: National Academy Press.

Treiman, Donald, and Patricia Roos. 1983. "Sex and Earnings in Industrial Society: A Nine Nation Comparison." *American Journal of Sociology* 89: 612–646.

Tyson, Laura D'Andrea. 1992. *Who's Bashing Whom? Trade Conflicts in High-Technology Industries.* Washington, DC: Institute for International Economics.

U.S. Bureau of the Census. 2000. *1999 Statistical Abstract of the United States.* Washington, DC: U.S. Government Printing Office [http://www.census.gov/prod/www/statistics-abstract-us.html].

U.S. Bureau of the Census. 2000. *Historical Income Tables from the March Current Population Surveys.* [http://www.census.gov/lines/income/histinc/fo2.html].

U.S. Council of Economic Advisors. 1998. *1997 Economic Report of the President.* Washington, DC: U.S. Government Printing Office [http://www.access.gpo.gov/eop/].

U.S. Council of Economic Advisors. 1999. *1998 Economic Report of the President.* Washington, DC: U.S. Government Printing Office [http://www.access.gpo.gov/eop/].

U.S. Department of Commerce. 1994a. *1987 Economic Census* CD-ROM vol. 1: Report Series 1E [MRDF]. Washington, DC: Bureau of the Census.

U.S. Department of Commerce. 1994b. *Regional Economic Information System* CD-ROM, 1969–1992 [MRDF]. Washington, DC: Bureau of Economic Analysis.

Waldinger, Roger. 1996. *Still the Promised City?: African Americans and New Immigrants in Postindustrial New York.* Cambridge, MA: Harvard University Press.

Waldinger, Roger, and Mehdi Bozorgmehr, eds. 1996. *Ethnic Los Angeles.* New York: Russell Sage Foundation.

Ward, Clare, and Angela Dale. 1992. "Geographical Variation in Female Labour Force Participation: An Application of Multilevel Modelling." *Regional Studies* 26(3): 243–255.

Ward, Kathryn, ed. 1990. *Women Workers and Global Restructuring.* Ithaca, NY: Cornell University Press.

Waters, Mary, and Karl Eschback. 1995. "Immigration and Racial and Ethnic Inequality in the United States." *American Review of Sociology* 21: 419–446.

Weinberg, Daniel. 1996. *Current Population Reports P60–191.* Washington, DC: U.S. Bureau of the Census [online service].

Weir, Margaret. 1992. *Politics and Jobs.* Princeton, NJ: Princeton University Press.

————. 1995a. "Property, Social Rights, and the Politics of Place in the United States." Pp.329–354 in *European Social Policy,* ed. S. Leibfried and P. Pierson. Washington, DC: Brookings Institution.

————. 1995b. "The Politics of Racial Isolation in Europe and America." Pp. 217–242 in *Classifying by Race,* ed. P. Peterson. Princeton, NJ: Princeton University Press.

Weir, Margaret, and Marshal Ganz. 1997. "Reconnecting People and Politics." Pp. 149–171 in *The New Majority: Toward a Popular Progressive Politics,* ed. S. Greenberg and T. Skocpol. New Haven, CT: Yale University Press.

Wellington, Alison. 1993. "Changes in the Male/Female Wage Gap." *Journal of Human Resources* 28(2): 383–411.

Williamson, Jeffrey. 1996. "Globalization and Inequality Then and Now: The Late 19th and Late 20th Centuries Compared." National Bureau of Economic Research Working Paper 5491.

Wilson, William Julius. 1987. *The Truly Disadvantaged.* Chicago: University of Chicago Press.

———. 1996. *When Work Disappears.* New York: Alfred Knopf.

———. 1997. "The New Social Inequality and Affirmative Opportunity." Pp.57–77 in *The New Majority: Toward a Popular Progressive Politics,* ed. S. Greenberg and T. Skocpol. New Haven, CT: Yale University Press.

———. 1999. *The Bridge over the Racial Divide.* Berkeley: University of California Press and Russell Sage Foundation.

Winant, Howard. 1997. "Racial Dualism at Century's End." Pp. 87–115 in *The House That Race Built,* ed. W. Lubiano. New York: Pantheon Books.

Wolff, Edward. 1995. *Top Heavy: A Study of the Increasing Inequality of Wealth in America.* New York: Twentieth Century Fund Press.

Wood, Adrian. 1994. *North-South Trade, Employment and Inequality.* Oxford: Clarendon Press.

Xie, Yu, and Emily Hannum. 1996. "Regional Variation in Earnings Inequality in Reform Era Urban China." *American Journal of Sociology* 101: 950–992.

Zukin, Sharon. 1991. *Landscapes of Power: From Detroit to Disney World.* Berkeley: University of California Press.

Index

aerospace industry, 45
affirmative action: defenders of, 5; and feminist agenda, 91; historical development, 180–81, 183–84, 186, 211*n*7–9; and occupational segregation, 113
African Americans: civil rights legislation, 180; in Dallas-Detroit, 52–53, 82–83; and deindustrialization, 169; in St. Louis, 45, 48, 49, 50. *See also* racial inequality
antidiscrimination strategies, 7–8, 177, 181, 184. *See also* affirmative action
anti-inequality initiatives: class inequality, 177, 178–79; and flexible employment, 169; racial inequality, 177–78, 180; and regional analysis benefits, 175–76. *See also* policy issues
Armstrong, Pat, 127, 138
Asians and inequality, 48, 57, 74, 169
Australia, occupational inequality in, 102
automotive industry, Detroit, 65
average gender wage gap, 119, 121, 141

Bernhardt, Annette, 146, 155
Blanchflower, David, 115–16, 133
Blau, Francine, 13, 32, 63, 64, 85, 103, 123, 129
Browne, Irene, 12

Canadian socioeconomic system, 127
capitalist welfare states, role of women in, 13
Card, David, 18
casualization of employment: data sources, 199; and gender inequality, 127, 129–30, 134, 135, 137, 153–54; impact of, 21, 98–99, 171; and low-wage labor market, 138; occupational segregation, 110, 111–12, 207*n*8; policy implications, 185; socioeconomic impact of, 9. *See also* flexibility in employment
Charles, Maria, 13
Chicago, inequality comparison, 31, 55, 57–58
Civil Rights Act (1964), 180
civil rights advocacy, 5, 180
class inequality: among women, 146–47, 148–49, 155–66, 167–68;

democracy, U.S. social, 4–5
Detroit: class inequality in, 53; comparison to national level, 49, 84–85; complexity of inequality in, 61–65, 68–69; economic restructuring effects, 43–44, 51–53; economy and labor force dynamics, 65–68; gender-class inequality, 69–72; gender-wage inequality, 72–74, 77–79; industrial-postindustrial factors, 76–77; racial inequality, 52–53, 74–76, 82–84; as subject of study, 31; supply-side analysis, 79–82
DiNardo, John, 66
discrimination: and high-technology industries, 50; initiatives against, 7–8, 177, 181, 184; and new inequality, 6; as source of inequality, 5. *See also* policy issues
division of labor, gender/racial, 12. *See also* occupational segregation

earnings. *See* wage inequality
economic issues: Dallas-Detroit economic profiles, 65–68; debate on prosperous economy, 211n13; and strategy of author's argument, 8–10; U.S. trends, 3. *See also* restructuring, economic
Economic Opportunity Act (1964), 180
education: as conservative cure-all for inequality, 4; economic restructuring effects, 53–54; and employment distribution in Detroit vs. Dallas, 66, 67; and gender wage inequality in Dallas and Detroit, 72, 74; hourly wage ratios, 124, 126; as solution to inequality, 33, 149. *See also* class inequality; *college entries*
employment: and cross-national research, 64; Dallas vs. Detroit, 66, 67; and immigration in Dallas, 84; vs. wage inequality, 62. *See also* insecure employment conditions; occupational segregation

Equal Pay Act (1963), 180
equilibrium theory, 151
ethnic inequality. *See* racial inequality
European vs. U.S. inequality, 62–63, 96, 138, 189, 206n2

Fagan, Collette, 93
fair-employment regulations, 180–81
family income inequality and gender differences, 147, 209n4
federal government, social democratic role of, 4. *See also* policy issues
females. *See* women, wage inequality among
feminist movement: criticism of postindustrial theories, 127–28, 143; focus on female composition in occupations, 87–88, 91; historical overview, 181; and social inequality, 14; and spatial analysis, 128
Ferber, Marianne, 103
finance, insurance and real estate (FIRE), 66, 113, 139–40, 199, 208n7
flexibility in employment: and gender inequality, 98–100, 127, 129–30; importance in inequality, 170–71; policy implications, 185; rise of, 183; wage level effects, 150–51, 153–54; within-group inequality, 166–70. *See also* casualization of employment
Fraser, Nancy, 14, 210n2
Freeman, Richard, 62, 66
free-market conservatism, 4

GDP growth, 211n12
gender inequality: casualization of employment, 127, 129–30, 134, 135, 137, 153–54; city comparisons, 45, 50–54, 55, 56–58, 65, 69–79, 83; and cross-national comparisons, 63, 97; definition, 204n5; flexibility in employment, 98–100, 127, 129–30; high-tech-

nology industries, 127–29, 139–41, 143, 171–72, 189–90; and importance of regional analysis, 85–88, 141–44; insecure employment conditions, 99, 130, 142–43, 190; methodology, 34–39, 210*n*15–17; in new social inequality, 170; policy implications, 5, 181, 185–86; and postindustrial economies, 80–82; vs. racial inequality, 7–8, 58, 87; service economy, 130–31, 207*n*4, 208*n*3; and supply-side explanations, 79–80. *See also* class inequality; occupational segregation; women, wage inequality among

German Democratic Republic, gender inequality in, 97

glass-ceiling effect, 53, 141, 167, 171–72

global cities and configurations of inequality, 54–58

globalization, 10–11, 205*n*10

Graham, Hugh, 211*n*7

Greenspan, Alan, 182

Handcock, Mark S., 146

Hannum, Emily, 18

Harrison, Bennett, 151

high-flexibility labor markets, 129–30, 150–51, 166–67. *See also* flexibility in employment

high joblessness. *See* unemployment

high-skill workers, demand for, 33, 45, 150, 152. *See also* education

high-technology labor markets: Dallas economic profile, 66, 68; data sources, 199; and gender inequality, 127–29, 139–41, 143, 171–72, 189–90; impact of, 21, 49; and labor demand for high-skill workers, 45, 150, 151–52; and occupational segregation, 114, 115, 117, 207*n*8; St. Louis, inequality study, 31, 44, 45–50, 53; wage inequality among women, 167–68

high-wage vs. low-wage labor markets, 120–21, 131–41, 151

hourly wages: comparison of averages, 78; by education, 124, 126; gender comparisons, 72, 73, 74; and labor market structures, 108; methodology, 34, 107; research focus on, 209*n*12

human-capital approach to inequality, 122, 123

immigration: data sources, 199; Detroit-Dallas analysis, 67, 67–68, 83–84; and gender inequality, 127, 130, 139, 144; and high-tech industries, 115; impact of, 9, 21, 171; in New York and LA, 56; and occupational segregation, 113, 116; regional factors in inequality, 209*n*6, 209*n*10, 210*n*18; research issues, 208*n*6; wage level effects, 153. *See also* Miami

import-sensitive manufacturing: data sources, 199; effect on men's inequality, 167; and gender inequality, 143–44; and low-wage labor market, 138; and occupational segregation, 116–17; wage level effects on men, 172

income. *See* wage inequality

independent contracting work. *See* insecure employment conditions

industrial economy: data sources, 200; and gender inequality, 130–31; and inequality in Dallas-Detroit, 76–85; wage level effects, 154, 168. *See also* Detroit; manufacturing labor markets

inequality, socioeconomic: complexity of, 58–59, 61–65, 68–69, 175, 178, 191–92; contributing factors, 3–6

informal self-employment. *See* insecure employment conditions

insecure employment conditions: data sources, 199; and deinstitutionalization of labor market, 98; elements of, 205*n*17; and gender inequality, 99, 130, 142–43, 190; loss of, 9; and new economic

order, 183–84; policy implications, 182–83, 185; and 1930s equality agenda, 179; wage level effects, 150–51, 152–54; within-group inequality, 168–70. *See also* flexibility in employment; immigration; unemployment insecurity, socioeconomic, definitional issues, 211*n*11. *See also* insecure employment conditions
institutional factors: decline of wage-setting institutions, 9, 62–63, 85–86, 98; deinstitutionalized labor market, 21, 98, 153; and postindustrial economy, 182
international competition, development of, 9
international factors in gender roles in labor market, 13–14. *See also* cross-national research on inequality
intersectionality of inequality, research goals, 14
intraoccupational wage inequality, 207*n*3

Japan, occupational inequality in, 96, 102, 103
Jargowsky, Paul, 19
Jencks, Christopher, 180
Jenson, Jane, 100
job classification systems, shortcomings of, 100
joblessness. *See* unemployment
job security. *See* insecure employment conditions

Kahn, Lawrence, 13, 32, 63, 64, 85, 123, 129
Kalleberg, Arne, 13, 92–93, 97, 102
Katz, Lawrence, 62, 66
Keynesian macroeconomic policies, 8, 179, 204*n*7
Krueger, Alan, 18
Krugman, Paul, 15

labor force dynamics, Dallas and Detroit, 65–68

labor markets: correlations of inequality over, 34–39; difficulties of establishing boundaries of, 15–17; and hourly wages, 109; and occupational segregation, 108. *See also* regional labor market analysis; *specific labor markets*
labor-market segmentation theory, 147
Larner, Wendy, 138
Latinas and African American Women at Work (Browne), 12
Latinos/Latinas: and deindustrialization, 169; in Detroit-Dallas study, 52–53, 67–68, 76, 83; in Silicon Valley, 57; in St. Louis, 48, 49
living standards vs. inequality, 204*n*4
local communities: as research subjects, 15–17; social action role, 11–12. *See also* regional labor market analysis
local/global continuum, 10–11
Los Angeles, inequality comparison, 31, 54, 55, 56
low-skill workers, 116, 130, 134–35. *See also* education; immigration
low-wage vs. high-wage labor markets, 120–21, 131–41, 151

macroquantitative vs. microqualitative approaches, 205*n*15
macrostructural studies of inequality, 122
males. *See* men, inequality among
manufacturing labor markets: and casualization of employment, 112; data sources, 200; Detroit and Dallas economies, 65–66; and gender inequality, 140; and service economy, 143–44; wage effects on men, 137–38, 154, 168. *See also* Detroit; high-technology labor markets; import-sensitive manufacturing
Markusen, Ann, 18, 206*n*3
McDowell, Linda, 100, 138
measurement methods. *See* methodology

median hourly wages by education, 124

men, inequality among: class inequality in Detroit-Dallas, 69, 70, 71; cross-national comparisons, 63, 64; high-flexibility labor markets, 154, 167–68; high-tech industries, 49, 152; industrial labor markets, 137–38, 154, 168; labor market structure, 162, 164, 165; scope of, 37, 41, 42–43; spatial elements, 172; wage structure, 80–82

mesocomparative method, 15–23

methodology: class inequality, 33–38, 35, 120; compensating differential, 209n5; data sources, 210n13; Detroit-Dallas analysis, 205–6n1; economic restructuring, 194; gender inequality, 34–39, 210n15–17; generalizability of Detroit-Dallas analysis, 84–85; mesocomparative, 15–23; microdata area map, 202; multivariate models, 196–98; occupational segregation, 103, 195–96, 207n5–6; regional labor markets, 31–34, 133–34, 193–94, 199–200; technical appendix notes, 212n1–4; variable interactions, 133; wage inequality, 194–95

metropolitan area, boundaries of, 16–17. *See also* regional labor market analysis

Miami: class inequality in, 46, 50, 53; economic restructuring effects, 43–44, 50–51; gender inequality, 139; racial inequality in, 48; as subject of study, 31

microdata area map, 202

middle class, 37, 181

migration, labor, to South, 65

Morris, Martina, 146

Morrison, Philip S., 16

multivariate models, 196–98

Nakano Glenn, Evelyn, 12, 13

national-level analysis: class inequal-

ity, 71–72, 122–28; inequality among women, 155–56, 157, 159; measurement methods, 32; occupational segregation, 95–103; vs. regional analysis, 6, 49, 84–85, 176, 210n1. *See also* cross-national research on inequality; United States

nation-state and globalization, 11

new social inequality, 5–6, 7–8, 170

New York City, inequality comparison, 31, 54, 55, 56

non-college vs. college-educated workers. *See* college- vs. non-college-educated workers

occupational segregation: casualization of employment, 207n8; cross-national vs. regional perspectives, 92–93, 95–103, 206n2; discrimination as source of inequality, 5; and feminist movement, 87–88, 91; and gender wage gaps, 103–18, 207n9–10; and hourly wages, 78; and immigration, 127; and individual characteristics, 206n1; inequality in Dallas-Detroit, 80–81, 82–84; introduction, 91–95; methodology, 103, 195–96, 207n5–6; policy implications, 184, 185, 186–87; and Sweden, 206n2

opportunity and 1960s equality agenda, 179–80

Oswald, Andrew, 115–16

part-time employment, 80, 153, 155, 210n14. *See also* insecure employment conditions

penalty, wage, 121

Piore, Michael, 11

place-based interest formation, 205n11

policy issues: and antidiscrimination strategies, 7–8; comparable worth, 91, 93, 96–97, 98, 113, 187; conservative vs. social democratic approaches, 4–5; in Detroit-Dallas analysis, 85–88; and economic conditions, 210*n*3; and flexible employment conditions, 169; historical view of inequality, 175–83; and occupational segregation, 112–13; research implications for, 183–92; welfare program implications, 206*n*5

politics of inequality: in Detroit-Dallas analysis, 85–88; historical analysis, 175–83; importance of institutions to women's status, 13; policy implications of research, 183–92; and strategy of author's argument, 8

post-Fordism, 100

postindustrial economy: class inequality in, 87; feminist criticism of, 127–28, 143; and gender inequality, 128–29; impact on inequality at urban center level, 54; and inequality in Silicon Valley, 56–57; lack of equalizing institutions in, 182; and occupational segregation, 101; shortcomings of, 125. *See also* Dallas; high-technology labor markets; service economy

poverty, and New Deal/Great Society, 181

premium, wage, 121, 148–49

privatization, conservative championing of, 4

productivity growth, 211*n*12

racial composition, Detroit vs. Dallas, 67, 67–68

racial inequality: anti-inequality initiatives, 177–78, 180; city comparison, 45, 48, 50–54, 55, 57, 74–76, 82–84; and class inequality, 188–89; definition, 204*n*5; and deindustrialization, 169, 170; and gender inequality, 7–8, 58, 87; measurement issues, 37–38; policy implications, 5, 187; Wilson's highlighting of, 187–88

Ragin, Charles, 17

"Reagan Revolution," 4, 10

regional labor market analysis: anti-inequality initiatives, 175–76; class inequality, 120, 125, 128–41, 150; configurations of inequality, 15–23, 29, 30; vs. cross-national research, 64–65, 92–93, 95–103, 206*n*2; Dallas and Detroit as study subjects, 9; gender gap over regions, 126; immigration, 209*n*6, 209*n*10, 210*n*18; importance of, 32, 39, 63–64, 85–88, 141–44; methodology, 31–34, 133–34, 193–94, 199–200; vs. national-level analysis, 6, 49, 84–85, 176, 210*n*1; occupational segregation, 97–102, 107–18; and value of urban case studies, 62; wage inequality among women, 150–66. *See also* temporal vs. spatial analysis; *individual cities*

research issues: and approaches to inequality, 64; economic restructuring role, 127; feminist research, 10–14, 12; occupational gender segregation, 91–95; structural sources for gender wage gap, 125; wage inequality among women, 145–49. *See also* methodology

Reskin, Barbara, 186–87

restructuring, economic: class inequality, 128–41; and configurations of inequality, 45–54; and deindustrialization, 137–38; elements of, 9, 179; and four-city analysis, 43–54; gender wage gap effects, 98–99; historical analysis, 181–82; impact on inequality factors, 102; methodology, 194; national level analysis, 122–28; and new inequality, 6–7; and sources of inequality, 178. *See also* flexibility in employment; insecure employment conditions

Roos, Patricia, 13, 186–87

Rosenfeld, Rachel, 13, 92–93, 97, 102

Rubery, Jill, 93

Sable, Charles, 11, 86
Santa Clara County, inequality comparison, 55, 56–57
security, job. *See* insecure employment conditions
segregation, employment. *See* occupational segregation
service economy: and casualization of employment, 112; data sources, 200; development of, 9; finance, insurance and real estate, 66, 113, 139–40, 199, 208n7; and gender inequality, 130–31, 207n4, 208n3; and high-tech industries, 152; lack of detailed job classification in, 100; and low-wage labor market, 138; and manufacturing, 143–44; and occupational integration, 101, 114–15; and unions, 189. *See also* Dallas
sex discrimination legislation, 181
Silicon Valley, 31, 55, 56–57, 151
skill levels: demand for high-skill workers, 33, 45, 150, 151–52; and wage trends, 122–25. *See also* class inequality; education
Smith, Barbara Ellen, 186
Smith, Shelley, 146, 155
social activism, local nature of, 11
social composition of inequality, 8–10
social democracy, U.S., 4–5
South, the, economic growth of, 65
spatial configurations of inequality, 15–23, 29–30. *See also* regional labor market analysis; temporal vs. spatial analysis
spatial-skill mismatches, 150
St. Louis, inequality study, 31, 44, 45–50, 53
structural perspective, 7–8, 12, 14. *See also* regional labor market analysis
supply-side analysis, 79–80, 149
Swedish occupational system, 96, 206n2

technology labor markets. *See* high-technology labor markets

Teixeira, Ruy, 149
temporal vs. spatial analysis: class-gender inequality, 127, 141–44; and gender inequality, 86–87, 99; and history of inequality politics, 175–92; inequality among women, 145; popularity of temporal analysis, 171; research questions, 44, 120–21; weaknesses of temporal approach, 122–25
temporary work. *See* insecure employment conditions
The Second Industrial Divide (Piore and Sable), 86
trade issues. *See* import-sensitive manufacturing
Treiman, Donald, 13
Tyson, Laura D'Andrea, 18

unconventional vs. conventional configurations of inequality, 111–17
unemployment: for blacks in Detroit, 83; class inequality, 132–33; Dallas vs. Detroit, 67; data sources, 199; and deindustrialization, 115–16; and gender inequality, 134, 135, 137; impact of, 21; and occupational segregation, 112–13; rates vs. reality, 182–83; wage level effects, 153
unions: Dallas vs. Detroit, 66, 67; and deindustrialization, 138; and gender inequality, 86; and gender sensitivity, 211–12n15; and high-tech industries, 45, 152; initiatives in service economy, 189; and insecure employment conditions, 153; and male wage structure, 80–82; wage premium, 181
United States: advantages of regional analysis in, 32; debate on prosperous economy, 211n13; decentralization of economy, 10; economic trends, 3; vs. Europe in inequality, 62–63, 96, 138, 189, 206n2; levels of inequality in, 203–4n2; measurements of labor market factors,

103; occupational segregation, 92–93; policy effects of economic restructuring, 182. *See also* national-level analysis

universal need vs. class language, 212*n*17

universal redistributive programs, 204*n*3. *See also* class inequality; policy issues

urban case-study approach, 15–17. *See also* regional labor market analysis; *individual cities*

wage inequality: vs. employment, 62; high-wage vs. low-wage labor markets, 120–21, 131–41, 151; methodology, 34–43, 194–95; postindustrial/industrial dichotomies, 76–85; U.S. levels of, 203–4*n*2. *See also* class inequality; high-technology labor markets; hourly wages; insecure employment conditions; occupational segregation; regional labor market analysis

wage-setting institutions, 9, 62–63, 85–86, 98

welfare programs, implications for, 206*n*5

Wilson, William Julius, 7, 170, 178, 187

within-occupation wage inequality, 99–100, 114

women, wage inequality among: and class inequality, 41, 42–43, 63, 70, 71–72, 170–72; complexities of inequality among, 13; high-flexibility labor markets, 166–67; high-technology labor markets, 167–68; importance of, 175; industrial economy, 168; insecure employment conditions, 168–70; policy implications, 190; regional analysis, 150–66; research issues, 145–49; wage structure, 39, 77–79. *See also* college-level effects on women; gender inequality

women's movement, 181

working class and gender inequality, 37. *See also* immigration; industrial economy

Xie, Yu, 18